Swift Blaze of Fire

Swift Blaze of Fire

Olympian, Cleric, Brigadista:
The Life of Robert Hilliard

Lin Rose Clark

THE LILLIPUT PRESS
DUBLIN

First published 2025 by
THE LILLIPUT PRESS

62–63 Sitric Road,
Arbour Hill,
Dublin 7,
Ireland
www.lilliputpress.ie

Copyright © Lin Rose Clark, 2025

10 9 8 7 6 5 4 3 2 1

All rights reserved. No part of this publication may be reproduced in any form or by any means without the prior permission of the publisher.

Quotation on page 15 from *Murphy* by Samuel Beckett, reproduced by permission of Faber and Faber, London. Quotation on page xiv from the song 'Viva la Quinta Brigada' reproduced here with kind permission from Christy Moore. Extract from Cork Grammar School song reproduced with the kind permission of Ashton School, Cork. Excerpt from Samuel Beckett's letter of 9 July 1935 by kind permission of the Estate of Samuel Beckett, c/o Rosica Colin Ltd, London; also by kind permission of the Samuel Beckett Collection, 9.5, Harry Ransom Center, The University of Texas at Austin.

A CIP record for this title is available from The British Library.

ISBN 978-1-84351-921-8
eBook ISBN: 978-1-84351-938-6

Set in 22pt on 12pt in Adobe Jenson Pro by Compuscript
Index by Fionbar Lyons
Cover design by Jack Smyth, jacksmyth.co
Printed and bound in Dublin, Ireland by Sprint Books

This book is dedicated to all those resisting fascism then and now.
And to Deirdre Davey

CONTENTS

Family tree	x
List of illustrations	xi
A note on names	xiii
Prologue	1

PART I — THE HILLIARDS OF KILLARNEY

Chapter 1: New capitalists	9
Chapter 2: 'A firm desire to do right'	17

PART II — SCHOOLDAYS IN TWO WARZONES

Chapter 3: Unsettled conditions	29
Chapter 4: 'Solidarity, spontaneity and direct action'	40
Chapter 5: A veritable hell	51

PART III — LITERATURE, GOD, AND THE STATE OF THE NATION

Chapter 6: 'The dead bodies of their own brothers'	65
Chapter 7: Rosemary	77

PART IV — THE BOXER

Chapter 8: 'The irishman worked hard and was dead game'	89
Chapter 9: Paris Olympics	97
Chapter 10: 'My friend'	103

Contents

PART V — MARRIED LOVE

Chapter 11: 'I wish I were a quarter good enough for you'   115

Chapter 12: Onward Christian soldiers   126

Chapter 13: A living force?   133

Chapter 14: Breakdown   144

PART VI — ANTI-FASCIST

Chapter 15: 'Why don't you kum back?'   157

Chapter 16: 'Prominent CP member'   167

Chapter 17: Civil war in Spain   175

Chapter 18: Madrigueras   186

Chapter 19: 'Teach the kids to stand for democracy'   197

Chapter 20: Jarama   204

Epilogue   213

Biographical chronology   222

Select bibliography   225

Notes   232

Acknowledgments   282

Index   285

I see this old bad order die

In a great swift blaze of fire,

A structure clear and mighty high,

Born in its funeral pyre.

Brendan Behan

FAMILY TREE

Family Tree of Robert Hilliard and Edith Rosemary Robins

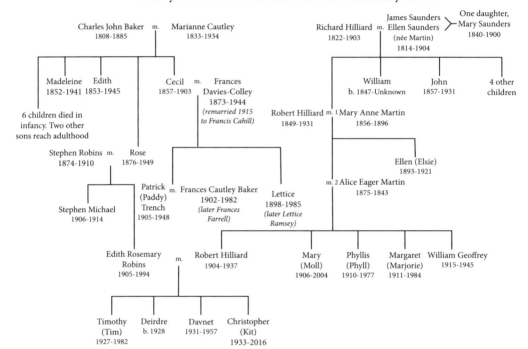

LIST OF ILLUSTRATIONS

1. Family portrait taken circa 1912. Left to right: Mary (Moll), Robert senior, Marjorie, Ellen (Elsie), Phyllis, Alice, Robert (Hilliard family photo).
2. Robert, circa 1914, aged about 10 (Hilliard family photo).
3. Irish Volunteers marching through Cork in 1917: Courtesy of Cork Public Museum
4. Robert at home in Moyeightragh, Easter 1916, with his younger sisters and brother. Left to right: Marjorie, Moll and Phyllis, with baby brother Geoff (born 1915) on Moll's lap. (Hilliard family photo).
5. Cork Grammar School Rugby Team, 1919-1920, reproduced with kind permission of Ashton School, Cork.
6. Aftermath of the burning of Cork on 11 December 1920, from Michael Lenihan Collection: Courtesy of Cork Public Museum.
7. British soldiers holding up a civilian, Dublin, circa 1920. Courtesy of Kilmainham Gaol Museum/OPW 19PC-1A46-25.
8. Pemba and Rosemary in 1905 (Rosemary's photo collection).
9. Michael, Rose and Rosemary Robins, circa 1910 (Robins family photo).
10. Rosemary with two of her samoyeds, circa 1922 (Robins family photo).
11. Robert (standing, centre, in white vest) and other Irish champion boxers. *Freeman's Journal*, 9 January, 1924.
12. Olympic team badge, 1924, stitched to Robert's blazer. Memorabilia kept by Rosemary Hilliard.
13. Bass beermat, 1928, bearing the slogan that Robert is often credited with devising: 'Great Stuff This Bass!' Reproduced with kind permission of Mitchells and Butler.
14. Robert's unruly hair is smoothed flat in this studio portrait, taken in 1926, the year of his marriage (Rosemary's photo collection).
15. Robert, Rosemary and baby Tim visited the Hilliard family in 1927. Back: Marjorie, Phyl, Moll; front: Geoff, Alice, Old Robert with Tim, Rosemary, Robert. (Hilliard family photo).

List of illustrations

16. Robert, shown centre right with boxing gloves, attended the 1929 event held in London by the (apparently exclusively masculine) Trinity College Dublin Dinner Club. Artist Fred May. Illustrated London News/Mary Evans Picture Library.
17. Robert's father holding Tim, 1927 (Rosemary's photo collection).
18. Robert with Tim at Kingswood Ruffs, circa 1929 (Rosemary's photo collection).
19. Tim and Deirdre in the garden at Kingswood Ruffs, 1929 (Rosemary's photo collection).
20. Deirdre looks on as Rosemary, pregnant with Davnet, mends Robert's torn trousers. Surrey Downs, June 1931 (Rosemary's photo collection).
21. Robert's letter to Tim and Deirdre from Dublin. Author's photo.
22. Outdoor Relief workers and supporters, Belfast, 4th October 1932: Chronicle/Alamy Stock Photo.
23. Rosemary recovering from Kit's birth (Rosemary's photo collection).
24. Davnet, Robert and Rosemary walking through Belfast to Kit's christening, Deirdre present but not shown. (Rosemary's photo collection).
25. Deirdre and Tim keeping their daily vigil for Robert at Brown's Bay, September 1934 (Rosemary's photo collection).
26. Weir Cottage, Ballinderry, 1935 (Rosemary's photo collection).
27. Optician's shop in Albacete: photo on reverse of Robert's new spectacles prescription, saved in his wallet in 1936 and sent to Rosemary after his death (Author's photo).
28.1 Robert Hilliard's last postcard to his family, written before the Battalion left Madrigueras for the front at Jarama, 24 January 1937 (Rosemary Hilliard's papers).
28.2 Robert Hilliard's last postcard to his family, written before the Battalion left Madrigueras for the front at Jarama, 24 January 1937 (Rosemary Hilliard's papers).
30. The hospital in Castellón where Robert Hilliard died (Author's photo, 2017).
31. The letter from King Street telling Rosemary of Robert's death, March 1937 (Rosemary Hilliard's papers).
32. Robert and Tim, Surrey, June 1931 (Rosemary's photo collection).
33. Historian Guillem Casañ stands above the mass grave in the Cemetery of San Josep, Castellón, where Hilliard now lies (Author's photo, 2017, reproduced with kind permission of Guillem Casañ).

A NOTE ON NAMES

This book refers to its protagonist as Robert Hilliard. Family members have always referred to him as Robert and Deirdre, his surviving daughter, cannot remember hearing him called anything else. In the letters that remain, he signs himself 'Robert', 'your loving husband Robert', or 'Daddy'. Some may have called him Bob in his lifetime and he is widely known as Bob Hilliard now.

PROLOGUE

This is how I found out my grandfather was killed in the Spanish Civil War.

One morning when I was about eight years old there was an exciting announcement in school assembly: our class teacher was going to show us her sides. I turned to stare at her. What did this mean? Was she going to undress? Later that day we were herded into an unfamiliar room. Our class teacher, fully clothed, hung up a white screen, drew the curtains to make everything dark and switched on an electric hum. A wobbly square of light appeared.

I had never seen anything like it. There were palm trees, blue sea and vivid sunshine, laughing grown-ups and children playing with an outsize beach ball in segments of red, green and yellow, silver fishes on a plate. This magic place, where all the colours were brighter, was where our teacher went for her holidays.

'Mrs Jackson showed us her sides,' I reported to my parents, as we sat around the tea-table that evening.

'Her what?'

'Her sides of Spain. Can we go there?'

My mother flinched. "No," she said, "we won't be going to Spain." My father said someone called General Franco had taken over in Spain twenty years earlier. Since then he had stopped the Spanish people voting for anyone else. It might look good in Mrs Jackson's slideshow, but for Spanish people who didn't want General Franco it was a cruel place.

Prologue

And that's when my mother said, "My father was killed there."

Later she tucked me up for the night and switched off the light, but instead of leaving she sat on my bed with her arm round my shoulders. My younger sisters were already asleep. The thin curtains let the moonlight through, and it fell across part of the wall and a corner of the room. Feeling safe in the curve of my mother's arm, I said, 'Tell me about your father who was killed in Spain.'

'He went to fight in the Spanish Civil War.'

I didn't know what that was, but the sadness in her voice made things I couldn't understand lodge in my memory.

'He was shot in the neck and died a few days later.'

I had seen people shot in cowboy programmes like *The Lone Ranger*, throwing up their hands and falling off their horses in instant black-and-white deaths. But this was real.

'He fought in the International Brigades,' she went on. 'People talk as if they were rebels, but General Franco was the rebel.'

'How old were you?'

'Eight.'

My age. 'So who looked after you?'

'My mother. Your granny. She looked after Uncle Tim and me and Auntie Davnet and Uncle Kit.' I had hardly ever met Uncle Kit, but playful, jokey Uncle Tim was a familiar figure. Auntie Davnet had died of polio when I was five; she was a remembered whirl of fair hair and smiling teeth and a crisp cotton dress that smelled of soap. Strange to think of these mighty figures as children. Now I knew their father had been killed in Spain.

I had also learned there was nothing I could say or do to comfort my mother.

My grandfather's name was Robert Martin Hilliard and there has always been a Robert Martin Hilliard-shaped gap in our family. As time passed my sisters and I heard more about him. It seemed he had a bewildering series of occupations. At one stage he was a Church of Ireland priest, so

Prologue

when our atheist father joked about marrying a vicar's daughter I clothed my mind's-eye grandfather in a white dog collar, like the local vicar. My mother said he was also a journalist and a boxer. Boxing was not his job, though – when boxing was on TV she would say, proudly, that he had been an amateur who boxed in the Olympic Games. In her opinion, amateur boxing was more sporting than professional, because amateurs wore thicker gloves and won by displaying skill rather than damaging their opponents.

Our grandfather was Irish, and our mother told tales of her own childhood in Northern Ireland, where he was sent after being ordained. The ugly part of his story was that he walked out on our grandmother and his four children to go to London; the sad part was that he died in Spain. Eventually I learned the name of the battle where he was shot, Jarama, and the year, 1937.

Tim and Deirdre (our mother), Robert Hilliard's eldest children, were shattered by his death. They had always thought he would come back. Long into adulthood, Deirdre was tormented by dreams that she was running to catch up with him in the street, only to find she was following a stranger – or worse, that he looked at her with no sign of love or recognition. Their mother transmitted a sense to her children that their father had dealt the whole family a crushing betrayal. Deirdre was left with irreconcilable contradictions. How could the affectionate, playful father she remembered walk away from her and her brothers and sister? How could he leave them so unprovided for that they had to do moonlight flits to escape unpaid bills, and often went short of food? On the one hand the International Brigades were a heroic undertaking; her father's readiness to fight Francoism was therefore heroic. On the other he had left his own children, and what kind of hero did that?

The effects of such an abandonment don't end with one generation. As a teenager I was acutely aware of our mother's unresolved unhappiness. It mingled with the resentments she shared with many women trapped in the role of 1960s housewife. Our house felt full of exploding emotions, making me eager to leave home and for a while putting Robert Hilliard out of my head.

3

Prologue

The Killarney department store came as a big surprise, standing out in the street, larger than its neighbouring shops, R HILLIARD AND SONS in impressive lettering across the front. Peering through plate glass, I could see no further than the window display of clothing, footwear and steam irons.

It was 1975 and I was a young teacher on my Easter holidays, hitchhiking and walking with a friend through Kerry and Cork. We had been trudging through Killarney, looking for the Killorglin road, when I saw the unexpected name. Was our family related to the Hilliards in this shop? I didn't go in. Tired and travel-stained after a day on the road, I felt too scruffy to present myself. We pressed on to the youth hostel, but the shop's image lingered.

During another of my 1970s visits to Kerry I wondered aloud to a stranger about the scarcity of people in the sweeping landscape – where *was* everyone? – and he described the events behind the long-deserted ruins and the haunted feel of empty places where once there had been inhabitants. His words brought back my mother's stories of a terrible Famine, evictions and mass emigration. Fragments of history, some from family members, some from strangers,[1] began connecting with my missing grandfather. That Killarney shop was central to his boyhood, I learned. His grandmother had walked hundreds of miles during the Famine to replenish its stock. He had swum in the Killarney lakes, fished in them, rowed boats across them, run wild on their margins with his sister Moll, and carried away from his childhood a lifelong yearning for the ecstatic self-forgetfulness that the lakes and the mountains brought.

After World War II, little was said or written in Ireland about Irish participation in the International Brigades. As this silence lifted, Robert Hilliard's repute grew. In 1984 singer-songwriter Christy Moore released his album *Ride On*, featuring the song 'Viva la Quinta Brigada', which commemorates the names of many fallen brigadistas. Here's the second verse:

> Bob Hilliard was a Church of Ireland pastor
> From Killarney across the Pyrenees he came,
> From Derry came a brave young Christian brother
> Side by side they fought and died in Spain.

Prologue

And then the stirring chorus:

'Viva La Quinta Brigada!
'No Pasaran' the pledge that made them fight.
'Adelante' was the cry around the hillside.
Let us all remember them tonight.'[2]

Suddenly every Christy Moore fan knew my grandfather's name and had heard of the anti-fascist cause for which he died.

Then, in 1988, Robert Hilliard's nephew Stephen Hilliard,[3] who like his uncle was first a journalist and later a Church of Ireland priest, published a piece about him in a magazine called *Resource*.[4] It dwelt on his exuberant friendliness and the way he made everyone laugh, quoting a fellow International Brigade member who knew him in Spain: '"One of the most amusing characters was … the Reverend R M Hilliard … his friends were of all classes. They liked him for his sense of humour and consistently cheerful attitude."'[5]

Stephen's article made clear Hilliard's lifelong refusal to conform. While still a schoolboy he 'liked to walk on the wild side', discarding the traditional attitudes of his Protestant family and supporting Irish freedom from British rule. Stephen told startling stories about his subsequent activities.[6] Even more striking was his effect on other people. Robert Hilliard was only thirty-two when he died, but Stephen was struck by the number of people who still approached him to say how vividly they remembered his uncle: 'He was clearly someone who made his presence felt wherever he went.'

The piece asked questions it couldn't answer. Why had Hilliard abandoned journalism in London to become a Church of Ireland priest in Belfast? Why, though acclaimed for his preaching, had he left his ministry only a few years later to go to England and join first the Communist Party and then the International Brigades? Was he ever a Christian Socialist at all, or was he rather 'a socialist, then a Christian believer, and then a socialist again?' Other questions were implicit in all this. Why, from his schooldays onwards, did Hilliard reject so many of the opinions and loyalties he was brought up with? Why turn his back on the ambitions he had been educated to fulfil? He acted like a driven man, but driven by what?

5

Prologue

Stephen's article however made me grasp an elementary fact. My grandfather was no icon, either of heroism or shiftless betrayal, but a flesh and blood human being, an everyman shaped by his times, and the earlier times that gave rise to them, trying to chart a course through an extraordinary period.

Through the years, my passive waiting for pieces to fit together became active research. I soon learned that different people had created impossibly divergent versions of him, filling gaps in what they knew with what they wanted to believe. Stories circulated which contradicted each other or defied verifiable facts. Parts of the family narrative were open to doubt: for instance, some family members, expressing vehement disapproval of his becoming a 'Red', fixed the onset of his communism at an implausibly early date. Others, including my grandmother Rosemary, his widow, had become reluctant to discuss him at all, fearing that a mythology was being woven round him. If the three-dimensional man were ever to be reclaimed, I would need to disentangle fact from invention.

Robert Hilliard was nothing if not engaging. People who never met him were tantalized by the mercurial swerves he made during his short lifetime; people who knew him were charmed by his humorous eloquence and stirred by the depth of his commitment to the causes he believed in; those close to him loved him – though for some, like my mother, that love had left a deep wound. There was a mystery here. A cloud of sorrow and grief and anger mingled with the esteem in which he was held. Robert Hilliard had set out to do good in the world, risking and losing his life for his beliefs, but had also inflicted great pain. I wanted to get to the bottom of it.

This is the story of a man whose irreconcilable personal conflicts grew out of the political struggles of his times. Only if viewed through the lens of those struggles does his life make sense; only then can it emerge as a coherent narrative rather than a series of mystifying still pictures. It's a narrative that's as much about the history that made him as the man himself.

It begins with his family. What were the conventions he flouted and why did his family espouse them? Who were they, and what had they wanted *him* to be?

PART I — THE HILLIARDS OF KILLARNEY

I

NEW CAPITALISTS

Robert Martin Hilliard was born on Thursday 7 April 1904, in a comfortable terraced house in Lower New Street, central Killarney.[1] His mother, Alice Eagar Hilliard (neé Martin), had been married for two years and this was her first child. The birth went safely and the baby was healthy, with eyes that soon turned grey-green and hair which showed signs of being fair.

Lying-in for a new mother who had domestic help could last for weeks. Alice's husband – also called Robert Martin Hilliard – kept at least one live-in maidservant, and she would also have had help from a relative, perhaps her aunt Margaret Martin, who had at one time lived with them as housekeeper.[2] There was much to do: keeping rooms warm and water boiled over coal or peat fires, the laundering of baby clothes and labour-stained bedlinen, and the preparation of nourishing meals as Alice fed her little boy. The house was a short walk from the Hilliard footwear factory, run by Alice's husband with his brother John, and the drapery and footwear shop run by John. Family members sent congratulations and paid visits.

Photos of Alice show her calm, steadfast smile and intelligent gaze. She was a well-read woman who liked children and got on well with them. My mother loved her dearly, remembering her as 'a very kind person, who read

Swift Blaze of Fire

me stories and was patient at all times.'[3] There was a child in the house already, eager to meet the new baby. Ten-year-old Ellen, known as Elsie, was Alice's stepdaughter. Her husband's first marriage had been to Alice's sister, Mary Ann Martin, who died in 1896. The child was named for her paternal grandmother Ellen (née Ellen Martin), co-founder of the family business. Alice had originally moved into the house as little Elsie's governess. The relationship with her pupil's father deepened until they were married in 1901, in another link between the Hilliards and the Martins.[4] Their union breached the law prohibiting marriage to a deceased wife's sister,[5] so young Alice and old Robert travelled to Jersey to tie the knot,[6] probably the longest journey either of them had ever made.

At twenty-nine Alice was older than the average first-time mother but her husband was much older still, fifty-five, born in 1849 during the Famine. Robert Martin Hilliard senior had waited many years for this son and marked the occasion by noting the date in the family New Testament. It probably seemed best to say little to his own mother, Ellen, about his hopes for baby Robert: they were unlikely to accord with her expectations.

Ninety-year-old Ellen felt profound satisfaction that her son Robert had at last produced an heir. After marrying into the Hilliard family in 1846,[7] she had regularly walked across the Derrynasaggart Mountains from Killarney to Cork and back, throughout the Famine years, to buy stock for the small shop which she ran with her husband Richard.[8] This shop, which sold leather, shoemakers' tools and haberdashery, was where the Hilliards' business had begun. Ellen had drilled it into her children that the family's commercial success was a hard-won thing, to be kept safe and passed on to their own descendants. They cherished the story of her 106-mile walks as they built the family fortunes on the foundations she had laid.

Ellen died in November 1904, having watched baby Robert survive the first half-year of infancy. She was buried next to her husband Richard, dead the year before, under an imposing slab in Killegy graveyard, a tranquil place with a hilltop view over Lough Leane. Other Hilliards also lie in Killegy, their graves marked by handsome inscriptions. The family had come a long way from relatively humble beginnings, but their prosperity had a price. Old Robert was keenly aware that the fulfilment of his mother's ambitions

New capitalists

had cost him his own. His story is worth telling if the hopes he formed for his newborn son are to be understood.

Succession to the family firm had not been straightforward. Ellen and Richard had intended their eldest son William, born in 1847, to take over the business. Their next son Robert was all set to pursue his love of classical studies at Trinity College Dublin, possibly to become a clergyman.

Robert duly left for Dublin and William learned the ropes of his parents' trade. When Ellen and Richard had started out there were dozens of shoemakers in Killarney, plentiful custom for their shop's leather and shoemaking tools, but by the 1860s machine-made shoes from English factories were driving these craftsmen into bankruptcy.[9] The Hilliards knew they must enter the manufacturing class themselves if they wanted their trade to survive. In 1868, when William was twenty-one, they opened their own factory on Killarney's High Street.

William had grown into a resourceful young man, the new broom whose task was to sweep the business into a mechanized age. At that time Hilliard employees[10] still joined soles and uppers together by punching individual holes with an awl and hammering tiny wooden pegs through each hole by hand. They started and ended work when they chose.[11] Each completed on average one pair of shoes a day; abysmal productivity compared with the output per worker in England. Over the next fourteen years the family installed new equipment,[12] against the will of many of the workforce, who were understandably reluctant to cede their skills to a row of machines.[13] The pressure to automate ratcheted up in the early 1880s when GB Britton of Bristol began importing boots made at mechanized benches. The Hilliards now had to introduce their own mechanized benches or go under.

Tectonic shifts were taking place inside Ireland's class structure, of which the Hilliard factory was a small part. The long-standing hostility of rural labourers to their landlords merged with the hostility felt by the rapidly growing urban working class to the new factory owners who grew rich by exploiting their labour. Combined nationalist and class rebellion found an early expression in the Fenian movement.[14] Only a year before

the Hilliard factory opened, the Irish Republican Brotherhood (IRB) –
foot-soldiers of the Fenians – had marched on Killarney, attempting to
capture it by force.[15] Although soldiers and constabulary scattered the IRB
before they reached the town, some of the anger which had fuelled the
Fenians came to the surface again in the Land Wars, fifteen years later.

These Land Wars, armed conflicts provoked by economic hardship,
began in 1882 and were soon fiercer in Kerry than anywhere else in
Ireland. Cutthroat competition in farming and the growth of a new class
of capitalist farmers was driving smaller tenant farmers off the land.[16] The
Irish National Land League[17] began its campaign for better tenants' rights[18]
by using peaceful methods such as rent strikes and boycotts,[19] but armed
government repression and the imprisonment of the League's leaders in
1881 forced the League underground, at which point many of its members
resorted to an older tradition of clandestine raids. Secret confraternities
('Moonlighters') launched armed attacks ('outrages') against individuals
among the new middle class. Landlords were one target; shopkeepers like
the Hilliards another, because 'the men of no property'[20] often owed them
money.[21] William and his parents were therefore imposing mechanized
benches – a radical, unpopular change – at a time of open class warfare.

What Ellen and Richard did not know was that William was leading a
double life.

He had secretly drawn close to Frances O'Keeffe, a young Catholic
woman working in the factory. During this critical time for the business,
Frances fell pregnant.[22] If or when word got out, her life as a respectable
woman was over in the eyes of Catholics and Protestants alike. For Ellen
and Richard, her religion, pregnancy and class profoundly threatened the
commercial and social relationships on which their upward social mobility
depended. It's easy to imagine the bitterness of the showdown where they
dismissed Frances and the scramble to hush it all up. William was told to
extricate himself from his disreputable affair.

But he refused, instead declaring he would marry Frances. This
was unthinkable for his parents. How could a pregnant, working-class
Catholic become their daughter-in-law? How could the product of his
shame become the family's legitimate heir? William must be driven out.

New capitalists

He packed his bags and sailed for New Zealand. Frances joined him for their wedding.

The couple had defied many taboos but each still clung to the one that ran deepest. When the baby arrived, Frances wanted a Catholic baptism, William Church of Ireland. While they argued, baby William died. The couple's misery seemed complete. They had lost home, family, friends, country, and now their baby too. Even this last taboo crumbled for William as he witnessed his wife's grief. Their next two children, both daughters, were baptized Catholics.[23]

William and Frances appear to have braved this tragedy and made an excellent fist of settling in a new country. According to the family narrative, William became a successful sheep-farmer.[24] He never saw his parents again, though he visited Ireland after World War I, when they were long dead, and told his story to other family members. He died in New Zealand, at an advanced age.

William's defection left Ellen wondering who would modernize the factory. She had little support from her husband, who turned sixty that year. It's said he had become 'a little fond of the bottle'[25] and he regularly disappeared on long salmon-fishing trips.[26] Nearly seventy herself, she considered her remaining five sons.

Robert was contentedly immersed in his studies at Trinity and had no wish to leave. Another son was preparing to qualify as a doctor, a third ran the family shop; neither of the two youngest was ready in Ellen's view to replace William on his own. She also had three daughters: her daughter by her first husband had married and left home in 1865, another daughter had died and the last was deaf-mute since childhood. Her hopes rested on her sons.

The moral pressure she exerted on Robert was too strong to resist. 'I can't manage without you,' he later quoted her as saying, 'you're the only one I can trust.'[27] He reluctantly left the academic life he loved and returned to Killarney to partner his younger brother John in running the factory. The two men collaborated cheerfully enough, at least at first. They established benchwork in 1884,[28] installed more machines[29] and

13

instituted regular hours: 8 a.m. to 6 p.m. on weekdays, 8 a.m. to 5 p.m. on Saturdays. The ready-made era had arrived and people who could never previously have afforded shoes were buying them. Thanks to the brothers' innovations the danger from English competition receded. The firm established a reputation for agricultural boots, their sturdiness reflected decades later in its international brand-name: 'Tuf'.

A charcoal portrait from a photo of Robert at this time shows a dapper man in a chalk-striped coat, with a jaunty smile and a trim moustache.[30] One of the first men in Killarney to use a penny-farthing bicycle, he eventually set up an agency for Raleigh cycles. In the 1880s he and John bought and let three houses in Hogan's Lane, central Killarney.[31]

With their new landlord status and growing wealth, the brothers would not have felt particularly safe. Moonlighters' outrages in Kerry were still rising: 339 instances[32] took place there between August 1885 and June 1886 alone. Cattle were 'hocked',[33] barns burned, money and guns taken and people shot.[34] Some shopkeepers were attacked for snapping up evicted farmland, or 'landgrabbing'. Robert and John appear to have held back from evicting tenants or acquiring property outside the town until the Land Wars died down. Whatever caution they exercised paid off: no outrages are recorded against the family.[35]

The Ireland of Ellen and Richard's heyday was slowly passing but their sons adapted pragmatically to the new one. The Land Acts of 1881–1903[36] gradually ended the Land Wars by allowing thousands more tenants, mostly Catholics, to buy out their rented land-holdings.[37] These changes in land ownership eroded the Protestant Ascendancy and added to the wealth of a growing Catholic middle class.[38] Leaders of the Land League found safe seats in Parliament within the Irish Parliamentary Party, abandoning demands for fundamental land reforms and instead joining the peaceful campaign for a form of devolution known as Home Rule.

Greater class mobility for a new layer of Catholic property and business owners brought new prestige to indigenous culture and a less agitational approach to much of the nationalist movement. The Gaelic revival, for which John Hilliard professed sympathy, demanded the renewed use of the Irish language, the respectful study of Irish literature and music, and the playing of Irish sports.

The Hilliard brothers thrived in the political climate of the 1890s and early 1900s. Widespread support for the Irish Parliamentary Party sat happily with self-enrichment and the pursuit of profit. Although the Gaelic revival and the Fenian tradition also fed new, more combative organizations, such as the Irish Socialist Republican Party, set up in 1896 by the revolutionary socialist James Connolly,[39] and Cumann na nGaedheal (later Sinn Féin), set up in 1900 by the socially conservative Arthur Griffith;[40] these were still only embryonic. Robert and John advanced their own interests with little opposition.

Court records show their readiness to take legal action against anyone who crossed them. For instance, they used a court order to force an indentured factory worker called Deborah Willey to continue working, against her will, when she wanted to leave her job as a cutter.[41] With the Land Wars safely over, they also used the courts to enforce a long series of evictions.[42] Further mechanization helped them hold down factory pay: when John stood for election to the town council he was accused of 'starving half Killarney'[43]; though that didn't stop him getting re-elected several times. The brothers bought and demolished numerous houses to expand the factory,[44] evicting tenants and occupying so much of the area that eventually Hogan's Lane was renamed Hilliards' Lane.

John Hilliard was an enthusiastic entrepreneur with an occasionally hot temper – in 1903, for example, he appeared at the Petty Sessions Court charged with using 'language and gestures' which were 'calculated to provoke a breach of the peace' (the charge was dismissed).[45] He soon took over the family's High Street shop from another of his brothers and rebuilt it on a larger scale.[46] In 1897 he purchased Castlelough, a lakeside mansion hotel.[47] Renamed the Lake Hotel, it did so well that in summer he farmed out his sometimes reluctant[48] children to his brother Robert and other family members. Eminent guests included the

Swift Blaze of Fire

painter-taxidermist Alexander Williams, whose landscapes and specimen trout still adorn its walls.[49] John eventually became the town council Chairman.[50] In 1907 Robert would be sworn in as a Justice of the Peace.[51] Both had become prominent local figures.

But Robert never stopped mourning his lost academic hopes or his time as a young student in Dublin. He would carry works by Virgil or Cicero in his pocket until the day he died, pulling them out to read when he got the chance. In a letter to his second son, written in advanced old age, he would confide that he still thought often of 'moving to Dublin altogether'.[52]

No child of his would suffer a similar disappointment, he resolved. Like many a parent made to abandon a cherished ambition, he decided his heirs must carry it out. Young Robert's horizons would not be limited by balance sheets, bottom lines or the littleness of a small town. He would study Classics, he would complete a degree at Trinity College Dublin, he would have the academic or professional career for which his father had longed. Nothing must stand in his way and no sacrifice was too great if it brought these things about. Old Robert's stern resolution on this score would dominate young Robert's early life.

2
'A FIRM DESIRE TO DO RIGHT'

A sepia photo of Robert junior, mounted on a pendant, shows him as a full-lipped toddler with a shock of wavy blond hair. It's hard to see whether he had yet developed the pronounced squint for which he later wore glasses. Alice had three daughters after Robert, Mary (known as Moll), Phyllis and Margaret (known as Marjorie). The couple's fifth and last child, William Geoffrey, would arrive in 1915.

Young Robert's formal schooling began at the local Church of Ireland national school. In a student debate, years later, he would joke that he was at the bottom of his national school class while the girls in the class were at the top.[1] In reality he came third in his infant class in 1910, albeit behind two girls.[2] His father was already tutoring him in Greek and Latin, imparting a lasting love of the classics and a foundation in philosophical argument. Moll shared these lessons and soon showed such a flair for languages that a governess was found to teach her French and German.[3] Unusually for those times, Alice and old Robert championed their daughters' education as vigorously as that of their sons.

Just how hard the old man drove all his children is shown by a letter written years later to his younger son Geoff at boarding school. He was scorching about Geoff's wobbly spelling: 'Such spelling as this disheartens me about you. Is it carelessness, or indifference, or some mental disease? It will come against you in afterlife, exposing you to failure and ridicule.'

The letter then corrects every single mistake in Geoff's last letter before jumping from good spelling to moral rectitude with a speed showing the importance of both in old Robert's mind: 'It [poor spelling] is disheartening to me and it deprives me of hopefulness as to your future. I would like to think of my son as being truthful and honourable, scrupulously so. Also as careful and industrious at the same time, generous as he could afford to be in money matters and desirous of helping others even at his own inconvenience. I would like him to have a religious sense of duty and to have a firm desire to do right.' Geoff kept this letter all his life, harshly critical though it was, passing it on to his eldest son, a sign of the weight the children placed on what their father said.[4]

My mother remembers Robert senior from childhood stays with her grandparents. Though only a toddler, she sensed the goodwill behind his rigorous exterior. He was:

> ... a very kind but very deaf old man ... He would take his teeth out and put them on the mantlepiece, then hawk and spit in the fire, where it would splutter and bounce from coal to coal to my great amusement and delight. He was always amiable but a bit scary, as he could not be talked to because he could not hear ... He tried to bridge the gap by taking me on his knee and letting me listen to his pocket watch and look at the workings inside, all shining gold; but he could not make real contact as we could not communicate. He seemed very tall to me, when he stood up, and he had very stiff and hairy trousers that tickled my legs when I sat on his knee. I think they would have stood on their own.[5]

Evidently the old man's trousers were as formidable and upstanding as he was.

Like her husband, Alice took her children's moral education seriously. When her son was ten she gave him a black leather-covered King James Bible, inscribing the flyleaf: 'Robert M Hilliard with Mother's love', and 'Prov.3

'A firm desire to do right'

Ch.5&6'. Those verses read: 'Trust in the LORD with all thine heart, and lean not upon thine own understanding: In all thy ways acknowledge him, And he shall direct thy paths.' She wanted him to plot his course by relying on God's commands rather than ideas he worked out for himself. It was a prescient choice of text. For years of his adult life Robert would oscillate between following his 'own understanding' and obedience to divine authority.

Young Robert Hilliard had boundless energy. He and his sister Moll swam in the lakes, roamed the countryside and played in the streets. When he had a new bicycle he shared it with Moll and the two of them took turns to hurtle down hills with the brakes off.[6] When he got into fights he asked her to hold his glasses; without them his eyes lapsed into their natural squint, so that opponents rarely knew where his fists would land. Robert was a shocking tease, even to loyal little Moll. He once led her over a series of ditches in the Muckross woods, leaping across with his longer legs and laughing as she fell into them and soaked her clothing with mud.[7] But Moll was a scamp too. One evening she persuaded a playmate to pee in a tureen of soup that they had found cooling on the windowsill of a Killarney restaurant. Afterwards the boy was racked with such guilt that Moll, all innocence, convinced him to confess. They went back and he owned up, but the owner begged the children to tell no-one because all the soup was served and eaten.[8]

There was much to enjoy in Killarney for children whose parents could afford to feed and clothe them. Travelling circuses featuring horseback stunts and the trapeze were one excitement; children would watch them set up their tents at Fair Hill, on the east side of the town.[9] The town hall hosted boxing events, which Robert may have watched. Dances were held at the dance hall near the Great Southern Hotel, in particular the annual International dance, attended by military men from England and other parts of Ireland. Children lined the road to watch grandly dressed visitors arrive in horse-drawn carriages and the young Killarney women coming on foot in their best clothes, some wearing dresses sent specially by relatives in the US. As the dancing began, the sound of waltz music echoed through the streets.

Swift Blaze of Fire

There were film shows twice a week in the upstairs room at Market Cross town hall, and when Robert was six years old the Kalem Film Company, based in New York, arrived to begin shooting what over four years became nearly thirty films set largely in and around Killarney, of which eight survive. *Come Back to Erin* (1914), for instance, includes footage of Killarney's annual livestock fair, which brought crowds of farmers from miles around to strike deals and socialize around the noisy cattle and sheep in their pens. Robert and Moll must often have watched the Kalem crew at work. Perhaps this early exposure to filmmaking was the start of the fierce enthusiasm for the movies that he would later express in the debating rooms of Trinity College.

A family portrait, taken in about 1912 when Robert was eight, shows him in a sailor suit and glasses. In everyone's family there are photos which we look back on with a sense of dramatic irony. 'Do you remember?' we say, 'that was before …'. There we sit in these pictures, so oblivious; little do we know. Alice, Robert senior, and five children regard us here with unruffled tranquillity, yet epoch-making events were happening or poised to begin. Within two years a world war would start; within ten years Ireland and the world would change so much that everything about the formally dressed figures in this sepia photo would look archaic. And, at some point between the two, the rather prim-faced little boy in the sailor suit would reject beliefs they all took for granted as they stood or sat there, gazing at the camera.

The convulsions already shaking Ireland and mainland Britain had begun in 1911 with The Great Unrest, a tide of strikes in key industries. In Ireland these were led by the Irish Transport and General Workers' Union (or ITGWU), founded by James Larkin and led by him and James Connolly. Connolly's vision of revolutionary workers' struggle cut across religious divides:

> The day has passed for patching up the capitalist system; it must go.
> And in the work of abolishing it the Catholic and the Protestant, the
> Catholic and the Jew, the Catholic and the Freethinker, the Catholic
> and the Buddhist, the Catholic and the Mahometan [Muslim] will

> co-operate together, knowing no rivalry but the rivalry of endeavour toward an end beneficial to all. For . . . socialism is neither Protestant nor Catholic, Christian nor Freethinker, Buddhist, Mahometan, nor Jew; it is only Human. We of the socialist working class realise that as we suffer together we must work together that we may enjoy together. We reject the firebrand of capitalist warfare and offer you the olive leaf of brotherhood and justice to and for all.[10]

This cross-sectarianism enabled the ITGWU to recruit Protestants in the north,[11] a nightmare for a government that feared unity between Protestant and Catholic workers above all else.

To head off the possibility of an Irish revolution, Parliament passed a Home Rule Bill in 1912,[12] which devolved a limited range of powers to a new Irish parliament. Though a modest measure,[13] it was too much for northern Irish unionist leaders. With British Tory support, they threatened armed revolt. Unionist MP Sir Edward Carson[14] pledged to oppose Home Rule by 'all means which may be found necessary'[15] and formed a private army, the Ulster Volunteers, later the Ulster Volunteer Force. By 1913 he was drilling over 100,000 men in the north. Irish nationalists countered by establishing their own Irish Volunteer corps up and down the country.

Nationalists in Killarney set up a company of Irish Volunteers in November 1913, in a building at the back of Upper High Street,[16] and the town swiftly became a hub of Volunteer activity. The Killarney men had almost no weapons but that didn't stop them drilling and marching. At four o'clock every Sunday morning the Hilliards, like other residents, would hear their trumpet sound as they began their dawn parade, with another parade in the evening. As numbers grew, they sent members out to start similar companies in other south Kerry towns.

Robert senior and John would have been anxious that the rising tide of strikes across Ireland during the Great Unrest should not reach their factory, and heartily relieved at news of the defeat of the Dublin Lockout strikes in 1913.[17] This defeat was a terrible setback for Irish labour.[18] It left strikers' families struggling to survive. James Larkin and James Connolly, the Irish workers' movement's leading organisers, now had a far weaker base.

Swift Blaze of Fire

Meanwhile the Unionist backlash was strengthening. In 1914, officers at the Curragh Camp, the main base for the British Army in Ireland, mutinously declared they would refuse to impose Home Rule. The head of the British Army promised not to give any such order.[19] Encouraged, the UVF bought a large supply of arms from Germany. The British government caved in. As World War I began in August 1914, Asquith passed a Bill to delay Home Rule until war ended.

The machinery of world war rolled into action. James Connolly was sickened by the spectacle of social democratic leaders across Europe, who had once argued that workers of the world should unite, calling on workers to march off and slaughter each other for the sake of competing empires. Many Irish enlisted but thousands of others were angry at the postponement of Home Rule and flocked instead to join the Irish Volunteers.

In the summer of 1914 the Killarney Irish Volunteers held a Great Oireachtas: a week of music, dance, signalling and drilling competitions, exhibitions and parades. People came by train from as far away as Dublin and Waterford. Bands played – 'brass, fife and drum, and pipers' – as thousands filled the streets to watch the Volunteers march past.[20] To the crowd's amazement the Killarney unit, 'led by Michael Spillane, son of an old Fenian,' held rifles with fixed bayonets.[21] The Kalem Film Company, which employed many Volunteers as extras, had provided them with weapons.[22]

Robert Hilliard senior was probably unimpressed. He had seen the Fenians and the Land League come and go and would have expected all this marching to die down sooner or later. Such predictions seemed borne out by a split in the Volunteer movement later that year. Thousands of Volunteers were persuaded by Irish Party MP John Redmond to halt demands for independence and support the war effort, trusting Westminster to bring in Home Rule when war ended. But these Redmondites never became a significant force in Killarney and volunteer membership only dropped briefly there. Killarney Volunteers continued to march and were highly successful at disrupting army recruitment meetings.[23]

Robert senior opposed Home Rule at any time, either in 1914 or at the end of the war. Six months earlier he had written to a local newspaper to

'A firm desire to do right'

say that in his view granting more men the vote[24] had 'brought to the top in our Councils the greatest mountebanks and most irresponsible persons in the community,' adding that he feared Home Rule would have similar effects.[25] When the week was over and the crowds gone, he ploughed on with plans for a new family home, completing the purchase in December 1914.[26] Ireland is divided into areas called townlands; both the new house and its townland were called Moyeightragh. It was a detached house on an acre of land near the edge of town, larger than their current home. The children loved it.

As young Robert grew older his insatiable energy attracted comment. He used to turn up at the Lake Hotel at all hours to play by the lakes with Robin, one of John's sons, who was two years younger. 'He's here again!' John's family would say, groaning because he came so very often.[27] The two cousins spent happy days fishing, sometimes from the lake shore, sometimes from a boat. Eels lived under the stones in the water by the hotel dump at Muck Sand and cousin Robin enjoyed spearing them with his mother's hatpin.[28] Robert also liked to explore the hotel on his own, finding his way to parts of it which would have been out of bounds had anyone known what he was up to. Inevitably his adventures led to a spectacular accident. Just before his tenth birthday in 1914, he fell through the skylight of the Lake Hotel kitchen roof.

The drama of Robert's fall has been recreated in countless family retellings. With a crash which shocked those present into statues, this flailing child burst in above their heads, the light catching his halo of fair hair and the shower of jagged glass fragments surrounding him as he descended the thirteen feet to the floor and landed, in his cousin Robin's words, 'on his arse.'

The event made such a big impression on Robin that in 2004, aged ninety-eight, he could still give me a vivid description of it. 'We thought the glass would kill him, if the fall didn't!' he said. Robert amazed everyone by getting up unharmed. His father noted his providential escape in the same New Testament where ten years earlier he had recorded his birth:

Swift Blaze of Fire

> Sunday 5 April 1914
>
> On this day my son Robert, playing on the roof of the kitchen at Castlelough [the Lake Hotel] with his cousins, fell through the skylight direct to the tiled floor. He received no injury though the height from which he fell was thirteen feet. Robert M. Hilliard.

Robin remembered things differently when he told the story ninety years later. According to him, Robert wasn't playing with his cousins at all; it was entirely his own idea to go on the roof and he was a very naughty boy. He interpreted the event as a signal that Robert was a born rule-breaker – a warning finger pointing towards his future delinquency in becoming a communist, or a 'Red', as Robin phrased it. To this day, the fall from the roof is one of the most frequent stories told about Robert by family members.

What lay behind Robert's childhood recklessness? It's not uncommon for young children to disregard their own safety but most of us are taught caution as we grow older by juvenile injuries and the fear of pain. For Robert, the lesson had not sunk in. He was brought up knowing he had a lot to achieve and perhaps this was the cause. Children living with psychological pressure can remain heedless of danger or pain, throwing themselves into challenges with a curious fearlessness, as if their minds are on something else. As we've seen, old Robert had his own dissatisfied inner voice and could be relentless in criticizing his children. Young Robert was brought up knowing that however well he did, and beloved though he was, he was not yet good enough. 'I will try to be better' was a phrase he would use in adult life.[29] It's easy to imagine him using it often in childhood as he strove to avoid disappointing his father.

He knew he must soon leave Moyeightragh. His father's next plan was to send him to Midleton College, a prestigious school founded in 1696 to educate the children of Church of Ireland families. The small town of Midleton was near Cork, so Robert would have to board. In September 1915 he mounted the steps of the school's imposing entrance, ready for his first term.

He didn't last long. His parents removed him at Christmas, with a speed suggesting he was too unhappy to continue. At least one other family member had serious problems at the school: his cousin Phil, sent soon afterwards, would complain into old age that its unsupervized dormitories allowed a culture of 'horrific bullying' which had left him 'black and blue'.[30]

In January 1916 Robert made a fresh start, this time at Cork Grammar School. He would remain there until he was sixteen. Throughout the aftermath of the Easter Rising in April 1916 and the revolution which followed, he would be living away from his family, first in central Cork and later in central Dublin, two cities at war. The turbulence of his schooldays would expose him to life-changing influences, and to experiences – often horrifying, sometimes inspiring – which his parents could neither foresee nor control.

PART II — SCHOOLDAYS IN TWO WARZONES

3

UNSETTLED CONDITIONS

Robert's time at boarding school had a decisive effect on the whole course of his life.

The Cork Grammar School building gave him an unpleasant sense of physical constraint. It was far smaller than Midleton College, box-shaped and built of tan-coloured brick, with a front door at pavement level, more like a house[1] than a school and too small for all the boys. There were no outdoor grounds where they could run about. Classrooms, dormitories and the rooms where the headmaster lived with his family were crammed into this one building. A recently added wing housed a science laboratory and a partly covered area used as a gymnasium and drill shed.[2] The land behind the school fell steeply away into an area known as 'the quarry', preventing further extension. There was a long-running plan to relieve the overcrowding by finding larger premises, but it never bore fruit, and during his time there Robert never reconciled himself to the lack of space. Three years after entering the school, he wrote a composition in which he 'dreamed' it had bigger grounds, a swimming lake and a large library.[3]

Wealthy, landed Irish Protestants sent their children to English public schools; their aspirational middle and lower middle-class counterparts chose schools like Cork Grammar.[4] Its stated raison d'être was preparing

Swift Blaze of Fire

boys 'for University, Army, Navy and Civil Service, Legal and Medical Professions and Mercantile Pursuits.'[5] Robert's parents hoped it would educate him for an academic or professional career in Ireland's British-run establishment. Enclosed in a separate network of Protestant 'schools, hospitals, clubs, youth groups and support services'[6], it did its utmost to function as if the rebellion gathering force in the city did not exist.

But the school's location and lack of grounds meant its pupils could not ignore what went on around them. It stood on a hillside, above and to the west of the main railway station, not far from a soldiers' home[7] and a Royal Irish Constabulary barracks. From its south windows the boys looked out across rooftops towards central Cork; from nearby St Patrick's Hill they could see Patrick's Bridge, crossing the River Lee and leading into Patrick Street, Cork's main avenue. At night, sounds of the city floated up to Robert's dormitory on the top floor with little to muffle them. As time went by, some of those sounds would become deeply disturbing to the worldview he had been brought up to hold.

Cork must have seemed vast to Robert, compared with Killarney.[8] A major port and naval base, it was also a centre of banking and industry. Robert, being a boarder, lacked day-boys' freedoms, though school excursions to the cinema, the municipal swimming baths or a hired field for sports lessons,[9] gave limited opportunities to observe more of the city. A nearby attraction was Thompson's bakery on the corner of York Street, which filled the air with tempting smells.[10] Also nearby was the arched gateway to the Christian Brothers' College, Cork's most prestigious Catholic school. It was a sore point that this college always thrashed Cork Grammar at rugby.[11]

Signs of war were everywhere. Half a mile uphill from the school stood the forbidding grey entrance to Victoria Barracks, Army headquarters for the whole province of Munster. Army vehicles passed near the school; soldiers, too, marching down the hill from the Barracks to the railway station, on their way to the Western Front. One motive for Irish men to enlist was that their wives – known as 'separation women' – received 12s 6d a week, with extra for children,[12] enough to keep a family out of the workhouse. Many paid a heavy price for this allowance. The Gallipoli campaign, just ending in January 1916, had been spitting out corpses and maimed men from the Royal Munster Fusiliers since the previous April, and there were plenty of injured soldiers on Cork's streets.

There were also the ragged, hungry and homeless. Malnutrition was rife and nearly one in eight Cork children died in infancy.[13] German U-boats had begun sinking Cork's shipping in February 1915,[14] causing severe food shortages which were aggravated by profiteering. The Grammar boys were better fed than many, but high food prices eroded the school's spending on everything else. The Head complained that 'it was difficult to get staff during the war and at our meagre salary scale'.[15]

Despite this widespread hardship, any talk of the war that Robert heard at school was supportive of the Allies. The Defence of the Realm Act (DORA) of 1914 prohibited 'the spread of false reports or reports likely to cause disaffection to His Majesty,' outlawing the expression of anti-war or anti-British feeling. Union Jacks fluttered everywhere, from Victoria Barracks to the Recruiting Office in Patrick Street to boats on the River Lee. Cork looked like a loyal city.

But this veneer of loyalism was cracking. On Friday 17 March 1916 the 4,000-strong annual St Patrick's Day parade marched through the centre of Cork. For the first time, it included no contingent of British troops. The Parade Committee had refused to permit their inclusion and instead allowed 1,000 Irish Volunteers to take part, 'many carrying rifles and pikes'.[16] The music of the bands would have reached Cork Grammar School. Did the boys notice the absence of British tunes and realize what it presaged?

The strain of two terms at different boarding schools is imprinted on Robert's face in a photo taken while he was at home for Easter, just after his twelfth birthday on 7 April. His father had his own anxieties that spring. James Connolly had brought the Irish Transport and General Workers' Union to Kerry the previous autumn and it was spreading.[17] To the Hilliards' dismay, their factory workers were joining it.[18] The family saw the ITGWU as a menace to prosperity.[19]

Swift Blaze of Fire

This was to be an Easter like no other. On Good Friday and Easter Saturday word spread in Killarney of extraordinary events. Sir Roger Casement, a British ex-consul, had been arrested in Tralee Bay, not thirty miles away, accused of trying to land a consignment of guns from the *Aud*, a German ship intercepted by the British Navy on its way to the Kerry coast. Rumour had it the guns were intended for a nationalist Rising.[20]

The news rapidly became even more astonishing. On the way to Cork Harbour under British Naval escort, the *Aud*'s German captain had scuttled the ship with the guns still on board, to prevent their capture.[21] Police and soldiers scoured the Tralee area for the Volunteers sent to meet Casement. On Easter Sunday, prominent Irish Volunteer Eoin MacNeill published a notice in the *Sunday Independent* countermanding the order for a Rising in Kerry, thus revealing that a Rising had been planned. And then, on Easter Monday, it began.

As it turned out, the Easter Rising chiefly took place in Dublin. Thirteen hundred or so rebels, drawn mostly from the IRB and the Volunteers but also including James Connolly and his Citizens' Army, occupied the Post Office in Sackville (now O'Connell) Street and other key locations. They issued a stirring Proclamation declaring Irish freedom and promising an Irish republic that would end religious and class injustices. After a week of fighting, superior British troop numbers and ordnance overcame the rebels.[22] The death toll was 116 soldiers, 16 police, 64 rebels and – after heavy British shelling – 254 Dublin civilians, with over 2,000 civilians wounded. The civilian suffering caused many Dublin bystanders to jeer the rebels when they were marched out of the Post Office and other strongholds. A total of 3,430 men and 79 women were interned and 92 condemned to death, though not all death sentences would be carried out.[23]

For most people outside the IRB, Irish Volunteers and Irish Citizens' Army, the Rising came as a total surprise. No surprise at all to some of the Hilliards' Killarney neighbours, however, since the smuggling of arms into Kerry had been central to the original Rising plan. Kerry Volunteers had been ready to join in, but MacNeill's press notice had thrown them on the back foot. Now soldiers and police began moving through the streets of Kerry towns, arresting suspects in Killarney and elsewhere.[24]

Unsettled conditions

Robert got back to school after the holiday to hear that Easter week had been a disaster for Cork's Volunteers.[25] Many had travelled to Macroom to join the Rising, only to be ordered home, where they barricaded themselves into the Volunteer Hall until persuaded by Cork's Bishop Cohalan to surrender. Disarmed, handcuffed and humiliated, they were herded into Victoria Barracks, up the hill from the school.[26]

Their bloodless defeat prompted widespread derision and shame, but the public mood changed when news broke of the execution of the Rising's leaders in Kilmainham Gaol, Dublin. Seven leaders were shot on 3 and 4 May, another six the following week. There was an outcry at the government's lack of even-handedness. Three years earlier Edward Carson and his Unionists had imported German guns, prepared for armed revolt and bullied the government into postponing Home Rule.[27] Army officers had mutinied in support. All had escaped punishment. By contrast, nationalists were being shot as traitors. Executions and internments continued despite the protests, and seventy-four more suspected Volunteers were arrested across County Cork.[28] Thomas Kent, a Cork Volunteer who had taken no part in the Rising, was seized after a gun battle and shot on 9 May at Victoria Barracks.[29] The sound of the firing squad may well have reached the school. It was a dark moment for the city.

James Connolly was the last Proclamation signatory to be shot in Kilmainham Gaol. Unable to stand because of a gangrenous leg wound, he was tied to a chair and shot on 12 May. Surviving Rising detainees were deported to Frongoch prison camp in Wales. Sir Roger Casement, imprisoned in Pentonville for organizing the shipment on the *Aud*, was a public figure with an illustrious past as a diplomat. The British authorities soured public opinion against him by releasing pages from his diary to out him as gay, before hanging him for treason in August.

Few Union Jacks flew in Cork now,[30] and Empire Day on 24 May was barely celebrated. The Irish National Aid Association (INAA) helped dependents of Easter week's prisoners and dead by selling thousands of posters and flags.[31] On 23 June a demonstration rampaged through the city centre,[32] furious at a proposal from Lloyd George (swiftly dropped), to partition the North from the South and give only partial Home Rule.[33]

Swift Blaze of Fire

Protests were increasing, often small and spontaneous: hissing the royal family on cinema newsreels; singing rebel songs in public; raising the illegal Irish tricolour flag; ripping down Army posters. The Royal Irish Constabulary (RIC) reacted with heavy-handed arrests and prosecutions for sedition.[34]

How much did Robert and his schoolfellows know of all this? They saw the INAA posters and flag-sellers when they went outside the school, the trail of damage left by protests, the torn-up paving stones outside the *Cork Examiner*, which supported the British war effort, the repeatedly smashed windows of the Army recruiting office. They heard newsboys calling headlines about the executions and rebel songs being sung or whistled, even if only under people's breath. It can't have been possible to overlook the atmosphere of growing defiance.

It has been said that boarding school causes psychological damage comparable to being taken into care, 'but with the added twist that your parents have demanded it.'[35] Wild child Robert, used to the freedom of Killarney's streets, lakes and mountains, found his wings well and truly clipped. He worked hard, however, and did well in most subjects. The boarders' routine began with an early period of schoolwork before the day boys arrived.[36] The school set high standards: during 1916 a Cork Grammar boy came first in all Ireland in Latin at the Intermediate examinations, and fourth in Greek.[37] The Head, the Reverend Claude Blakeley Armstrong, had been a notable Classics scholar at Trinity College Dublin. Robert's classical studies flourished in this atmosphere. An avid reader, he was also good at English and developed a glib, zestful writing style. He enjoyed algebra and years later would charm his future wife by teaching her quadratic equations.[38] Divinity and science were subjects which his parents urged him to take seriously, but he became conscious of a clash between the two. He would later recall his school science lessons as he swung in adult life between belief in scientific empiricism and faith in divine revelation.[39] The school's other subjects were French, music, drawing, and commercial studies.[40] This last mattered to the school because 'for every student who went on to university ten went into business,'[41] but Robert knew his father wanted him to take a more academic path.

Full of energy, Robert did well at sports. The school had no tradition of boxing – his love of it would develop later[42] – but offered hockey (designated the school game in 1909),[43] cricket and rugby. These were sports associated with class privilege and loyalty to Britain, unlike the Gaelic sports played in most Irish schools.[44] Rugby pitted Robert against far more heavily built players but he found ways to work around this disparity and it became his favourite sport. He liked to play fly-half,[45] a position compatible with a small, wiry physique, and earned a place on the school team. However sports lessons and matches were never enough to exhaust a boy used to roaming the Kerry countryside. Very likely he was one of the pupils who scrambled into the out-of-bounds quarry behind the school, 'perform[ing] in it hair-raising Alpine feats'.[46]

One feature of the school's privileged social position was the militarization of school life. Many boys were from army families. All boys learned Swedish drill,[47] a British Army exercise regime. The school magazine's Roll of Honour recorded ex-pupils and ex-teachers killed or injured in action[48] and the school song included a briskly stoical reference to their deaths:

> We've toiled in many cities and we've sailed on many a sea
> We've fought the Hun in Flanders ... and some of us have died
> Yet our hearts are ever ringing to the murmur of the Lee
> And the good old School is still our pride.[49]

The Head held a Territorial Army commission and commanded the school's Officer Training Corps (OTC), which had its own rifles and military equipment.[50] Robert put off joining the OTC for three years, though he soon joined the Scout Troop.[51] It met half a mile away in South Mall and offered escape from the cramped school with the hope of summer camps.

Sombre announcements of past pupils and teachers killed or injured at the Front became ever more frequent that year. Robert saw boys around him hit by grief as they lost brothers and fathers. It became obvious that the war was going badly for the Allies. On 1 July 1916 hundreds of Irish soldiers were killed and thousands wounded at the Somme. In the holidays he found Killarney reeling at the number of its dead. At least sixty men from Killarney would be killed in the course of the war,[52] many of them at Gallipoli or the Somme. Support for the war was collapsing. By 1917 only 5 per cent of Irish men had enlisted, compared with 17 per cent in England, Wales and Scotland.[53] The sense of crisis pervading Britain and Ireland ended Asquith's prime ministership in December 1916. Lloyd George formed a coalition and began releasing Frongoch prisoners. These changes came too late to stem the tide of war disillusionment.

That disillusionment fed nationalist feeling in Ireland. Robert would only ever have heard nationalists described as 'Sinn Féiners' or 'Shinners', regardless of their affiliations, though the Easter Rising had been led by Volunteers and James Connolly's Irish Citizen Army, not Sinn Féin. The government and press gave Sinn Féin credit for it however, by lumping all nationalists together under their name, and this boosted the party electorally. In February 1917 Sinn Féin won its first Commons seat, at the Roscommon by-election.[54]

No school, however rarefied its internal atmosphere, could have stopped Robert or the other boys from becoming aware of the brewing storm. The school could not seal itself off, for example, from the wave of strikes which began to sweep Cork and the rest of Ireland during 1917. As news sank in of the revolution taking off in Russia that year, workers' power suddenly began to look achievable to many workers across Europe.[55] In the eyes of the British government, Bolshevism was a real and terrible threat. Thousands of workers joined the ITGWU; by the end of 1917 it had 4,000 members in Cork. Strikes repeatedly disrupted daily life: building workers, tram workers, bread van drivers, wool mill hands, gas plant staff, dock labourers and many more went on strike, or threatened to.[56] Even the privileged Grammar boys learned how effective strikes could be when the school's coal and bread deliveries were disrupted or the trams used by day-boys failed to run. With the growth of Russian soviets, or

Unsettled conditions

workers' councils, the word 'soviet' entered the language of Irish revolt. During the Irish revolution, there would be at least 100 self-dubbed soviets as workers took control of workplaces or towns. Not all strikes were successful, but many more were than before the war. So many men were at the Front that a unionized workforce could sometimes win its demands with a strike warning. This in turn encouraged more strike warnings and more strikes.

Marches and demonstrations often started at the railway station, not far from the school, making a noisy background to some of the boys' lessons. The increase in such marches and the ferocity of the riots in which they sometimes ended were another signal of a mounting rebellion. As each gathering assembled the hubbub grew, until the band struck up and the crowd set off along King Street (now MacCurtain Street) for the city centre, passing close to Cork Grammar. When the RIC tried to break things up, the pandemonium could last late into the night. From February 1917 onwards, Volunteers flouted the DORA by restarting parades.[57] The crowds which these events attracted were winning control of the streets away from the police.

The biggest disturbance Robert heard that year was the 'Battle of Patrick Street', on Saturday and Sunday 23 and 24 June 1917.[58] It began at the railway station with a 10,000-strong march to welcome released republican prisoners. Bands played as the marchers moved towards the city centre. Separation women attacked them outside the Soldiers' Home in Glanmire Road, scuffles broke out and shots were fired. Saturday ended in riots, which lasted until midnight. On Sunday, further clashes with separation women and an attack on the recruiting office led to a battle of unprecedented intensity with police around Patrick's Bridge and in Patrick Street. Demonstrators stoned police, police used bayonets and rifle butts and there was gunfire from both sides. One man, bayoneted by police, bled to death. The windows of thirty-four businesses were smashed. Eventually army vehicles thundered by near the school as soldiers joined the fray from Victoria Barracks. Their machine guns scared the rioters away, but disturbances rumbled on for days.

Any illusion that they were secure from the hostilities outside was lost for Robert and his school-fellows on Sunday 2 September 1917, when Irish Volunteers penetrated the school itself.

It had been a rowdy weekend. The previous evening a crowd hundreds strong had attacked three women and their American escorts outside the nearby Palace Theatre[59] and rioted for hours in Patrick Street. Similar noisy clashes were starting as the boys went to bed on Sunday night. While the school supposedly slept, Volunteers broke in, raided the Officer's Training Corps armoury and stole all the school's weapons. One estimate of their haul was 'about fifty Lee Enfield and Martini Henri rifles, as well as revolvers and even a quantity of swords.'[60] Daniel Healy, one of the Volunteers involved, later gave this account to the Irish Bureau of Military History:

> In September, 1917, a very successful raid for arms was carried out at night on the grammar school, Sydney Place, off Patrick's Hill, Cork. In this school there was an officers' training corps for young Protestants. ... About twenty of our lads took part in the raid which resulted in the capture of about thirty [sic] rifles. ... There was no interference from any enemy force. ... The guns were safely removed to a temporary hiding place.[61]

The raiders had entered using a duplicate key for the street door which had been prepared from an impression made by Con Twomey, a man hired to do a painting job at the school premises.[62] Discovery of the security breach came at eight o'clock next morning, when the armoury door was found forced open. The school magazine's report tried for a light-hearted tone: 'We heartily congratulate the boarders on their plucky attempt to capture the thieves, especially those of the dormitory which overlooks the armoury. They would certainly have succeeded in not only recovering the arms but capturing the thieves had they not been asleep.'[63]

In reality, given the noise that night, the boys in that dormitory may well have been awake, terrified into silence as they listened to the intruders' stealthy moves only yards away. Their nerves were tested further the next night by more King Street clashes and shouts of 'Up Dublin!' and 'Up the Huns!' An American officer later commented, 'The Sinn Féiners made quite a row.'[64]

Unsettled conditions

Many boys' next letters home must have alarmed their families. Cork Grammar was already in trouble and this raid did not help. Boys were being removed from the school. Academic standards slipped as it struggled to keep students and an adequately qualified staff: 'The difficulty of retaining good staff, the unsettled war conditions and the general unrest in the years after the Easter Rising no doubt contributed to the fall in examination results ...'[65]

Trying to regain control[66] as disturbances continued that autumn,[67] the RIC arrested the city's leading republicans,[68] who went on hunger strike. Angry crowds gathered outside the men's prison, forcing their release in November. That same month another crowd welcomed a freed republican prisoner at the station before marching up Patrick's Hill. Led by the Brian Boru pipers' band, which used loud two-drone warpipes, marchers headed for the band's meeting rooms in Hardwick Street, down the road from Cork Grammar School, where they clashed with the RIC. The boys would have heard the blaring bagpipes in the narrow street give way to thuds and screams as stones flew and the RIC bludgeoned marchers with batons and rifle butts, injuring sixteen. The noise must have been deafening. A group of senior police later broke into the band's rooms, smashed the instruments and assaulted a nearby Irish language class, hospitalizing several students with severe injuries.[69]

Robert went home at Christmas at the end of a momentous year. During 1917 Cork had seen a massive resurgence of strikes, a large proportion of Cork people had turned against the war, Volunteers and the ITGWU were defying the DORA to march through the city, Sinn Féin had celebrated wins in four by-elections[70] and the police were losing control of the streets.[71] It was a far cry from the calm, loyal place his parents had believed they were sending him to when they withdrew him from Midleton. The social order he'd been brought up to serve was coming apart at the seams.

He was still only thirteen. Whatever insecurity or distress he experienced, whatever his misgivings about the future, it's unlikely he felt able to confide them to his parents, who were investing a great deal in his education and wanted him to stay at Cork. The conflicts going on in young Robert's mind would intensify as the Irish revolution began in earnest.

4

'SOLIDARITY, SPONTANEITY AND DIRECT ACTION'

In Killarney for Christmas, Robert would soon have heard from his shopkeeping family that Volunteers were bypassing shopkeepers, distributing food to ease the desperate shortages:

> When the farmers stopped bringing potatoes into the town this was a blow to the poor people ... So Spillane and O'Sullivan [Michael Spillane and Michael O'Sullivan, leading local Volunteers] detailed Volunteer officers to collect them and bring them in to the Volunteer Hall and sell them at cost price .... The butchers, who were never very Irish, were sending the meat to England. Spillane and O'Sullivan ... told them unless they kept sufficient meat for their ordinary customers they would see that the meat was dumped into the river at Cork.[1]

Robert returned to school in January 1918 to find milk and potatoes in short supply and no butter or bacon at all.[2] No doubt anxious parents sent food parcels when they could. The Famine of the 1840s was within living memory, and in the rebellious atmosphere of 1918 plenty of people were prepared to use direct action to prevent its repetition. Cork's trade unionists and Volunteers patrolled docks, railways, slaughterhouses and

'Solidarity, spontaneity and direct action'

butchers' shops to enforce a ban[3] on meat exports.[4] Food depots were set up[5] to stop farmers using scarcity to push up prices. These measures had an effect.[6] Food was still scarce, but the city escaped outright famine.[7]

Such direct action from below added to the sense that the British state was losing its grip, a sense which grew stronger in April 1918 as the government discussed the conscription of Irish men,[8] prompting a furious backlash. Clusters of fearful but defiant people gathered in the streets awaiting developments. Many wore badges saying 'Conscription? Not damn likely.'[9]

In the middle of this crisis, Cork Grammar School's OTC (re-armed since the previous year's raid) held a field day in Ballincollig, near Cork, returning by train. With astonishing insensitivity, those in charge detoured the boys through Patrick Street instead of going straight back to the school. As a result they were sworn at and attacked (the word 'blessings' in this school magazine report is of course ironic): 'we ... finally marched at about two hundred paces to the minute [sic] through Patrick Street, where we came across a crowd anxiously awaiting the latest news of conscription. Needless to say they showered pieces of wood and their ... blessings on our heads.'[10]

Robert was not yet an OTC member but would have heard all about this confrontation. It showed the city's mood. The school's day-boys could travel to school in civilian school uniform without harsh words or missiles being thrown at them, but the sight of these privileged mini-soldiers quick marching round the city centre had pushed people too far.

On 15 April Parliament passed the legislation[11] which enforced Irish conscription. Cork's city leaders protested; churches prayed; a surge of recruits joined the Volunteers;[12] but what halted conscription in its tracks was a general strike, called by the Irish TUC. On 23 April everything stopped. Throughout the country, 'Railways, docks, factories, mills, theatres, cinemas, trams, public services, shipyards, newspapers, shops, all were affected, even the Government munitions factories, and the stoppage was complete and entire.'[13]

In Cork up to 30,000 people signed an anti-conscription pledge at probably the biggest meeting so far in the city's history. Women pledged

Swift Blaze of Fire

not to take the jobs of conscripted men. All the usual sounds of a working city were stilled and everything ground to a halt.

Tellingly, the strike included a number, albeit limited, of Ulster workplaces. The Unionist newspaper *The Irish Times* described 23 April as 'the day on which Irish Labour realised its strength.'[14] The government understood at once that it had lost a crucial battle. That night Sir Henry Wilson, an Irish Unionist who was Chief of the Imperial General Staff, wrote in his diary: 'Lloyd George was full of abuse for Ireland and said he wished my d[amne]d country was put at the bottom of the sea.'[15]

Irish Labour had indeed realized its strength. Irish conscription was a dead letter.

Suddenly the streets around Cork Grammar School were busier than ever as military traffic in and out of Victoria Barracks increased. The government would be unable to fight the war if general strikes spread to Britain or other parts of the Empire. This remarkable display of Irish working-class solidarity posed a genuine threat to British imperialism globally. As twelve thousand more troops poured into Ireland, Cork swarmed with soldiers and armoured cars. Royal Defence Corps units guarded the railways.[16] The government issued an Empire-wide proclamation stating that Irish rebels were conspiring with Germany in a 'German Plot'. There were raids, mass arrests, internments and deportations to England without charge or trial.[17] Prisoners rounded up in Co. Cork and Kerry were brought to Cork by rail. In yet another defiant demonstration near the school, a large crowd gathered at the station to cheer them as they were taken to Cork Gaol.[18]

Repression deepened on 23 July when Sinn Féin, Cumann na mBan,[19] the Volunteers and the Gaelic League were all banned. The next day all gatherings, including trade union and sporting events,[20] were also banned unless they had a police permit. Police broke up any meetings they found – though there were a great many they did not find[21] – and arrested those they caught. This one-sided ban forbade Irish sports but not 'British' ones.[22] Robert and his schoolfellows could play cricket, hockey and rugby without

'Solidarity, spontaneity and direct action'

permits but there were ugly scenes as police rounded up and assaulted men and boys at hurling matches. On 4 August the Gaelic Athletics Association defied the ban by holding matches at three o'clock in every Irish parish. Attended by an estimated 100,000, these marked the beginning of the end for the restrictions.[23]

British measures were hardening attitudes. That autumn Lord French, Lord Lieutenant of Ireland, began an all-out recruitment campaign. Cork echoed to military parades, recruiting leaflets fell from the sky in a series of airdrops, there were shows of 'thrilling lantern slides from the front' and a clock was stuck up outside the GPO to tally recruits.[24] It all failed hopelessly. Cork provided only 12 per cent of its target.[25] The second (and last) recruiting meeting was howled down.[26]

French's efforts did however succeed in raising pressure to join the OTC in schools like Robert's. The school magazine records that he joined that autumn. A photo among the school records taken in 1919 shows the OTC drilling in a field; they wear breeches and puttees, carry wooden practice rifles, and their faces are grave.

Robert would discover eighteen years later in Spain that the International Brigades saw OTC experience as an asset. Perhaps his schoolboy training was one of the things in his mind when he wrote to his wife before the Battle of Jarama, 'I think I am going to make quite a good soldier.'

Cork Grammar School sent the boys home for eight weeks when the 1918 influenza pandemic struck Ireland in mid-October, giving the Christmas holidays an early start.[27] Robert spent Armistice Day on 11 November in Killarney with his family. Only Protestant church bells rang in celebration, though the sense of relief was widely shared. In the snap general election that followed the Armistice, Sinn Féin won nearly three-quarters of Irish seats.[28]

With the school closed there could be no Speech Day.[29] Robert nevertheless had a prize to bring home: the Dill Medal for Classics.[30] This was a pewter disc, engraved with a laurel wreath, Robert's name and the year. His parents were proud of it and so was he, proud enough to keep it into adulthood. His wife, my grandmother, gave it to me not long before she died.

43

Swift Blaze of Fire

Tensions rose further within the school in 1919. Robert and his schoolfellows were penned into the school building but the arms raid had shown that those who might be hostile to them were not necessarily penned out. There were more gaps in the familiar faces around Robert as more boys left the school, withdrawn by anxious parents. Many Protestants were leaving Ireland, and the exodus from Cork was especially large.[31] The military occupation of the city fuelled two forms of revolt: armed nationalist conflict and a further build-up of strikes and occupations by Cork's workers. Both impacted on everyone living there, including boys at the school.

In Dublin on 21 January 1919 Sinn Féin inaugurated an independent Irish Parliament, Dáil Éireann, which promptly declared Irish independence.[32] The same day, Volunteers seized a cart of gelignite near Soloheadbeg, Co. Tipperary, killing its police escort.[33] Sinn Féin was quick to dissociate itself from the shootings,[34] which highlighted the gulf between its focus on the dignified apparatus of a new state and the Volunteers' efforts to kick-start a guerrilla war.[35] Four days after the first Dáil meeting, a general strike spread across Belfast,[36] drawing in both Protestant and Catholic workers and 'present[ing] Dublin Castle with its most fearful moments'.[37] For three to four weeks the city was under workers' control,[38] run by the strike committee.[39] There was mass unrest all over Britain, too, including a mass strike on the Clyde in Scotland. British state power was starting to look decidedly shaky. As intelligence officer Basil Home Thomson said, 'During the first three months of 1919 unrest touched the high-water mark. I do not think that at any time in history since the Bristol Riots we have been so near revolution.'[40]

Robert probably heard frequent mention of 'Bolshevism' at this time. More general strikes were bringing whole cities and even the whole of Ireland to a halt. On 13 April 1919 the Trades Council of Limerick also began a general strike. Workers' councils governed the city for a fortnight and declared it the 'Limerick Soviet'.[41] On 1 May a general strike in Southern Ireland celebrated Mayday.[42] Again workplaces in Cork fell silent, with 8,000 workers demonstrating outside the ITGWU offices.[43] In Belfast,

'Solidarity, spontaneity and direct action'

100,000 Protestant and Catholic workers marched together under union banners and red flags.[44]

From autumn 1919 onwards, Dublin Castle clamped down even harder with thousands of raids,[45] trials held on often arbitrary charges, attacks on civilians, suppression of newspapers, the banning of the Dáil,[46] and the burning of properties.[47] The Irish Republican Army or IRA, as the Volunteers were now known,[48] began a policy of ambushing and killing RIC members[49] and the Dáil called a boycott of the RIC.[50]

Staff at Cork Grammar struggled to maintain normality. Whatever Robert felt about the turmoil in the city, he worked hard. At Easter he won the Lord Bishop's Prize for Divinity, another achievement to delight his parents. In summer 1919 he published a story in the school magazine called 'A Glimpse of Future Grammar'. It tells of a potion offering travel to the future – 'You may be sure I drank without hesitation' – and continues with a tour of the future school. He finds a plaque listing the school's war dead, a new boarders' building and new playing fields. 'At the back there was a large artificial lake where boys were accustomed to swim during the hot weather. It also had a large library, containing an extensive collection of books.' The school was actually saving up for the memorial plaque,[51] new boarding house and playing fields,[52] but the swimming lake and large library were Robert's own inventions. He was still homesick for Killarney and its lakes and, with his love of reading, longed for a bigger and better library than the school could offer.

In its efforts to keep order, the school sometimes resorted to severe canings. The autumn (Michaelmas) issue of 1919 saw publication of Robert's poem 'Corporal Punishment', in which a boy is beaten until he shrieks with pain, can hardly walk and goes home weeping. The poem shows scant sympathy however: children were expected to endure such beatings with humour and bravado. Robert turns the boy's suffering into jokey doggerel: 'And then the cane goes up and down – / The yells can be surmised./Ah, Readers! do have pity for/The lad that is chastised. At last the painful work is done/The boy bewails his fate/As he goes home in agony/With slow and limping gait.'

45

Swift Blaze of Fire

Although the school debating society had discussed in 1916 whether corporal punishment should continue,[53] Robert's poem didn't question it. Unlike the child in his poem, he couldn't go home to be comforted if he was beaten and had to cope on his own, forcing himself to smile. He would use laughter all his life to face down fear or pain. No doubt other boys learned the same harsh lesson; denial of one's own miseries is after all part of what boarding schools teach.

Fighting in Cork grew even more fierce from January 1920 onwards. The IRA seized weapons by attacking RIC barracks in the surrounding towns, driving police forces to take refuge in Cork city. Increasingly police attacked civilians. On 11 March the IRA shot policeman Timothy Scully in Glanmire, northeast of Cork. RIC officers retaliated by attacking civilian homes in the city. On 19 March the IRA shot RIC Constable Joseph Murtagh as he returned from a funeral and the next day a gang of men with blackened faces shot dead the newly elected Mayor of Cork, Tomás MacCurtain, in front of his family. The coroner's verdict concluded that MacCurtain was 'wilfully murdered under circumstances of most callous brutality; that the murder was organised and carried out by the Royal Irish Constabulary, officially directed by the British government'[54] – something most people had worked out for themselves.[55] The whole city stopped for his funeral on 22 March and thousands of grim-faced mourners thronged the streets.[56]

The day after the funeral Robert and the rest of the school rugby team played a Junior Cup match against the Christian Brothers' College. Headmaster Armstrong had once described these arch-rivals as 'much too heavy and old for us',[57] but this time the Grammar School boys were the victors. A team photo shows Robert sitting cross-legged next to the enormous trophy, looking smaller and younger than most of his teammates. He must have been far smaller than opposing team members. Returning from the match the boys wanted to sing and cheer, but the staff had learned after the OTC incident to ensure pupils showed respect for the feelings of Cork's citizens: '... on the drive back to the school we were unable to exercise our lung power to its full extent, on account of the City's mourning for the late Lord Mayor.'[58]

'Solidarity, spontaneity and direct action'

That same month a new police force arrived to support the RIC, nicknamed the 'Black and Tans' after the mixed colours of their uniform. To this day their name is synonymous with terrorism against civilians.[59] Their Cork headquarters was in Empress Street, 500 metres from Cork Grammar School, so the boys saw plenty of them. The new force carried out random beatings, tortured, raped,[60] murdered, looted and burned down homes and businesses.[61]

Robert's sister Moll had by this time enrolled at Rochelle School in Cork. Some distance from the city centre, with extensive grounds, her school was shielded from the many signs of conflict to which Robert's was exposed. However on a train journey to Killarney, Moll endured such humiliating treatment from a group of Black and Tans that Alice and Robert senior decided there must be no repetition and arranged for her to spend future holidays with a friend.[62] The Hilliards were loyal to the Crown, but to the Crown's forces their daughter was just another Irish girl, a fit target for terrifying abuse. The implications weren't lost on Robert. Years later he would tell his wife and children about the absolute fear the Black and Tans inspired.[63]

He published another poem, called 'The Daily Round', in the spring 1920 issue of the school magazine. The school needed to create an impression of unruffled continuity, so Robert's trite lines were probably just what the magazine was looking for. Robert tells of 'day-boys coming, clean and bright/With satchels full, and hearts as light/As anyone could wish for' and – despite the repression of non-'British' sports gatherings – breezily describes how 'At Rugby then 'tis next we meet/In any kind of rain or sleet/And do our very best to beat/Whatever teams oppose us.'

But the contrast between the tone of these verses and events around the school was glaring. The boys must often have smelled smoke, heard screams and explosions, felt the vibrations of vehicles from the nearby Barracks or RIC headquarters and wondered what would happen next.

The school had lost its headmaster when Armstrong left in 1919 for a new job in Dublin. Two temporary heads came and went before the arrival later in 1920 of Houston Larmour Doak, a young classicist and published

Swift Blaze of Fire

poet. Doak's brief headship coincided with the most violent period of the independence struggle, which 'made for a tense background to [his] tenure there'.[64]

Yet again, Cork came to a standstill[65] on 13 April 1920 when an indefinite national general strike began in support of sixty-six prisoners[66] held without trial in Mountjoy Prison, Dublin, who were on hunger strike for political status.[67] Workers' councils took over the administration of towns and cities in many parts of Ireland.[68] In Cork the Trades Council took charge of bread distribution.[69] Huge crowds gathered outside Mountjoy Prison. By 15 April the authorities were obliged to release the prisoners.[70] More strikes followed: dockers refused to unload armaments for Crown forces and rail workers refused to transport military cargoes, armed soldiers or more than twenty military personnel even if unarmed.[71] It became common to see groups of soldiers stranded on station platforms.[72]

Revolt even reached the RIC. Policemen mutinied in Listowel and Killarney when new broom Divisional Commissioner Smyth[73] announced a shoot-to-kill policy against any civilians who failed to raise their hands when ordered: 'You may make mistakes occasionally and innocent persons may be shot, but that cannot be helped and you are bound to get the right person sometime. The more you shoot the better I shall like you and I assure you that no policeman will get into trouble for shooting a man.'[74] The RIC men who leaked Smyth's chilling speech[75] must have known they were signing his eventual death warrant. Over a thousand men left the RIC in the subsequent three months.[76]

Robert's last summer term at Cork Grammar was a time of spiralling violence. IRA member Sean Healy, who in 1920 lived undercover in York Street, close to the school, describes the sounds to be heard in this part of Cork at night:

> ... we listened to the rumbling of the British Curfew lorries outside. Boisterous voices of the English soldiers could be clearly heard in the night air as they were holding up and interrogating some poor unfortunate citizen who happened to be on the street. An occasional shriek could be heard from somebody who was being beaten up by the 'Black and Tans.

'Solidarity, spontaneity and direct action'

The noises from the throbbing engines were frequently interspersed with shots from rifles and revolvers, fired by the soldiery. Even the public service clocks and street lamps were used as practice targets by some of the forces of 'Law and Order'.[77]

A deafening explosion shook the school on 1 July as an IRA bomb detonated at the RIC station, round the corner in King Street. The building was gutted. The next day the IRA hijacked an Army vehicle at nearby Glanmire Road station. On 12 July three Cork RIC stations were burned, two of them close enough for the boys to see the flames.[78]

On 17 July the IRA at last caught up with DC Smyth at Cork's exclusive County Club, and shot him.[79] Gunfire echoed through the city that night as soldiers and Black and Tans, intent on revenge, took over the streets, shooting at random, killing one man and wounding about forty more.[80] Shootings of ex-servicemen and civilians continued during clashes on 18 July.

Robert was sixteen when he left the school. Facets of his adult self were already emerging: Classics and Divinity student, highly competitive sportsman, confident writer, eloquent joker who tried to laugh off his own anxiety or pain. He was indelibly marked by his time in Cork. Strikes, demonstrations and the spirit of revolt had generated a heady mood: 'there is no denying the extraordinary class triumphalism that gripped the people ... This counter politics stood for the rejection of capitalism, and the celebration of solidarity, spontaneity and direct action.'[81] The school had not been able to insulate him from this current of 'solidarity, spontaneity and direct action'. Despite the atrocities of the Black and Tans and the constant nervous tension of life in a place of violent conflict, Robert had found something inspiring in those years.

What process would turn this son of a factory-owning, bourgeois family into a man who would one day march through Barcelona, revelling in the fact that the working class had taken power there? It's not far-fetched to suppose the seeds of this process lay in Cork. His intellectual development in that city coincided with the spectacle of working people repeatedly taking control and winning victories.[82] It also coincided with the

49

Swift Blaze of Fire

onset of a regime of state repression so brutal that despite his upbringing and boarding school conditioning he was revolted by it. In 1920 Robert was still only a half-formed thing, certainly not yet a conscious socialist, as his debating contributions at Trinity College Dublin would soon make clear. But at some less conscious level he was making a significant shift. When he met his future wife, four years after leaving Cork, he told her he had started to become a socialist when he was sixteen.[83]

5

A VERITABLE HELL

Robert's father had enrolled him for a 'finishing' year at Mountjoy School in Dublin, the city where he himself had once dreamed of a different life. The old man remembered a place of scholars, poets and playwrights, gracious eighteenth-century terraces and famous public houses where men of learning exchanged witticisms, with the stately Liffey flowing through its heart and the Wicklow hills in sight. Dublin still boasted all those things but had also kept its reputation for squalor.[1] Most Dubliners' homes were decaying and overcrowded. When Robert arrived in 1920 it was still scarred by the Easter Rising. Though rebuilding had begun,[2] the GPO was a ruin behind its fire-stained façade and there were many empty spaces and bullet-pocked walls.

Above all it was an occupied city, patrolled by armoured vehicles and tense with sudden gunfire. From July 1920 another new force, the Auxiliary Division, appeared on Ireland's streets, a heavily armed paramilitary unit recruited from British officers. Like the Black and Tans, the 'Auxies' were infamous for their brutality and readiness to kill. IRA fighter Dan Breen describes the non-stop searches in Dublin by the Army, Black and Tans, Auxiliaries and RIC:

> It was quite a common thing for a pedestrian to be held up and searched six or seven times in one day. The Crown forces jumped off lorries and searched and questioned passers-by. They boarded tramcars and 'frisked' every passenger. They surrounded whole blocks of buildings and, for days on end, kept a cordon drawn tight while every house was searched from cellar to attic.[3]

There were covert operations too. An intelligence-led death squad of British agents, based in Dublin Castle and known later[4] as the Cairo Gang,[5] had been carrying out targeted assassinations for months. In Dublin as in Cork, explosions, gunshots, screams and the sounds of forced entry might pierce the air at any time, day or night. For Robert the stress of life in a city under occupation was all too familiar. His new school, like his last, was close to the city centre. He had only to step outside to see the khaki uniforms and guns and sense the febrile atmosphere generated by searches, raids and killings.

Mountjoy School, at 6–7 Mountjoy Square North, had opened in 1896. Mountjoy is one of Dublin's loveliest Georgian squares, four sides of 1790s Palladian redbrick with gardens in the middle. When Robert boarded there the square had a faded air and was a locus of political activity, home to socialist activist Delia Larkin[6] and socialist playwright Sean O' Casey (the Black and Tans raided his flat while Robert was a pupil at Mountjoy School[7]). During 1919 the Dáil had met clandestinely a few doors along from the school.[8] Several key IRA meeting places lay within a half-mile radius: for example, Shanahan's pub at 134 Foley Street[9] and an outfitters at 95 Talbot Street[10] were places where IRA men were sheltered, Devlin's pub in Parnell Square was an HQ for IRA chief Michael Collins, who often slept there,[11] and a stable in Great Charles Street was an IRA arms dump.[12]

Robert joined a class of twenty boys in Mountjoy School's oldest year group. His parents paid an entrance charge of ten shillings, fees of £18 8s 2d per term, plus 16s 8d for laundry and medical care and 23s 6d for 'extra' subjects – though French, science and games don't seem like extras to us today.[13] The total was £21 8s 4d, about £966 per term in today's money and

A veritable hell

a big outlay for his father, who had five other children to provide for. Some boys paid additional sums for new sporting items such as games caps and cricket trousers but Robert did without.

Mountjoy School, like Cork Grammar, was proud of its high academic standards and its service to the British armed forces: 500 past pupils had enlisted during World War I, with seventy-four killed. The Head, Reverend William Anderson, all twelve staff and the 200 or so students were members of the Church of Ireland. The school was partly funded from endowed land and property, managed by a Board of Governors who had no scruples about discriminating against Catholic tenants.[14] As with Cork Grammar, there was a gulf between the traditionalist ethos of Protestant loyalism within the school and the fracturing of the social order outside it.[15]

That fracturing became even more violent over the autumn of 1920 as the forces of law and order sacked, shot up and wholly or partly burned down twenty-four Irish towns. IRA commander Tom Barry described the methods used by the Auxiliaries in these operations:

> Men and women, old and young, the sick and the decrepit, were lined up against the walls ... No raid was ever carried out by these ex-officers without their beating up with the butt ends of their revolvers, at least a half-dozen people. . . . on more than one occasion . . . they stripped all the men naked ... and beat them mercilessly with belts and rifles.[16]

Two atrocities had an impact on Robert in his first term at Mountjoy School, one in Dublin and one in Cork. The first soon become known as Bloody Sunday.

On the morning of Sunday 21 November, at various Dublin addresses, the IRA shot between fourteen and twenty men identified to Michael Collins as members of the government death squad run from Dublin Castle.[17] News of the shootings reached Dublin Castle as fans were pouring into the city to watch Dublin play Tipperary in a Gaelic football match at Croke Park. The stadium was half a mile from Mountjoy School, across a canal, close

Swift Blaze of Fire

enough for the stands to be within earshot of Mountjoy Square. About 5000 spectators crowded in, many from Tipperary, oblivious of either the IRA shootings earlier that day or the Crown forces' determination to impose a collective punishment.

Soon after the game began at 3.15, eighteen Crossley tenders (armoured vehicles) carrying police and Auxiliaries drove down Russell Street, passing near Mountjoy School, and spread along Russell Street Bridge and Jones's Road, adjoining the stadium. Some of these forces entered the ground, others began firing from the road. In less than five minutes, they discharged 228 rounds of small arms fire and fifty rounds of machine-gun fire. Spectators and players took a few seconds to grasp that they were the targets. Seven people died at the scene, including two children. Two others died in the stampede to get out, scores more suffered bullet wounds, many serious, and five people died of wounds afterwards. No policeman or soldier was injured.[18]

A quickly-held enquiry, in camera, concluded that spectators began the firing and that the RIC returned fire without orders. In effect this exonerated police and army officers, though their testimony was frequently contradicted by spectators. Cross examination was not permitted. The enquiry's conclusions were reported on 8 December 1921 but the government withheld release of the evidence and proceedings until 2000, nearly eighty years later. To this day we have no comprehensive, reliable account of events in the stadium on Bloody Sunday.[19]

Everyone in Mountjoy Square on that day, including boys at the school, must have heard the gunfire and the not-so-distant screams. Some spectators were shot as they tried to escape over the stadium walls. The tenders blocked access to Russell Street, so few if any of the fleeing and injured would have made their getaway past the school; nevertheless it must have been obvious in the Square that an act of atrocious, terrifying violence was taking place on the other side of the canal.

It's only possible to speculate what account of events Mountjoy School's masters gave their students that day. Whatever they said, we may be sure that Bloody Sunday would have been fresh in Robert's mind when he learned of the burning of Cork three weeks later.

54

A week after Bloody Sunday, the IRA ambushed a patrol at Kilmichael, Co. Cork, and killed 17 Auxiliaries. Robert may have heard in a letter from home that all of Munster (southwest Ireland) was placed under martial law as a result.[20] Then, on the evening of Saturday 11 December, the IRA killed one Auxiliary and wounded another twelve in a grenade attack at Dillon's Cross in north Cork. The Auxiliaries' revenge was swift. They set fire to homes in the Dillon's Cross area and afterwards ran amok, torching central Cork. One Auxiliary who took part wrote to his mother: 'Many who had witnessed scenes in France and Flanders say that nothing they had experienced was comparable with the punishment meted out in Cork.'[21]

Whole streets were levelled and buildings in other streets gutted. People were pulled from their beds and shot out of hand. Shops were looted and burned; thousands lost their livelihoods overnight. The City Hall and Carnegie Library were destroyed along with Cork's public records. The arsonists spared Cork Grammar School but not all the buildings nearby. The night sky over the city was red with flames. Next day the city centre looked as if it had been bombed.

Reports were on every newsstand in Dublin by the following Monday. 'Cork city in flames!' the newsboys of the *Irish Independent* sang out, 'Night of horror!' Robert's first thoughts must have been of Moll, still in Cork at Rochelle School. Was she safe? He was unlikely to have known that she was until he got home for Christmas some days later. What else did he think of as he contemplated those descriptions of familiar places, now razed, blackened and smoking, in the city where he had lived a quarter of his life?

His mental tumult while travelling home can't have been improved by the presence of soldiers, now able to travel by train. They cast a threatening pall over the journey and endangered passengers by turning trains into a target for IRA attacks. Union leaders had ended rail workers' long refusal to carry soldiers and military materials earlier that month.[22] For those opposed to British rule, the train drivers' boycott had boosted morale and exemplified the effectiveness of collective action. Calling it off was a depressing blow to the independence struggle. IRA attacks on individual trains would be far less effective than the boycott and would cost civilian lives.

Killarney was no longer the place Robert remembered from his childhood, where he could run about freely as if in a vast playground. He found members of the Crown forces tyrannising over the local population. One account tells of Auxiliaries searching every man or boy who entered or left Killarney during much of that autumn, detaining them for hours.[23]

Five days before Christmas a group of Auxiliaries smashed shop windows and forced their way into all the shops in Killarney, looting whatever they wanted.[24] This included the Hilliards' main shop, where they looted blankets.[25] The authors of this fear and destruction were making sure of their own supply of Christmas spirit in Killarney's public houses. They would 'put a bomb on the counter and then call for what they wanted, needless to say without paying, the bomb being apparently intended as a threat if they weren't served'.[26]

In such an atmosphere it was difficult for Robert or anyone else in the family to enjoy Christmas.

It's hardly surprising that something was seriously amiss with Robert in the spring term, physically or psychologically or both. He'd already been absent from lessons more often than any other boy in his class during the previous term – three days in September, six in October, a day in December – but that spring the school register records that his absences rose to a startling eighteen days, most of them consecutive. No-one else in his year group came close, so there was no school epidemic of illness.[27] He had robust health as a rule and it would have been almost impossible for a boarder to malinger or truant. Whatever the cause, it must have aroused concern at school and at home.

Robert had spent most of his schooldays away from his family in two out of the three most violent cities in Ireland.[28] So far he had coped with the constant alarms generated by living in the midst of hideous conflict. Now he had cause to worry about his family as well. It's highly likely that the tensions were at last taking a toll on his health, including his mental health. If one possible explanation for this spate of absences is a physical illness, another is that a period of acute emotional distress made him unfit for lessons.

A veritable hell

Adolescence can hardly have made things easier. School records suggest it caught up with him in a rush that spring. It's a period when rapid physical change can trigger depression and anxiety as well as rebelliousness. The school charged his parents for so many new clothes that term – jerseys, knickers, stockings – that he must have had a major growth spurt. Dancing shoes costing 8s 11d brought his footwear and clothing charges to the highest of any boy in his year.[29]

Robert was the only boy in his class charged for dancing shoes. There's no recorded bill for school dancing lessons, so he appears to have had them elsewhere, or was perhaps invited to the home of a school friend where he had an opportunity to learn. His wish to go dancing suggests a blossoming interest in meeting women and girls. Apart from the Matron,[30] the school was an all-male zone, but learning dances like the waltz and the foxtrot allowed him to gaze at, touch and talk to female partners. Newer, more risqué dances like the tango were catching on fast in Dublin and no doubt he wanted to try them too.[31] The urge to throw off his troubles by doing something exuberantly physical was typical of Robert. Months later, at Trinity College, he would describe dancing as 'the joy forever'.[32]

How far did he take his quest for release and excitement? If dancing shoes suggest a wish to meet women, he could meet them in the street. Three hundred yards south of Mountjoy Square was the Monto,[33] the biggest red-light district in Europe. James Joyce wrote of it as 'Nighttown' in *Ulysses*: it was the 'squalid quarter of the brothels,' located in a 'maze of narrow and dirty streets,'[34] visited by the schoolboy Stephen Dedalus in *Portrait of the Artist*. The brothels, run by famous madams like Betty Cooper and May Oblong, operated openly: 'Oh, there was about seven or eight kip houses, we used to live next door to them. Oh, they were grand-looking girls, seventeen, eighteen, maybe twenty. The kip houses were just ordinary houses, but you seen the men going in and out, in and out. The men'd come in with big cars, big shots . . . businessmen, British soldiers, officers in the army, British generals. Big shots!'[35] The school's location meant Robert saw prostitutes; turning the idea of

Swift Blaze of Fire

visiting them into reality would have been difficult,[36] but perhaps not impossible.

Both sides of the independence struggle escalated their terror tactics in 1921, with hundreds of attacks and counter-attacks in Dublin between March and June. On the British side there were shootings out of hand, torture, house-burnings, thousands of internments without trial and convictions under martial law, often followed by hangings. Military vehicles carried civilian hostages as human shields.[37] The IRA mounted ambushes, shootings, grenade attacks and eventually house-burnings and hostage-taking.[38] The dumped bodies of more than seventy men and women were found between January and April 1921, shot by one side or the other.

Street clashes and ambushes took an increasing toll of civilian lives, and not just in Dublin.[39] There was nowhere Robert could feel safe. On 21 March the Kerry IRA attacked a train at Headford Junction, near Killarney, killing three civilians as well as an estimated twenty soldiers and two IRA members. Robert was not on this train, but he would have been on another like it at around this time, travelling home for the Easter holidays. The knowledge that he could be killed in a similar attack must have added to his parents' anxieties.

Back in Killarney, old Robert Hilliard's world had turned upside down. He believed in law, order, and a 'religious sense of duty',[40] but the Crown forces who were supposed to defend law and order were destroying lives and taking private property. His work as a Justice of the Peace had long been impossible. The IRA in Killarney had set up their own Parish and District Courts to hear local cases, some of them brought by ex-members of the RIC or even Lord Kenmare.[41] At the same time IRA units were burning down Protestant mansions in County Cork and Kerry and had recently begun demanding food and sometimes billets from loyalist Protestant homes. IRA commander Tom Barry explains this new billeting policy, which he oversaw in West Cork but which also occurred elsewhere: 'from February 1921 … Whenever possible British loyalists' houses were

A veritable hell

used as billets for the flying Columns and our own people got a chance to recover … in certain cases, the discipline and good behaviour of the IRA Column made non-supporters become our good friends.'[42]

There's a family story that Robert fed the local IRA men at Moyeightragh. Some versions say he repeatedly invited them round for a meal. Given Barry's account, what seems more probable is that an armed IRA unit arrived while Robert was at home for the holidays and demanded food at gunpoint.[43] If so, the family had little choice but to comply. Robert's nephew Stephen Hilliard tells the tale as he would have heard it from Moll and her sisters: 'On at least one occasion[44] … he fed the local IRA men downstairs in the kitchen of the family home in Killarney, leaving his nervous parents upstairs with strict instructions not to come down while he was entertaining these particular visitors!'[45]

Evidently Robert's first concern was for the safety of his parents and presumably his younger siblings: they must be taken upstairs out of harm's way. Returning to the kitchen he was likely to find boys his own age or little older among the IRA unit, some faces possibly known to him since early childhood. Perhaps he was already consciously sympathetic to the nationalist cause, given what had been going on around him in Cork and Dublin, or perhaps he was leaning that way – or perhaps, indeed, this breakfast at Moyeightragh was an example of the process described by Barry, where members of the column won a new 'friend'. Whether or not it was this encounter which tipped the balance, within a few months Robert would be making his mark in Trinity College debates as an outspoken nationalist.

Robert's growth spurt must have slowed over the summer term since there were no more charges for new clothes. However other extra bills suggest wayward behaviour. He was the only boy charged for replacing broken glass and the only boy needing 7s 6d in extra cash and a guinea in 'pocket money', largeish amounts in those days.[46] Whatever his reasons for needing extra money (they're not recorded), bad behaviour on his part would have been sternly punished. Anderson was a relatively liberal-minded Head, but harsh punishments were as much part of life at Mountjoy as at

Cork. He caned another boy so severely at about this time – eight cuts across the back, shoulders and arms – that the boy's mother sent a furious letter complaining of her son's 'bare-back flogging' and withdrew him. The school saw such canings as perfectly normal.[47]

It became evident that while the nationalist side weren't losing the war they also weren't winning. A waning of militant labour movement action didn't help. Strikes almost halved to 119[48] in 1921 when a slump hit Britain and Ireland.[49] As strikes and mass action ebbed, so did the particular kind of solidarity and optimism they bred. Keeping that spirit alive required union leaders to lead vigorously, avoid needless concessions and spread solidarity action. Instead they fell in behind Sinn Féin, who did not support strikes[50] and at worst actively discouraged them.

This is not to deny the high level of working-class support for Sinn Féin and the IRA. In the May 1921 election, 124 Sinn Féin MPs were elected unopposed.[51] Working women and men gave shelter and food to the IRA and passed them intelligence at great personal risk. But increasingly independence was being fought for in their name, by a minority of armed combatants, rather than by a mass workers' movement on its own behalf. It was now a war of attrition, inflicting grotesque suffering on civilians, with a vast imbalance of forces and materiel between the two sides. It might go on indefinitely if neither side called a halt but without the mass involvement of Irish labour it became hard to see how there could be outright victory. Sinn Féin's attempts to mount big, conventional attacks were going disastrously wrong. An IRA onslaught on Dublin's Custom House saw two civilians and six Volunteers killed, twelve Volunteers wounded, and up to a hundred[52] captured.[53] Conventional (rather than guerrilla) battles pitted the IRA against the best-resourced empire on the planet and they could not win them. IRA leader Michael Collins had remarked some time earlier, 'Well, we'll see which wears out first, the body or the lash.'[54]

The British government planned to break the impasse by keeping the North within the UK while securing a regime in the South that it could do business with. It had already recruited a new, sectarian Ulster police force.[55]

A veritable hell

In June 1921 it opened a new Northern Irish Parliament.[56] Sinn Féin's lack of interest in workers' struggles – for example failing to support the Belfast shipyard strike in 1919 – had left many Northern Protestant workers feeling they had nothing to gain from independence. This in turn left a vacuum for Unionist sectarians to fill, making British divide-and-rule easier. Having paved the way for partition, the government offered Sinn Féin a truce, allowing negotiations for a possible treaty to end the conflict.

That summer term was critical for Robert. He had to justify his parents' investment in his schooling by gaining a Reid Sizarship to Trinity College Dublin. This was a scholarship covering annual college fees and 'commons' (living expenses) for students who passed an entrance exam and whose families could demonstrate a limited income.[57] Robert bought extra books (the school charged 3s 10d for them) and buckled down to work.

On 11 July 1921, to general rejoicing, the British government signed a truce agreement with Sinn Féin. IRA leader Michael Collins was despatched to London with Arthur Griffith and treaty negotiations began within a week.

In the same month Robert passed his Reid Sizarship exam and was formally admitted to Trinity College Dublin. Aged only seventeen years and seven months, he would begin undergraduate life in October. As he would soon make clear, he had been changed utterly by his years at school in two war zones, radicalized into an ardent opponent of British rule in Ireland.

PART III — LITERATURE, GOD, AND THE STATE OF THE NATION

6
'THE DEAD BODIES OF THEIR OWN BROTHERS'

'With the first shot of the Civil War, the Irish counter-revolution had begun.'

Kieran Allen, *1916 – Ireland's Revolutionary Tradition*[1]

In later years Robert would look back on his time at Trinity College Dublin with longing: '... when I was at College I had in me the power to [do] good work. I don't mean just good writing and that sort of thing – I mean that I had in me the power to be a force for good in the world.'[2]

Filled with confident optimism, he moved into his new college room. Fellow student Lionel Fleming, who arrived in 1922 and later became a good friend, scornfully compared Trinity's shabby accommodation to 'a stage setting for a Sean O'Casey play,'[3] but Robert was only too pleased to leave school dormitories behind.

His tutor was Harry Thrift, MA, FTCD, a physics lecturer whose real interests were rugby (he was capped for Ireland eighteen times) and cycling. James Joyce had renamed him 'Shrift' and included his second place in Trinity's 1904 quarter mile cycling handicap race in *Ulysses*. If Robert hoped for helpful advice from 'Shrift' he was disappointed, as he was 'a perfunctory lecturer and indifferent tutor', with a 'peppery, somewhat bullying manner'.[4] Robert was expected to attend divine service every Sunday in the College Chapel, turn up for evening roll call and ask permission if he stayed out late (not always enforced).[5] He must attend 'Commons', a formal evening meal every weekday for Scholars, Fellows, Sizars like himself, other College members and guests. Female students were not permitted to attend. A bell rang at six o'clock and the meal began fifteen minutes later, with a Latin grace and the ceremonial slamming of the hall doors.

Despite the rules and rituals and his disappointing tutor, Robert, like his fellow students, found college life wonderfully easy-going after boarding school. Fleming describes the pleasure of feeling like 'ordinary men-about-town' when they went outside, 'at full liberty, either to get drunk in the pub round the corner or to pick up a prostitute', adding: 'few of us did either.'[6] Samuel Beckett, who entered Trinity in Robert's third year, would have disagreed: student drinking and brothel-visiting feature in his *More Pricks than Kicks* stories. Certainly some of Robert's contributions to debates testify to a growing love of drinking.

At last Robert was free to express his beliefs. There was nothing to stop students 'discussing literature, God, and the state of the nation, up to four in the morning,'[7] Robert's morning lie-ins matched his late nights and a family story tells of his father paying a surprise visit and his anger at finding Robert still in bed at a late hour.[8] Students' excited discussions reflected the intellectual upheavals going on at Trinity, where venerable certainties were being challenged as rarely before.

In Robert's father's day, Trinity had been dominated by Classical Studies and Divinity, its reputation personified by the eccentric figure of John Mahaffy, classicist, doctor of Divinity, Ancient Historian and the College's provost for five years until his death in 1919. By 1921, when Robert arrived there, Mahaffy's contempt for modern science and view of ancient Greece as the source of all civilized achievement[9] were still

'The dead bodies of their own brothers'

part of Trinity's intellectual furniture, but more scientific, less traditional academic approaches were also gaining support. Old prejudices were giving way to the pragmatic need for the college to relate to the likely prospect of Irish self-rule. In the year before Robert's arrival, a straw in the wind was the establishment of a Thomas Davis Society, named after the founder of Young Ireland and a gathering place for republicans.[10]

Fleming noted that though Trinity still 'bore the strong stamp of the Anglo-Irish gentry' there were three growing minorities: Catholics, sons of Northern Irish manufacturing families and the 'sons of ... Protestant shopkeepers of the south, who we (if we had been land-owners in Kenya instead of Ireland) might have described as "poor whites".'[11]

Being a 'poor white' may have sharpened Robert's determination to challenge the conservatism still much in evidence at the College. To this end he frequented the Classical, Historical and Neophyte Societies and soon attracted notice for his roistering enthusiasm in debates. *TCD*, the college magazine, reported at least twenty-one debating contributions from Robert in his first year.[12] A fellow student described him as 'a youth of seventeen, flaxen-haired and bubbling over with energy.'[13]

He quickly signalled his nationalism and anti-imperialism. In his first reported speech in November 1921 he spoke of 'the tolerance of the Irish Party', referring to the old Irish Parliamentary Party's over-willingness to tolerate deferment of Home Rule.[14] Soon afterwards in 'an excellent maiden' speech to the Classical Society he deprecated Aeneas, founder of the Roman Empire and an emblem of imperialism, calling him 'a wretched hero.'[15]

His first speech from the platform rather than the floor defended popular cinema, opposing a motion that 'This society disapproves of the hero worship of cinema stars'. The three most successful films of 1921 were Charlie Chaplin's first feature, *The Kid*, and two films starring Rudolph Valentino, *The Four Horsemen of the Apocalypse* and *The Sheik*. All three had gravely alarmed conservative opinion,[16] but the growth of this new medium delighted Robert. He argued for a thousand times more film enthusiasts, a billion rather than a million: 'Where now a million worship,' answered Hilliard/'If I'd my way, I'd like to see a milliard.'[17]

During his first year Robert took a consistent stand against cultural conservatism, speaking against motions which lamented the growth of 'inferior' literature, 'defective' modern education, the 'excessive' interest in athletics and the 'craze' for dancing. His zeal for modernity may be why he has been described in a number of accounts as a 'Marxist and an atheist' at this time, though *TCD*'s many reports of his speeches give no evidence of either belief.[18] What does emerge is that anyone hand-wringing over popular culture might find themselves up against Robert.

The exception to all this was his backward attitude to women, in which Robert was a product of his single-sex education and his times. He spoke against a motion condemning Cambridge's refusal to grant degrees to women,[19] and like other undergraduates made sexist jokes in some of his debating contributions.[20] Women had been admitted to Trinity to take degrees since 1904,[21] but still weren't allowed to join the major societies. Nor could they enter Trinity after 6 p.m., be members of the Common Room or elected Foundation Scholars or Fellows.[22] Life must have been difficult for female students, including Moll, who would follow Robert into Trinity in 1924. Male students saw women as a different breed; for example, an anonymous *TCD* article that term claimed that an equal education for women would create 'an abnormal, neuter type of human being.'[23] Robert wanted eventually to form a close relationship with a woman and in December supported a motion that 'There is nothing so sweet in life as love's young dream,'[24] apparently hoping one day to enjoy that dream himself. But Trinity gave him and his peers few opportunities to relate to women as equals[25] or even make friends with them.

In December 1921 news broke that Sinn Féin's negotiators Michael Collins and Arthur Griffith had signed a Treaty with the British. Its terms caused uproar. The bitterest blow for republicans was that it brought no republic. A new 'Free' State of twenty-six counties would remain in the British Empire, Britain would maintain three naval bases there and Dáil deputies must swear loyalty to King George. Six Northern counties would still be part of the British state.[26] At Trinity the Treaty had wide support but in Killarney at Christmas Robert found furious dissension.

It can't have been easy getting there. Railways were in chaos and roads were even worse, with trenches from pre-Truce ambushes lying unrepaired.[27] He found Killarney divided. His parents wanted peace because war was disastrous for business; they would therefore have leaned towards the Treaty, despite sharing other southern Protestants' anxieties about partition.[28] The *Kerry People* reported that the Sinn Féin Club unanimously opposed the Treaty but a week later the Club's chairman insisted it had reached no such decision.[29]

While debate raged, Treaty provisions became faits accomplis. In January the Irish Free State's Provisional Government was installed at Dublin Castle and the Dáil ratified the Treaty. Sinn Féin's leaders split and Treaty opponent Éamon de Valera, the Dáil's President, resigned. Labour and trade union leaders declared neutrality, paralysed by a wish to placate both wings of Sinn Féin. In practice, neutrality meant acquiescing to the Treaty. Partition would disastrously worsen sectarian divisions in the North and Northern Catholic workers were already losing jobs, homes and lives in a wave of Unionist pogroms – but Labour leaders stayed on the fence.[30]

The British military left Killarney in January. The IRA were supposed to take over policing[31] but both its pro- and anti-Treatyite members were preparing for civil war. Anti-Treatyites were already training in an IRA camp close to Killarney at Aghadoe.[32] Local republicans estimated 1,000 Kerrymen would take up arms against the Treaty if called on.[33] Talk spilled into action in February 1922, when thirty armed men took a large quantity of weaponry in a raid on Castleisland Barracks, fifteen miles from Killarney.[34] By then Robert had returned to Trinity.[35] He had made his own views clear to his family: he was against the Treaty.

Robert's first reported speech of 1922 was uncompromisingly anti-imperialist, in support of a motion 'That this [Historical] Society favours a grant of complete independence to Egypt'. Britain was in the

Swift Blaze of Fire

process of granting Egypt nominal independence after an uprising in 1919,[36] but planned to keep troops there and control its politics. Robert quoted Thomas Davis and drew analogies between Egypt and Ireland. Tempers ran high; another speaker became 'hysterical and almost unintelligible' at hearing criticism of the British Empire – but Robert won the agreement of half the audience and the motion passed with the Chair's casting vote.[37]

During the next week Robert took a clear stand against the Treaty in a debate on the motion 'That this Society welcomes the ratification of the Irish Agreement of December 6th 1921': 'Mr R M Hilliard declared that England would never have dared to renew the war on Ireland after the Truce. We would have attained independence merely by sitting still and not signing the Treaty.' Whether or not he was correct in this assessment, his stand was a brave one, given that the only other person voting with him was a diehard Unionist.[38]

Robert's readiness to overturn Trinity's shibboleths extended to his classical studies.[39] The assumptions of traditional classicists about ancient Greece had been fundamentally questioned for several years by a school of thought which applied archaeological discoveries to the study of the classical world, stressing the mystical and ritual qualities of ancient Greek religion as actually practised[40] and the power of Greek myth to express the unconscious mind. It's unclear whether Robert read the writings of Jane Harrison, who pioneered this line of scholarship, but he certainly read her collaborator Gilbert Murray, author of *Euripides and His Age* (1913) and many other works. Murray translated Euripides (a dramatist Robert especially loved), Aeschylus and other ancient Greek writers; Robert would later give some of Murray's translations as love-offerings to the woman he married, telling her how important they had been to him.[41]

Robert delighted in making fun of what was pompous or censorious[42] but there was usually something heartfelt at the core of his arguments. When he opposed a Neophyte Society motion that 'the present craze for dancing is a sign of the degeneracy of the time', for instance, *TCD* reported that 'Mr Hilliard fears to hide "the joy forever" by abolishing dancing.'[43] At first sight Robert was referring to Keats's *Endymion*: 'A thing of beauty is a joy forever', but it's likely that behind this line in his mind (and possibly Keats's) would have stood a choral lyric from *The Bacchae*, by Euripides. Gilbert Murray's translation of this lyric begins 'Will they ever come to me, ever again,/The long long dances,/On through the dark till the dim stars wane?'[44] It ends: 'And shall not Loveliness be loved for ever?' – a line which has also been translated as 'A thing of beauty is a joy forever'.[45] *The Bacchae*'s protagonist is Dionysus, god of wine, fertility and religious ecstasy. In defending dancing, Robert was not only defending the Dionysian tradition, whose devotees gained wisdom through rituals of dance, self-abandonment, drinking and music, but also his own wild streak, the release he found in drunkenness, his delight in the absurd and his sense that to behave respectably at all times would be to lose part of his identity.

Ireland was hurtling towards civil war that spring. The IRA had split into two factions: one for and one against the Treaty.[46] Not all opposition to the Treaty came from the IRA. Despite ineffectual national leadership, some Irish workers were still mounting successful strikes and occupations, declaring local workplace soviets and calling for a workers' republic.[47]

James Connolly had accurately predicted in 1914 that separating Ulster from the rest of Ireland would bring 'a carnival of reaction both North and South'.[48] The hideous carnival was already underway as the logic of impending partition took effect in the North. The IRA continued to attack policemen while death squads, composed in part of Ulster Special Constabulary members, carried out atrocities against Catholic civilians. On 24 March 1922 a group of armed men smashed their way with a sledgehammer into the home of the Catholic McMahon family, who had no links to the IRA, killed their father, four of his sons and a family friend, fatally wounded another son and assaulted a female family member. There were protests throughout Ireland. In Killarney, Robert senior and John Hilliard were among the signatories of a statement, signed by local Protestants, 'condemning the cruel murders perpetrated on the McMahon

Swift Blaze of Fire

and other families in the North, which have filled us with deep grief and horror … and we hereby denounce sectarian strife of all kinds and long to see complete unity.'[49]

The split in the IRA over the Treaty went to the top. Robert arrived home at Easter to hear that the anti-Treaty Éamon de Valera had visited Killarney on 18 March and given a bloodthirsty speech, in which he said his supporters must be ready to 'march over the dead bodies of their own brothers.'[50] On 14 April (Good Friday) news broke that 120 armed anti-Treaty IRA men had occupied Dublin's Four Courts. Michael Collins visited Killarney on 22 April to speak in favour of the Treaty. Anti-Treatyites issued threats against those planning to hear him, burned down the platform erected for him, and met him at the station with submachine guns. He had to hold his rally in the grounds of a Franciscan friary.[51] Anti-Treatyite Robert probably didn't attend. Back in Dublin for the summer term he again threw himself into debating.

He responded to a motion on 24 May 'That the present foreign policy of France is subversive of European peace' by again basing his arguments on an anti-imperialist position: 'Mr Hilliard darkly hinted that oil was the cause of the troubled waters in Europe at the moment. France does not want to be dependent on England for fuel in the next war.'[52]

The background to this was the carve-up of the Middle East between France and Britain by means of the secret Sykes-Picot agreement, exposed in 1917, and the Balfour Declaration of 1916, which was partly designed to strengthen Britain's position on the Suez Canal. Then, as now, the politics of the region were dominated by imperialist powers jockeying to control the region's oilfields. Robert was right to foresee another war. This speech and his earlier speech about Egypt were by far the most radical he is reported as making at Trinity.[53]

There was a fresh election on 16 June.[54] An entertaining anecdote in an *Irish Times* column written twenty-two years later in 1944 by Robert's friend Bert Smyllie claims Robert voted for the anti-Treaty Sinn Féin faction 'seventeen times before breakfast', using his college room-mate's identity.[55] Describing Robert as 'a fierce republican', Smyllie tells how the room-mate,

'The dead bodies of their own brothers'

an 'almost offensively ardent' Treaty supporter, was, as a result of Robert's deception, 'arrested on claiming the vote to which he was fully entitled.'[56] It's a great tale, but my mother has never believed it. She points out that the baby-faced Robert didn't look eighteen, and certainly not the voting age of twenty-one, so he was unlikely to convince a polling station to allow him to vote even once let alone seventeen times. No doubt this election saw fraud, but if multiple voting had been as easy as this, voting numbers would have exceeded the 62.5 per cent recorded. Perhaps Smyllie inflated the tale as years passed, or perhaps Robert had told his friend a shaggy dog story.

In the event, both pro- and anti-Treaty Sinn Féin candidates won fewer seats than in the January elections.[57] Labour did better than expected: all but one of eighteen Labour candidates were elected, on a ticket demanding a worker's republic.[58] Support for this demand was shown by a wave of new soviets and strikes by gas workers, rail workers, creamery workers and others.[59]

When two IRA members assassinated government adviser Sir Henry Wilson in London on 22 June, the British government's impatience turned to fury.[60] An ultimatum was issued: the Free State government must impose the Treaty at once or Ireland faced a full-scale invasion.[61] The Free State did as it was told. Britain provided two eighteen-pound field guns, later four, with instructions to bombard Dublin's Four Courts, where the anti-Treatyite republican garrison was still holed up. As the first shells fell, on 28 June, the Irish Civil War began. For the second time in six years, buildings in Sackville Street burned and Dublin echoed to the boom of field guns as two sides fought to control the city. The republican garrison surrendered on 5 July.

The British government bankrolled mass recruitment to the new Free State National Army and provided it with more guns and field artillery. As Free State troops gained control of the rest of Ireland they crushed all direct action by Irish workers, forcibly ending workers' occupations in Tipperary in July, driving occupiers out of creameries, tearing down the brave signs declaring 'We make cream not profits' as they marched further south and west, and harshly suppressing all remaining strikes and local soviets.

Swift Blaze of Fire

The Irish counter-revolution had arrived. With British help, Arthur Griffith's vision of a new Irish state, with its class relationships kept intact, was being rammed by force of arms down the throats of the Irish working class. By the end of July, Free State troops controlled all the South except Munster and parts of the west. By mid-August the conventional phase of the Civil War was over.[62]

Robert could no longer reach home by train.[63] To force the Free State Army onto roads, where they were easier to attack, anti-Treaty forces had blown up stations, bridges, rolling stock and the hub at Farranfore, north of Killarney, cutting off the whole area. Even if Robert and Moll could find a way to travel it was dangerous to try. Mail trains had stopped; Robert's family news came by phone or telegraph. He almost certainly had to spend the summer holiday in Dublin.

Free State troops landed on the Kerry coast in August, and took Killarney. Anti-Treatyites reverted to guerrilla methods and the Free State grew more ruthless. Torture, killing and dumping bodies became commonplace. A draconian Army (Emergency Powers) Resolution was passed by the Dáil on 18 October. Often referred to as the 'Public Safety Act', though it does not appear in the Irish statutes book, it permitted Military Courts to order the execution of anyone helping the anti-Treatyites.

The longest anti-Treaty resistance in Ireland would be in Kerry, where civilians suffered terrible effects. On 9 September 1922 republican forces recaptured Kenmare, Killarney's nearest port, stopping landings of food and gaining enough weaponry to fight until the spring. Over the winter, attacks on road convoys stopped any food reaching Killarney. People of all classes endured acute shortages. The *Cork Examiner* wrote of Killarney's 'pitiful plight' as it suffered 'genteel starvation.'[64] Shops closed; businesses failed. The Hilliards' finances came under pressure[65] and Robert senior sold some of his interests to his brother John. He would keep his son and daughter at Trinity – nothing must interfere with their studies – but money was short.

As Robert's second Trinity year began in the autumn of 1922 there were still clashes in Dublin. Lionel Fleming records how the superficial

'The dead bodies of their own brothers'

calm could erupt at any moment: 'The city was generally peaceful, but when things happened they happened fast. All at once a man would start running down the street, pursued by detectives with pistols in their hands. Or a bomb would suddenly be thrown at a lorry.'[66]

Paddy Trench, an outspoken anti-Treatyite republican like Robert, entered Trinity that October. Their on-off friendship would last Robert's lifetime. A keen motorcyclist, Trench claimed to have carried despatches to republican forces in the southwest during his first college year (with Alec Newman, later an *Irish Times* journalist, riding pillion)[67] and 'along with other students' to have engaged in 'clashes with the Dublin Metropolitan Police'. To prove it, he kept a captured police helmet and knuckledusters in his rooms.[68] Robert may have been one of the 'other students' in these scuffles;[69] he may also have helped the anti-Treaty cause in other ways.

For instance, Johanna Mary Cogley, giving evidence in an interview in 1946 for her military service pension application, stated that he took 'quite a few' guns, including a Parabellum (a semi-automatic Luger pistol) and some revolvers, from the Trinity College Dublin Officers' Training Corps and passed them to her husband for IRA use: 'I know there were a deal of guns out of Trinity from the OTC and I remember those guns coming in. There was a little man called Hilliard used to get them.' She went on to describe Robert, accurately enough, as 'a small, fair man'. The interviewer injected doubt about the source of the weapons – 'You wouldn't be sure they came from Trinity College ...?' – but also asked leading questions – 'Was he a Kerry man?' and 'Was that more in the Civil War?' (as opposed to the War of Independence, before Robert was at Trinity) – which show that by 1946 the idea that Robert had helped the republicans during the Civil War was already in circulation.[70]

However at the Historical Society on 15 November, Robert expressed disenchantment with both sides. He was 'heavily sarcastic about both Free Staters and Republicans, Capital and Labour, but befriended the plain people.'[71] Though he was still a republican, anti-imperialist and anti-Treatyite, this report shows he saw neither faction of Sinn Féin as serving the 'plain people's' interests. Since he was also 'heavily sarcastic' about

Swift Blaze of Fire

'Capital and Labour', we can infer that he did not yet identify 'the plain people' with 'Labour' or the working class. That his ideas about class were still unformed is borne out by his contributions to other Trinity debates about class issues.[72]

From late 1922 onwards, Robert began to drift away from the debating societies. Ironically this was just as he became recognized as something of a debating star. The Neophyte Debating Society awarded an annual silver medal for Oratory for the best speaker, with votes cast at each meeting. During 1921–22 Robert was the only Junior Freshman among the top scorers. In November he was one of six candidates unanimously elected to the Society Committee.[73] The post required a commitment he no longer felt. The certainty that the Treaty would be imposed and the brutality of both sides in the Civil War were destroying the optimism he had felt during Ireland's revolution. His debating contributions would tail off in 1923 before stopping altogether.

Instead he was training hard with Trinity's Boxing Club. On 7 December 1922 he entered – and won – the Club's Novices' competition at bantamweight.[74] My mother still keeps his medal, an ornate piece of metal inscribed 'Novices Bantamweight' and 'TCD Boxing Club 1922'.

Robert had a wiry physical resilience and tolerance for hard knocks, reinforced by years of playing rugby and other school sports against bigger opponents.[75] He was fiercely competitive and enjoyed performing to a crowd. Boxing appealed to his urge to live on the edge. John Le Carré has observed that 'if you live with danger long enough, you do indeed get used to it – even, Heaven help us, dependent on it'.[76] Robert had become used to the adrenalin-fuelled state of mind bred by the violent, unpredictable events going on around him since he was twelve years old. Boxing suited him perfectly and he threw himself wholeheartedly into a schedule of vigorous training.

As Robert moved into this new phase of his life, an English teenager with a very different background began paying visits to her aunt-in-law in Dublin. She found these visits exhilarating and returned to England keen to come again. She and Robert had never met, but their lives would soon converge.

76

7

ROSEMARY

In 1910 my English great-grandmother Rose Melicent Robins left her two young children in the care of her sisters and travelled to Port Herald (now Nsanje), in Nyasaland (now part of Malawi). Her husband Stephen was Assistant Resident[1] to the Governor of the British Protectorate of Nyasaland, and he was to meet her there. Her journey was long: a steamer down the East African coast, a series of smaller boats up the Zambesi and Shire rivers and an overland trek in fierce heat, carried part of the way on the shoulders of Africans in a conveyance like a sling. Rose's impatience to rejoin the husband she deeply loved grew as she made her journey. From Port Herald they would return to their home in Ngara, near Kasungu, 380 or so miles to the north.

It was the second time she had travelled there. As the steamer moved through the Suez Canal and crossed the Equator she remembered the first, made when they were just married. Stephen Robins, sixth of eleven children of a Hampstead barrister, was sent off to be a sailor by his parents but after two seafaring jobs took an administrative post in Nyasaland. He met Rose Baker while on leave in England. They were both brought up to put duty to family and Empire before personal happiness, and their relationship had been full of waiting. Engaged in 1900, Rose had been persuaded by her forceful sister Madeline to wait four years while Stephen's career advanced. They married at last in Guildford, Surrey, in 1904, and left together for Africa.

Retracing that journey now, Rose remembered the hardships and excitements of her newlywed life. The humid climate had damaged her European clothes and termites had eaten her carefully wrapped wedding dress. She still kept the journal in which she had recorded the hippos and crocodiles they saw on their river voyages and the nights when Stephen stayed outside until dawn, gun cocked, waiting to shoot the man-eating lions which raided the settlement after dark.

How short it had been, that first period of time together. She had given birth to their daughter Edith Rosemary, always known as Rosemary, at the Kasungu Mission on 20 April 1905. Stephen and Rose were devoted parents and for the first year of Rosemary's life, as Stephen wrote to his mother, they were 'two very happy people'.

Central to colonial administration[2] and Stephen's job was the collection of taxes. Stephen was dependent[3] on the help of a man called Pemba, who accompanied him on tax collecting and hunting expeditions and acted as his intermediary and interpreter. Both Pemba and one of his two wives, whom the couple called Ruth,[4] also looked after Rosemary. A picture shows Pemba looking sorrowful and abstracted, with a plump, contented Rosemary on his lap. Rose shared the unthinking racism[5] of the colonial class to which she belonged and it would never have occurred to her that her infant child's emotional security could rest in large measure on her bond with these early carers. This bond was abruptly severed when Rose became pregnant again and decided she must return to England until the babies were older. Taking Rosemary, she returned to her mother's large house, Kingswood Hanger, in Surrey.

And there Rose had waited again, for Stephen's posting to end or for Rosemary and the new baby, Michael, to be old enough for her to return. Stephen visited when he had leave. He and Rose exchanged passionate letters and he wrote often to tell his children that Daddy would soon be home for good.[6] Now Rosemary was five and Michael four. Rose missed them every day of her voyage and knew they missed her, but could wait no longer to be with her husband. Her eagerness intensified as she endured the slow final trek.

When at last she arrived, Stephen was nowhere to be seen. Bewildered, she asked to be taken to him, and was led to a heap of freshly dug earth, marked with a wooden cross. He had just died, of blackwater fever.

Rose undertook the journey back to Surrey in a state of shock. There she broke the news as best she could to Rosemary and Michael. All they had left of Stephen were his letters, each of them saved, Rose's photos and his African trophies. Rose arranged the trophies in Kingswood Hanger's many rooms: lion skins with snarling faces on the floor, an elephant's foot in the hallway, a set of hippo's teeth on the wall.[7] She kept one photo of him in a separate envelope, stripped to his waist, arms folded against his trim torso, smiling gently as she pointed her camera.

The family had lost its breadwinner but were comfortably off. Stephen left a pension, there was income from investments and there was also inherited money. Rose's father Charles Baker, who had been registrar to a clerical charity,[8] had inherited money from his own father, Sir Robert Baker, Chief Magistrate of London and Treasurer of the Inner Temple during the reign of George IV. Charles Baker had fathered Rose as an old man and died when she was very young; his widow, Rose's mother Marianne, had bought Kingswood Hanger with the money he left. This large house was now home to Marianne, Rose, Rose's older sisters Madeline and Edie, and the two children.

Rose hoped for great things from her cherished son Michael. She planned to send him to Dartmouth College, and his godfather, Admiral Oliver Leggett, promised to help him in a future naval career. But Michael suffered from a grumbling appendix, and in those days appendectomies were too dangerous to perform except in emergencies. In 1914, when he was seven, Rose again left the children in the care of her sisters to attend a funeral. While she was away they began a game of knights in armour, with dustbin lids as shields and bamboo canes as spears. One of Rosemary's spear-thrusts missed Michael's dustbin lid, prodding him in the stomach.

Swift Blaze of Fire

He doubled over, screaming as his appendix ruptured, and died soon afterwards of sepsis.

Rose had lost her husband and her son. In this crisis she turned again to her duty. She trained as a Red Cross nurse and then, as World War I began, moved to a boarding house in the Wirral, taking her daughter with her. Rosemary was sent to a local school and Rose got a job deciphering messages for the Liverpool Censorship office. Here she tried to recover from her grief while decoding secret communications, ironing out documents written in invisible ink and making sense of waterlogged letters recovered from torpedoed ships.

Rosemary, meanwhile, was trapped in a private hell. Her father was dead. Her brother was dead. Uprooted in infancy from her earliest carers in Ngara, she was now uprooted from her Surrey home and every familiar face. Her mother was all she had left, yet Rose worked long hours and she saw little of her. She was only nine years old and had no control over any of this. All she knew was that she must be good and not complain. Worst of all, she could not stop reliving her brother's agonizing death. She believed it was her fault, and her days and nights passed in a state of guilty horror. It would last a lifetime, and she would still be talking of it to her daughter Deirdre (my mother) when she was an old woman. Some part of her could never grasp that she was not to blame, that Michael's appendix had been so severely infected it could have ruptured at any time. A dark sense of her own sinfulness mingled with her loneliness and grief.

Realising that Rosemary was wretched living in the Wirral, Rose sent her back to Surrey as a weekly boarder at Tormead School, Guildford, where she could go home to Kingswood Hanger at weekends. Unsurprisingly, she remained an insecure, fey child, with easily hurt feelings. When Rose became engaged to an officer fighting in France, Rosemary re-entered a whirl of misery. The news of this man's death in an explosion on Armistice Day came as a great relief, tainted by more secret guilt: how could she rejoice at yet another loss for her mother?

With the war over, Rosemary might have expected to live with her mother again, but in 1919 there was yet another uprooting. Rose decided that a girl of Rosemary's temperament should mix with both boys and girls rather than inhabit an all-female environment. She sent her off to board at St George's School in Harpenden, one of the first co-educational boarding schools in England. As always, Rosemary was a docile pupil – her school reports portray her as diligent, a good influence, obedient – but she developed a mysterious illness which affected her physically and mentally. The symptoms were weakness and an overwhelming need to sleep. Either because she didn't understand her own feelings, or because she kept them to herself, nobody could diagnose the cause. She didn't recover until St George's sent her home in 1921.

During her schooldays Rosemary had enjoyed some happy moments and made a few friendships which would last into adulthood, but she emerged from them in an estranged, vulnerable state. She now lived in a household composed mostly of elderly women, all very set in their ways. Her grandmother, born Marianne Cautley in 1832, was of sound mind but preferred to ignore the passage of time, referring to Rosemary's aunts as 'the girls', although they were in their late sixties. She wore Victorian shawls, lace collars and lace caps, which gave her the air of a benign time traveller from a long-ago age. Aunt Madeline, born in 1852, was an energetic woman who read the left-wing *Daily Herald* and believed in votes for women and the health-giving properties of honey and lemons, either eaten or rubbed into the skin. Proud to describe herself as a socialist, she gave away much of her income to the causes she supported. In the previous century she had cycled around in bloomers, or travelled in her own 'health caravan', visiting the poor and full of bright ideas to help them survive, such as stuffing their clothes with newspaper in cold weather. Later she nursed wounded soldiers sent back from the Boer War. Rose's other sister Edie, born in 1853, was a devout Christian. My mother recalls her gentleness and her smell of lemon verbena soap and lavender water. She had a supply of chocolate drops, which she called 'would-you-likes': 'Would you like a would-you-like?' she used to ask Rosemary, who never forgot it; in old age she would ask her visiting grandchildren the same question.

Swift Blaze of Fire

Kingswood Hanger had been an impressive establishment before the war but Rosemary became aware as she grew older that Charles Baker's money was ebbing away. Its loss was accelerated by a disastrous investment recommended to Marianne by a relative. There were other, more successful investments (Rose had shares in a South African goldmine and the Premier Oil and Finance Company) but the house's glories were dimming. Gone were the tennis matches, the parties on the lawn, the throngs of guests dancing on the polished floors. The quarters for a nanny and servants, the coach house and the stable stood empty and Rose let the coachman's flat to a Gomshall baker. The garage held a few old bicycles and a rotting governess cart. My mother remembers the eerie atmosphere of the outdoor pergola, with its 'skulls of many kinds of antelope and deer brought back from Africa, set on wooden shields hanging round the walls, with skin shields and spears ... there were spiders' webs with little cobbles of dead flies hanging from them, trailing from the beams of the roof.'[9]

Gone, too, were the live-in servants of Rosemary's early childhood. A Mrs Downey came in to help Rose clean and a war veteran called Mr Upfold helped Marianne with the garden. The lack of electricity added to the sense of a dimming past. When dusk fell Rose lowered gas lamps from the ceiling, lit them and hauled them up again. There was only one flush lavatory. Earth closets around the house gave off what my mother calls 'a certain smell': buckets set in holes in the ground, topped by lidded wooden seats, they had to be kept closed to hold at least some of the smell inside. A handle released earth into the hole after use. Mr Upfold emptied the buckets.

Rosemary read avidly and liked writing imaginative stories. Someone gave her a Samoyed dog, said to be from the same stock as that used on Scott's expedition to the Antarctic, and she began breeding them in kennels erected on Marianne's lawns. As she grew older, Rose felt her daughter should be getting more fun out of life, and laid on excursions to the West End for plays and musicals like *The Timberton Follies*.[10] But Rosemary was starting to chart her own course, one which would take her instead to London's East End. Influenced by her Aunt Madeline and her own desire to do good, she became passionate about the plight of the poor and at

1. Family portrait taken circa 1912. Left to right: Mary (Moll), Robert senior, Marjorie, Ellen (Elsie), Phyllis, Alice, Robert (Hilliard family photo).

2. Robert, circa 1914, aged about 10 (Hilliard family photo).

3. Irish Volunteers marching through Cork in 1917: Courtesy of Cork Public Museum

4. Robert at home in Moyeightragh, Easter 1916, with his younger sisters and brother. Left to right: Marjorie, Moll and Phyllis, with baby brother Geoff (born 1915) on Moll's lap. (Hilliard family photo).

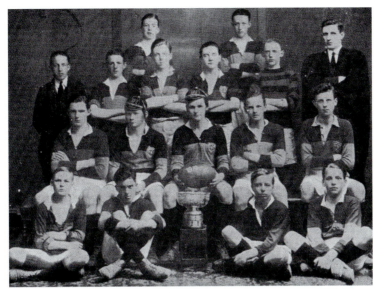

5. Cork Grammar School Rugby Team, 1919-1920, reproduced with kind permission of Ashton School, Cork.

6. Aftermath of the burning of Cork on 11 December 1920, from Michael Lenihan Collection: Courtesy of Cork Public Museum.

7. British soldiers holding up a civilian, Dublin, circa 1920. Courtesy of Kilmainham Gaol Museum/OPW 19PC-1A46-25.

8. Pemba and Rosemary in 1905 (Rosemary's photo collection).

9. Michael, Rose and Rosemary Robins, circa 1910 (Robins family photo).

10. Rosemary with two of her samoyeds, circa 1922 (Robins family photo).

11. Robert (standing, centre, in white vest) and other Irish champion boxers. *Freeman's Journal*, 9 January, 1924.

12. Olympic team badge, 1924, stitched to Robert's blazer. Memorabilia kept by Rosemary Hilliard.

13. Bass beermat, 1928, bearing the slogan that Robert is often credited with devising: 'Great Stuff This Bass!' Reproduced with kind permission of Mitchells and Butler.

14. Robert's unruly hair is smoothed flat in this studio portrait, taken in 1926, the year of his marriage (Rosemary's photo collection).

15. Robert, Rosemary and baby Tim visited the Hilliard family in 1927. Back: Marjorie, Phyl, Moll; front: Geoff, Alice, Old Robert with Tim, Rosemary, Robert. (Hilliard family photo).

16. Robert, shown centre right with boxing gloves, attended the 1929 event held in London by the (apparently exclusively masculine) Trinity College Dublin Dinner Club. Artist Fred May. Illustrated London News/Mary Evans Picture Library.

sixteen joined the Labour Party. This led to her meeting Muriel Lester, at which point her life was transformed.

Muriel Lester, born in 1883, was a Christian socialist. The daughter of a self-made Essex businessman, she had abandoned an opulent lifestyle to work with women in Bow, East London. At the meetings she organized, working-class women drank tea, socialized and listened to music; they also discussed industrial law and their workplace rights, the need for women's suffrage, the dangers of alcohol and – above all – the Bible. For Lester, 'our religion touched life at all points and made sense out of it'.[11] She argued that poverty was caused by inequality rather than any wickedness or irresponsibility on the part of the poor. In 1915 she and her sister Doris founded Kingsley Hall in Poplar, East London, a 'People's house' for working people and those who campaigned for them (Gandhi would stay there in 1931). It ran a nursery, social and cultural events, holiday schemes and Sunday services, and had close links with East London suffragette groups.[12]

The wave of strikes and unrest across England and Ireland in the years after the Russian Revolution, which 'touched the high-water mark'[13] in 1919, swept a big Labour majority onto Poplar Borough Council. The new mayor was Lester's friend, fellow Christian socialist George Lansbury. The new councillors were mostly local working people. They improved public health by building homes, compelling landlords to carry out repairs, planting trees, giving out cheap milk to babies and pregnant women, opening bathing and laundry facilities, and treating TB in a new centre.[14] Results were impressive: infant mortality, for example, would fall from 124 per thousand births pre-war to 60 by 1923. Poplar also introduced a minimum wage,[15] with equal pay for men and women council workers, and began building better roads and sewage works.

All London boroughs had to contribute sums taken from the rates, known as precepts, to cover the spending of centralized bodies such as the London County Council and London's police, water and Poor Law hospital authorities.[16] Centralized spending was therefore pooled, with wealthier

Swift Blaze of Fire

boroughs helping out the poorest. By contrast, local expenditure made necessary by joblessness and hardship largely fell on individual boroughs and was met from local rates. In the poorest boroughs such expenditure was high, so that total rates in poor boroughs were often far higher than in wealthy ones. There had been talk of rates equalization, but in practice little happened.[17] This was resented as unfair by working people because, when they could find jobs, the profits of their work enriched the wealthy. As Lester put it, workers 'drove their trains, kept their drains in order, unloaded their fruit at the docks and manufactured their goods'[18] – and all on poverty pay. Why shouldn't London's wealthy pay a pooled charge to equalize the costs of social welfare?

Then as in our own time, councillors tended to dilute their principles once in office, adapting to squeezed budgets by focusing on bureaucratic manoeuvres to achieve small gains. Poplar was different. Councillors there were determined to keep their election promises, and it alarmed the government. Hoping to bring them to heel, in January 1921 the government withheld from Poplar a previously promised central grant. The council found itself running out of money. After failed deputations to Ministers and much debate, councillors responded in March by denouncing the rates system as unjust and refusing to levy the precepts.[19] In September thirty Poplar councillors were jailed for this refusal.

Lester brought Rosemary into the tide of protests and demonstrations which thronged the streets in response to these jailings. A huge campaign forced the government to release the councillors after six weeks, or face a mass rent strike across the East End. After their release the councillors maintained their refusal to collect the precepts and their defiance won the day. A Metropolitan Common Poor Law fund was set up and London councils like Poplar received a substantial increase in their poor relief. The Poplar victory is still cited today, because it shows that government austerity can be successfully resisted by a genuine mass movement.

After this victory Lester became an Alderman.[20] As chair of Poplar's Maternal and Child Welfare Committee she championed many of the far-sighted Poplar measures which later became national policy under the welfare state, such as the issue of free milk to pregnant women and children. Rosemary by this time stayed regularly in Kingsley Hall as Lester's friend. Lester's socialist friends became her friends too, including Elsie and Doris Waters, later the comedy act 'Gert and Daisy', and their brother Horace John Waters, better known as actor Jack Warner.[21]

There was a big Irish community in East London, many of whom took an impassioned interest in Irish politics.[22] Hanna Sheehy-Skeffington, widow of Francis Sheehy-Skeffington, an Irish radical shot by a British officer in the 1916 Rising, had stayed with Lester when visiting England[23] and Lester had supported protests against the Black and Tans. Rosemary learned at Kingsley Hall about the brutality endured by the Irish during the War of Independence.

Rosemary was one of the companions who carried Lester's speaking platform and collected money when Lester spoke at Victoria Park and Speaker's Corner in Hyde Park. She adopted her friend's way of referring to Christ as a working man – 'the Carpenter' – and embraced her Christian Socialism, though not her Baptist faith (she remained in the Church of England). There were major setbacks in Poplar after 1921 as the tide of mass resistance ebbed, but Rosemary stayed loyal to Lester and the Christian socialist cause.[24]

Her life was opening out in other directions too. She had begun visiting her aunt-by-marriage, the artist Frances Baker, who lived at 80 Merrion Square in Dublin. This Georgian square had long been a haunt of Dublin's dramatists, painters, critics, poets and scholars. Oscar Wilde was born and had lived there, WB Yeats still lived there, James Joyce had met Nora Barnacle there for their first date on the first Bloomsday; it was a place where the living celebrated a convivial creativity amid echoes of the iconic dead. Frances Baker's friends and artistic collaborators included her neighbour, the painter and writer George Russell ('AE'), the nationalist activist, politician and artist Constance Markievicz[25] and the writer James Stephens. Baker had two daughters from her first marriage, to Rose's brother Cecil Baker who had killed himself in 1903 while suffering from a depressive illness. The elder of these, Lettice Baker (later the photographer

85

Swift Blaze of Fire

Lettice Ramsey), had been educated in England at Bedales and Cambridge and had paid a number of visits to Kingswood Hanger. Though seven years older than Rosemary and a far more confident, self-reliant character, she became her friend. Frances Baker's second husband, Francis Cahill, was a doctor. His amateur involvement in Dublin's artistic and theatrical life added to the vibrancy of the gatherings at their Merrion Square house, where they 'entertained lavishly' and 'regaled their guests with music after dinner'.[26]

In appearance Rosemary was by now a very pretty young woman with dark hair and eyes and a delightful smile. Since the activism in Poplar she had become less outwardly shy, but her friendship with Muriel Lester had, if possible, intensified her religious piety. Emotionally fragile, she had always found it hard to relax or lose herself in the sheer joy of living. Staying with Aunt Frances was therefore a revelation. Rosemary disapproved of the bohemian attitudes to sexual morality she often encountered in Merrion Square but thoroughly enjoyed the wit and laughter that flowed within her aunt's circle and their boisterous delight in literature and art. Every time she boarded the ferry to Dublin, she was filled with excitement at the prospect of meeting more of these fascinating people.

PART IV — THE BOXER

8

'THE IRISHMAN WORKED HARD AND WAS DEAD GAME'

Throughout 1923 Robert spent much of his time in the gym, an echoing room smelling of wintergreen and dotted with swing balls, speed balls and punchbags of varying weights. On arrival he would bandage his hands to protect his knuckles before taking a pair of boxing gloves from the shared pile. One training session might be an hour or two of skipping, press-ups and other exercises, followed by shadow boxing before a mirror; another might be bag work, ball work and sparring in the ring. A stop-clock tracked times. He prepared for the ring by putting in a gum shield, greasing his eyebrows to keep the tender skin above his eyes slippery and walking his leather boots through a tray of powdered resin to prevent sliding on the canvas.

Some sparring partners liked to take liberties but Robert learned to dodge the blows and give as good as he got. When the sparring was over, the trainer would rub both fighters down with the pain-easing wintergreen salve whose vaguely medicinal scent overwhelmed all other odours in the room. The gym's camaraderie was a balm to Robert of a different kind. Seasoned boxers kept an eye on novices like him, encouraging them and

Swift Blaze of Fire

offering tips in a new language of hooks and crosses and jabs that he was eager to learn.[1]

His family's situation and the hardship in Killarney were sources of nagging anxiety all through that autumn and winter. He couldn't go home for Christmas in 1922. The Kerry rail network was still impassable and anti-Treatyite attacks were regularly undoing every attempt to repair it. He could travel to one of Kerry's harbours by sea (his friend Fleming took a ship to Cork for Christmas),[2] but the next leg of the journey was dangerous; for weeks the roads between Killarney and the coast had seen both military and civilian food convoys come under fire. There had also been local attacks and reprisals on individual travellers. The Hilliard family were especially on edge after the Lake Hotel's ostler, Mike Price, narrowly escaped being shot. When the rail bridge at Mallow was blown up, Price had the job of transporting cartloads of leather to the Killarney factory from Fenit. As he approached Brennan's Glen on one of these journeys, a bullet, fired at him, passed between his arm and his body, killing the horse behind.[3] In this climate it's unlikely Robert's parents would let either Robert or Moll attempt the journey.

Robert still opposed the Treaty but as we have seen had become critical of 'both Free-Staters and Republicans' by November 1922. Such dismay at both sides' disregard for ordinary people was widespread in the southwest, summed up in an anonymous *Cork Examiner* piece: 'We expected that the government would come to our assistance sooner by protecting us and putting an end to the warfare waged against us by people who should devote themselves to helping us rather than starving us.'[4] Now Robert had to wait in Dublin as the anniversary of the Treaty came and went, knowing that Killarney remained cut off and Christmas there would be a desperately lean occasion.

On 16 January 1923, a convoy of 100 horses and carts carrying food at last reached Killarney. Anti-Treatyites reacted with a flurry of destruction on the railway network[5] and two lethal assaults on railwaymen. On 18 January they derailed a troop train on its way to Listowel, tumbling it down an embankment. The driver and fireman were crushed and scalded to death.[6]

Five days later Daniel Daly, a railwayman, was shot through the heart at Tralee station and his colleague Daniel Lynch was shot in the arms.[7] It was widely assumed that this, again, was the work of anti-Treatyites. Railwaymen had been heroes of the Irish revolution, running the gauntlet of beatings and death threats at gunpoint while staying steadfast in their refusal to drive trains carrying soldiers. Tactics which targeted them provoked widespread revulsion.[8]

Nevertheless anti-Treaty feeling continued to run high in Kerry, reflected in the food and shelter given to the anti-Treatyite IRA by ordinary people, and the slowness of the Free State forces to win control there. With the superior resources and firepower provided by British money, everyone knew the Free State would eventually win, but victory would be long delayed.

On 6 February the first two trains carrying passengers and mail got through to Killarney. Postal communications to Dublin gradually resumed and Robert was at long last able to get regular news of his family by letter. Even then the Civil War in Kerry was not over.

Robert took time out of the gym for a few more debates in early 1923 before losing interest altogether. On 5 February he spoke against a motion disapproving of 'all secret societies, especially those of the type of the Ku Klux Klan'.[9] Colonial repression in Ireland had frequently forced the struggle for national liberation into operating through secret societies. Any republican would oppose this motion, which apparently sought to tarnish all such organizations by association with the KKK.

His pessimism in other debates reflected the low mood induced by the Civil War. On 12 February he supported a motion 'that our modern civilisation is on the decline',[10] and a week later another that 'Ireland offers no prospects for a man with a university education'.[11] Soon after that he opposed a motion for Irish reunification, a decidedly odd position given that he was a republican anti-Treatyite.[12] His eagerness to defend modern culture had been replaced by a dreary feeling that both 'civilization' and his future career in Ireland were taking a wrong turn.

His fascination with boxing drew him to one more debate that spring. On 5 March the Neophyte Debating Society discussed the motion 'That this Society welcomes the staging of the Siki–McTigue fight in Dublin.'[13] On 17 March – St Patrick's Day – Mike McTigue, an Irishman, was due to challenge Louis Mbarick Fall, a black French-Senegalese fighter who for boxing purposes called himself Battling Siki. Fall had won the world light-heavyweight title in a match against the great Georges Carpentier of France, knocking Carpentier out cold. The referee claimed he'd tripped him, initially awarding the match to the unconscious Frenchman on the floor, and Fall had gained the title only after the ringside judges overruled this unfair decision. Soon after his victory the British Home Secretary provoked an outcry by invoking the British boxing colour-bar (in existence since 1911) to prevent him from fighting on the British mainland, on the grounds that 'contests between men of different colours' aroused 'bitter and even dangerous social antipathies.'[14]

The Neophyte debating room filled up with noisy, excitable students, all aware that the boxing world's gaze was focused on Dublin. The debate was marred by racism, such as the grotesque suggestion that a black boxer was less than human: a 'Mr WS Mcguinness (visitor) compared the black man to a horse'. Part way through, Robert and a friend made a dramatic entrance: 'At this point two "ladies", claiming to be honorary members, entered and caused some slight excitement …'[15]

Looking to raise a laugh, Robert and a friend had arrived dressed as women. Unsurprisingly this added to the febrile atmosphere. *TCD* reports that Robert spoke up for Battling Siki – '"MISS" Hilliard … wanted the "underdog" to get a chance' – but he was evidently in a light-hearted mood and this doesn't sound like the ringing defence of Fall's human rights that the occasion called for.

Battling Siki/Louis Fall deserved better than the treatment he got in Dublin. On 17 March he lost his title to McTigue, after twenty rounds, in a highly contentious decision on points. He left for the US, where his boxing career went rapidly downhill. In December 1925 he was found shot dead, lying in the snow.

'The irishman worked hard and was dead game'

News from home remained grim. Spring 1923 saw the worst atrocities yet in Kerry. On 6 March anti-Treatyites lured Pat O'Connor, a local lad who had enlisted in the Free State Army, to Bairinarig Wood in Knocknagoshel with a story that it contained an anti-Treatyite arms dump. It was a booby trap, and the 'dump' was mined. O'Connor and four other soldiers were killed in the explosion and another lost his legs.[16] The next day the Free State army tied nine republican prisoners to a landmine at Ballyseedy Cross, near Tralee, and set it off. The remains of eight of them had to be picked out of the trees and ditches; the ninth – blown clear – escaped.[17] On 12 March five republican prisoners in Cahersiveen were shot in the legs and then blown up with a landmine.[18] These were only some of the murderous reprisals taking place in Kerry. Those at risk on both sides often felt compelled to emigrate to save their own lives. The *Cork Examiner* reported on 3 April that thousands were emigrating from West Kerry, more than for several years. But the war was in its last throes. On 30 April the anti-Treatyites declared a ceasefire. On 24 May all anti-Treaty units were told to dump their arms.

Robert was in Dublin during the last months of the Civil War, where he trained intensively. He sparred in the gym, did long runs and joined the Trinity Hurling Club, a public marker of his republicanism. He would gain his hurling colours in February the following year.[19] In the Trinity College Races of April 1923 he was first in the one-mile handicap race and fifth in the two-mile handicap, respectively described as 'a fine race'[20] and 'a good race'[21] by the *Freeman's Journal*.

Irish welterweight champion Mike Ronan became the Boxing Club's trainer in May 1923, and TCD noted that his small size would enable him to spar with the 'lighter members' of the club.[22] Robert was one of these lighter members and over the next year he went from strength to strength. He was an instinctive performer, popular with spectators because he carried his air of humorous energy into the ring. Even when a blow troubled him he kept smiling,[23] and newspaper reports show he swiftly gained a reputation for being a tenacious, 'game' fighter. The flow of adrenalin conferred immunity

Swift Blaze of Fire

to pain and fear while each match lasted. If he won, he felt an exhilaration nothing else could match; if he lost, or if he woke next day to rope burns on his back, bruises or stiff muscles, it only made him want to train even harder.

By 19 May 1923, Robert had boxed his way to the semi-finals of the All-Ireland Amateur Boxing Championships, held in the Everyman Theatre in Dublin's Rotunda. He went through the semi-final on a bye[24] before winning the final in front of a noisy crowd of 250 or so, doing most of his scoring in the second and third rounds.[25] His victory made him All-Ireland Amateur Bantamweight champion. It was only six months since he had won the Novices' award.

A month later he was knocked to the canvas in the third round of the Irish Inter-Varsity Boxing contest between Trinity College, Queen's Belfast and University College Dublin. He got up, fought on and won, but *The Irish Times* called him 'a lucky winner'.[26] Spurred on, he was running again by 20 June, in a Junior League Athletic contest, coming first in a three-mile race. Term was ending, and with the Civil War over, he could at last go back to Killarney for the summer holiday and show off his medals.

If his parents feared all this talk of boxing meant his studies were suffering, they were right. His final Freshman examination, nicknamed 'Little-Go', came and went in September 1923. He either failed to turn up for it or took it and failed. He could not qualify to start the Junior Sophister curriculum until he passed. Robert would be permitted to sit the Little-Go exam again in the spring or summer of 1924, but for now he must remain a Freshman, going to 'such lectures as the Senior Lecturer [might] consider advisable',[27] and lagging seriously behind.

That autumn, however, he concentrated on boxing instead of studying. On 6 December he went to the Universities', Hospital and Cadets' Championships in London, competing against doctors, soldiers and students from seven universities.[28] He had gained weight, so boxed at featherweight against heavier fighters.[29] *The Irish Times* reported that 'The Irishman worked hard and was dead game,'[30] but succumbed to 'a better boxer' in the semi-final. Determined to lose the extra weight, he went straight back to running on his return and in the St James's Gate Harriers' Invitation Race on 15 December, came ninth out of eighty.[31]

A flurry of symbolism marked the end of British rule in Ireland. Red pillar boxes were painted green, army uniforms dyed green, with new buttons showing a harp, British postage stamps over-printed with the words 'Saorstát Éireann' (Free State of Ireland), and English placenames replaced by Gaelic ones. Boxing was seen as an important part of encouraging a sense of nationhood. The government gave the Army Athletics Council[32] £17,000 for boxing equipment and training, appointing Tancy Lee, former British professional champion,[33] as their instructor.

The Paris Olympic Games were due to start in May 1924. A newly formed Olympic Council of Ireland (OCI) held its first meeting in December 1923 and planned to send the first-ever Irish teams. To boost national unity these teams would include competitors from both North and South, Protestants and Catholics, Free-Staters and republicans. When the OCI assembled a panel of the great and the good to help them, it included Sir Robert Tate, Lecturer in Classical Composition at Trinity and a familiar figure to Robert. Trinity buzzed with talk of the Olympics. If a boxing team was going to Paris, Robert wanted to be selected. He trained even harder.[34]

Robert's social circle was expanding. Early in 1924 he was invited to a dinner party at 80 Merrion Square, as a guest of the artist Frances Baker, probably introduced by his friend Paddy Trench, who was a talented artist and part of Frances Baker's circle (Trench would later marry Francie, Baker's younger daughter).[35] Another guest was writer James Stephens, who sat next to Rosemary Robins, Baker's young niece, who was visiting her aunt from Surrey.

Rosemary was charmed by James Stephens and later said he had 'the kindest face and brightest twinkling eyes you have ever seen.'[36] She told him she had enjoyed his book *Deirdre*, a tragic story retold from Irish legend in which a young girl dashes her own brains out after a forced marriage to a man she hates. Stephens laughingly predicted she would marry an Irishman and name her daughter Deirdre after the book. When dinner was over he introduced her to the handsome, lively young boxing champion from Trinity College.

Both Rosemary and Robert loved books and writing and they found plenty to talk about. Robert – as always – had a great desire to amuse, and Rosemary a great willingness to be amused, but each also sensed the other's underlying seriousness. Politically discouraged himself, Robert was struck by Rosemary's commitment to the causes she cared about. This beautiful woman had shown herself ready to stand up for her beliefs. For Rosemary, who had so often felt guilty and unworthy, it was a heady sensation to read the admiration in his eyes. He may have told her about Killarney; perhaps she had noticed his accent. She told him about her home in Surrey, including the address. They were both very young, Rosemary eighteen and Robert nineteen. Neither of them foresaw how significant this meeting would prove to be.

9

PARIS OLYMPICS

Money, training space and resources were in short supply for the Irish Olympic teams. The Olympic Council of Ireland held its first fundraising public meeting at the Mansion House on 19 March 1924. Trinity College entered into the spirit by granting the OCI use of the Trinity College Park for training athletes after 6.00 p.m., and giving its own Boxing and Gymnastics Club £20.2s.0d for an instructor and equipment.[1]

On 7 May initial playoffs for the Irish Olympic boxing team took place at the Gymnasium in Dublin's Portobello Barracks. According to *The Irish Times*, Robert and his opponent were the stars of the event: '... the best bout of the night was the 10-rounds Bantam contest between R M Hilliard, of Dublin University, and Volunteer[2] D Flaherty of Cork ... Hilliard put up a plucky showing, using his right and left to the greater advantage, but he lost by a small margin after a rattling good display.'[3] The *Freeman's Journal* agreed and wrote that Robert had 'displayed the best science'. Robert and Volunteer Daniel Flaherty were now rival frontrunners for Olympic selection.

The final Olympic selection matches coincided with a series of hard fights for Robert in May and early June and were made even more challenging by

Swift Blaze of Fire

a trouncing he had taken in an especially demanding fight on 29 May.[4] After four days to nurse his bruises, he scored a double triumph in two consecutive matches at the Dublin University Boxing Championships on 2 June, winning both the bantam and featherweight Dublin University titles.[5] These victories meant he now held three titles.

Two days later he was in the ring again for the Irish Amateur Boxing Association Championships. There was a lot at stake as the winners would be selected for the Olympic team besides becoming IABA champions. Robert won in the first and second rounds on 4 and 5 June.[6] The semi-final and final took place on 6 June. Public suspense was building, and there was a large crowd. By this time Robert was 'stale', meaning his body and brain were suffering from too many fights too close together, but he remained very determined and won the semi-final after a 'close contest'.[7] The all-important final followed on that same night and to cap it all he was up against Daniel Flaherty. It was a hard-fought match, but Robert won on points and kept his title. All the newspapers remarked on his staleness, though *The Irish Times* described their encounter as 'a rattling good mill'.[8]

Astonishingly, Robert went on to fight the Intervarsity contests on the next day (also at Portobello) and even more astonishingly competed at two different weights. This time he'd pushed it too far. In the featherweight match he stubbornly 'carried the fight to his adversary'[9] but was easily beaten. Another boxer had to stand in for him in the bantamweight match. No matter; Robert had boxed eight matches in ten days, won six, gained two titles, successfully defended another title and earned selection for the Olympic Games, an astonishing tally of achievements.

Every other Olympic qualifying match except the heavyweight[10] had been won by a soldier. The Army newspaper *An t-Óglách's*[11] reporter had supported Flaherty for the bantamweight selection and resented Robert's victory, opining that Flaherty had 'decidedly hard luck'[12] in losing to Robert. At a fundraiser held soon afterwards on 27 June, again at the Portobello Barracks, Robert lost to Flaherty. This same reporter praised every other boxer who took part, taking care to encourage all the losers except Robert, about whom he was scathing:

Paris Olympics

O'Flaherty outpointed Hilliard in every round. Both boys had met in the final of the Amateur Championship. Hilliard succeeded in catching the Judge's eye then, but his opponent on Friday night made the task of the Judges easy by holding the upper hand all through. Hilliard in our opinion looked to be in bad shape. Let us hope that Friday's lesson will awake in him the necessity of training conscientiously for his Paris undertakings.[13]

At some point that month the decision was taken that Daniel Flaherty would go to Paris as well as Robert. The Army reporter would also travel with the team.

A party of eminent individuals assembled on the warm, sunny evening of 6 July 1924 at Westland Row Station, Dublin for a ceremony in which J.J. Healy, Secretary of the Irish ABA, presented the members of the Irish Olympic Boxing and Water Polo teams with the Olympic Tournament medals issued to mark their membership of the Irish team.[14] Tancy Lee, the Army boxing instructor, was to accompany the boxers. The heavyweight champion, O'Driscoll, had withdrawn. The teams were waved off on the 8.10 p.m. train, scheduled to travel all night and reach Paris, via Folkestone and Boulogne, next day.

Robert had never been to France; indeed his only other trip abroad had been to London the previous year. The team was due to come back on 22 July but he wouldn't be with them. As he looked out across the sunset-tinted waves of the Irish Sea he thought about the tent he'd packed in his luggage and a bold plan he was forming for what to do next.

The Irishmen were headed for the biggest Olympics there had ever been. There were forty-four nations taking part, up from twenty-nine in 1920. Competitors' exploits would be reported around the globe. This was the year when Harold Abrahams and Eric Liddell won the gold medals that inspired *Chariots of Fire*, Benjamin (later Doctor) Spock rowed for the US, and Johnny Weissmuller, sporting the muscles that would one day equip him to play Tarzan in a series of movies, won four medals for swimming. It was also the year many modern standards and customs began: the Olympic

Swift Blaze of Fire

pool length, the Olympic marathon length, the Olympic village, a cannon salute, a flypast, the release of doves.

The Games' amateur ethos had more to do with the 'gentleman sportsman' ideal than any classless meritocracy. Olympic competitors were all unpaid but not equally funded. Most were male, nearly all were white, and they tended to come from gilded backgrounds, pursuing sport while studying at prestigious universities in Europe and the US. The wealthier nations had spent incomparably more than Ireland, whose teams had to manage on a shoestring. As these Games' scale dawned on the Irish contingent, so did the sparseness of their resources.

Ireland's five all-male teams were competing in athletics, boxing, football, lawn tennis and water polo. The athletics team were already in Paris, the only Irish team present at the official opening ceremony on 5 July.[15] The footballers had already gone home, having lost to Holland in the second round. The Irish attaché in France, a Mr McDevitt, met the boxers at the Gare du Nord and took them to the Prince Albert Hotel, in the Rue Saint-Hyacinthe near the Louvre,[16] where they and the athletics team filled the hotel's modestly sized bedrooms.

Robert was in several ways the odd man out among the boxers – he was the only civilian, the only college boy and almost certainly the only Protestant – but he had always been a gregarious character and no doubt tried to fit in. Having fought so hard for his team place he would have followed the training regime with a will. The boxers' bedtime throughout their stay was 10.30 p.m. They rose at 7.30, took Mass at 8.00 in the Madeleine Church (Robert, as a Protestant, was presumably excused), ate breakfast at 9.00 and then ran for two hours in 'a beautiful park'. Lunch was at 1.00 and from 2.00 to 4.30 they trained in the gym at the National Sporting Club de France, a splendid government building with a boxing hall big enough for 2000 spectators. At 5.30 they had a massage, and dinner was at 7.00.

That was the schedule in theory. In practice, limited funding made it hard to follow. They had been given only £12 for lunches and transport, leaving nothing for fares, so had to walk everywhere. They soon discovered that their hotel was several kilometres from either their training gym or the boxers' arena near the Eiffel Tower. As they footslogged through the dust and fumes of a July heatwave, it was galling to be passed by buses and taxis carrying other nations' teams. They would be forced to waste much training time walking the city.

The Army reporter's articles impart a sense of grievance over this and much else too, like having to buy his own lunches when the French reporters had theirs paid for, and the heat, which made it harder to train. He decided French food was 'the wrong sort', being 'soft and sloppy' – though Daniel Flaherty must have liked it, as he quickly put on too much weight and was disqualified when the contests began. Most of all the reporter lamented the 'meagre patronage so grudgingly given' to the Irish teams. The boxers were only too aware of this lack of money but kept their hopes high. In the event they acquitted themselves well.

The boxing began on 15 July at the Vélodrome d'Hiver on Rue Nélaton. Each match was three rounds long. Maurice Doyle, the Irish featherweight, came close to beating the US champion Fields and was 'cheered to the echo' by spectators (Fields went on to win the final). Welterweight Patrick Dwyer boxed against the wonderfully named Basham of Great Britain and beat him, delighting the Irish party.

Robert had to wait two days for his own turn and during that time several of his team mates were defeated. Friday 18 July saw him enter the ring at last, up against Benjamin Pertuzzo, the Argentine champion. His opponent was too strong for him but he refused to give in and lasted the full three rounds. The *Irish Independent* said he was 'outclassed', but took his punishment 'in game style, and was smiling at the end of the third gruelling round.'[17] Predictably, the *An t-Óglách* reporter took a much more dismal view: 'Hilliard, Irish Bantam Champion, was outpointed by the Champion of the Argentine. The bout was by no means spectacular, neither man impressed the spectators. The Argentinian was beaten on the following day rather easily.'

To dismiss the Argentinian as 'beaten ... rather easily' was unfair to both him and Robert. Pertuzzo's vanquisher was Salvatore Tripoli of the USA, a formidable adversary who went on to win the silver medal. All

Swift Blaze of Fire

remaining Irish boxers were defeated that same evening or on Saturday 19 July, though Dwyer reached the semi-final and only lost when his opponent headbutted him in a flagrant foul.

Robert had worked extremely hard to win his team place and like the others had arrived in Paris full of hope. It was humiliating to be eliminated so swiftly. He was left with the feeling that his best had not been good enough, and in later years would be modest to the point of sheepishness about his part in the Olympics.[18]

That Friday evening he comforted himself by turning his thoughts to the possibility of a very different encounter. For months a glow of hopeful, tender excitement had been gathering radiance in his mind. As the fighting adrenalin drained away and his bruises began to throb, he packed his luggage, resolving to leave Paris first thing in the morning. He travelled non-stop the next day, from the Gare du Nord to Calais or Dunkirk and the Dover ferry, then a train to London and another one to Gomshall, Surrey, arriving the evening of the day he had set out.

Night had fallen when he set off across the North Downs. The moon was on the wane but still bright. A brief heatwave had broken two days earlier in Surrey with a downpour that had left the air cool.[19] It was less than a mile from Gomshall station to the address he was heading for at Kingswood Hanger. He found a large house, set in gardens, woodland and an orchard.

All the lights were out. The hour was too late to wake the house's occupants by knocking. Instead he pitched his tent under the moonlit apple trees on the damp grass, crawled in and slept.

10

'MY FRIEND'

It was Rosemary's formidable Aunt Madeline who discovered Robert's tent in the orchard next morning. Family tradition has it she ran into the house calling out that a 'strange, wild Irishman' was camped outside, asking for Rosemary. No-one thought any the worse of Robert for his eccentric arrival. Rose invited him in and made him welcome. Her neat entry in the house Visitors' Book shows he stayed three more nights.[1]

Robert had brought a present for Rosemary from Paris, a miniature edition of Omar Khayyam's *Rubaiyat*, in French,[2] wrapped in an envelope on which he'd written '*Amica mea*' – 'my friend'. Rosemary would treasure the book all her life. Shortly before her death she passed it to her daughter Deirdre with a note explaining why, despite everything, she still held it dear.

Robert wrote later that 'it was Rosemary's ... love of all beauty and all creatures ... that caused me to love her'.[3] He saw her socialist beliefs as an expression of this generalized love. His own opinions started falling into place as she set hers out. Years afterwards Rosemary said to my mother that Robert told her he had started to become a socialist when he was

Swift Blaze of Fire

sixteen. This does not square with the absence of socialism in his debating contributions while at Trinity, but does make sense if he was reflecting back on the past and reinterpreting it in the light of a present epiphany.

It was when he was sixteen in Cork, after all, that the Irish workers' struggle had been at its height. The demonstrations and strikes he had witnessed there were motivated by class anger as well as nationalism. Marchers and strikers had demanded social justice and an end to inequality as well as Irish self-determination. Social justice was also the cause for which the Poplar councillors had gone to prison. Listening to Rosemary he made the link between the two. This was a cause which straddled the Irish Sea and united the interests of working people everywhere. Already a republican and an anti-imperialist, he now became conscious of his own socialist ideas.

The version of socialism which Rosemary espoused and which Robert now found so persuasive was not Marxism, though his family in Killarney would have seen little difference. It was an idealist version of socialism based on moral imperatives rather than a materialist version based on Marxist dialectics. Rosemary's faith in the Labour Party meant that while honouring the achievements of the Russian Revolution (Labour had opposed war on Russia in 1920) she believed a more just society would come from above, through Parliament, albeit a Parliament influenced by mass campaigns. This was very different from Marx's revolution from below. Ramsay MacDonald had become the first Labour Prime Minister in January that same year. Rosemary and her Labour friends were full of optimism about what his party could achieve in government. Robert, politically disorientated by the cruelties of the Irish Civil War and the imposition of the Treaty, found it wonderful to hear about the Poplar councillors' principled leadership and the class solidarity which had won the day, and soon shared her faith in Labour.

It was even more wonderful to find in Rosemary a sympathetic listener to whom he could at last confide the traumatizing events of his schooldays. She later told my mother of his passionate anger about the Black and Tans' atrocities, opining that those years had forced him to 'grow up too early'.

'My friend'

Rosemary was reticent about specifics and there's one story my mother never heard the whole of: it concerned 'a hanging child'. Who the child was, or what was meant by hanging, she never learned, but the phrase conjures a nightmare image, like one of Goya's *Disasters of War*, and my mother gathered that this memory held a particular horror for Robert.

His confidences helped to draw Rosemary very close. How could they not fall in love? He was attractive, eloquent and funny. Nothing in her life had prepared her to withstand his irrepressible energy and humour or his readiness to adore her. He found her beautiful as well as admirable. Rosemary's face in those days was touchingly young and artless. In later years she often had a guarded, hurt expression, but at twenty she trusted Robert absolutely.

Kingswood Hanger, with its large, tranquil rooms, its library overflowing with old and new books and its hospitable atmosphere, provided the setting for a bewitching few days with Rosemary that ended all too soon. On the morning of 23 July Robert packed his belongings and made his way back to Gomshall Station. Back in Dublin and short of money, he looked for a job. On 2 September an advertisement appeared in *The Irish Times* for Avoca School, in Blackrock on the edge of Dublin, announcing that 'R M Hilliard (Sizar T.C.D)' was now sharing the teaching of languages with the Headmaster, a Mr A A MacDonogh BA (MacDonogh described himself as an MA in later adverts).[4] Robert's was the only name mentioned besides the Headmaster's, suggesting MacDonogh considered him a major reputational asset.

This was supposed to be Robert's final year at Trinity. He had at last passed the Little-Go exam in April and in July 1924 Trinity's calendar listed him as a Junior Sophister. To become a Candidate Bachelor and take his degree, he now had to catch up fast with the studies he'd missed and attend a minimum number of Senior Sophister lectures by July 1925. It was unfortunate for him that his tutor was the 'peppery' Thrift, who had no interest in pastoral care. A more sympathetic tutor might have helped him. As it was, he made a poor job of all his commitments, whether teaching,

105

boxing or studying. He cannot have lasted long at Avoca School as his name never reappeared in their advertisements. Having gained weight and lost fitness, he was so conspicuously out of form at featherweight in the Eastern Command Boxing championships in November that the *Freeman's Journal* coverage of the event was headlined 'Hilliard Disappoints'.[5] Although he joined the college's Boxing Club Committee and attended the Club's October AGM, there's no sign he played a significant role. And he certainly did not prioritize his studies. Some behaviour suggests he was losing the plot altogether. At a Neophyte Society meeting in November the chair fined him three times (fines were issued for unruly or poor conduct).[6]

The upcoming Intervarsity Championships brought a ray of light: if he were selected, his fares would be paid to London, allowing him to visit Rosemary. He returned to the gym with renewed vigour, boxing well enough in the trials on 1 December to be selected. The *Freeman's Journal* praised his 'skill, pluck and ability to absorb punishment', noting that he 'fought considerably better' than in his last major contest. Four days later in London, both *The Irish Times* and the *Freeman's Journal* thought him unlucky to lose the semi-final. After the match he went straight to Kingswood Hanger for a delightful four-day visit. Given the state of his finances he probably spent Christmas with his parents in Killarney. Did he tell them about Rosemary? They wanted to hear their son was on course to gain a degree. It was not an assurance he could honestly give.

During the following year everything else in Robert's life gave way to his overwhelming longing to be with Rosemary. If he was looking for further self-justifications for becoming one of Ireland's many emigrants, they weren't hard to find. It was fast becoming a claustrophobically illiberal country.

Under the new Irish state, big business, including big farmers, came first and people's needs came last. Minister of Industry and Commerce Patrick McGilligan even said he was ready to bring back famine to further his policies, asserting that 'People may have to die in the country, and die through starvation'.[7] Twenty-five years earlier James Connolly had issued a sarcastic warning that if Ireland's capitalists went unchallenged, independence would bring no relief for workers:

> After Ireland is free, says the patriot who won't touch socialism, we will protect all classes, and if you won't pay your rent you will be evicted same as now. But the evicting party ... will wear green uniforms and the Harp without the Crown, and the warrant turning you out on the roadside will be stamped with the arms of the Irish Republic. Now, isn't that worth fighting for?[8]

Ministers seemed hell-bent on making Connolly's predictions come true. President Cosgrave was on sick leave, and Vice President and Minister for Justice Kevin O'Higgins was the effective head of government. A ruthless counter-revolutionary, he had confirmed the death sentences of seventy-seven republican prisoners during the Civil War,[9] including the best man at his own wedding. O'Higgins loathed any sign that the lower orders were getting uppity, denouncing the

> attitude of protest, the attitude of negation, the attitude sometimes of sheer wantonness and wayward-ness and destructiveness which ... has been ... a traditional attitude on behalf of the Irish people.[10]

He replaced elected judges and the republican courts in 1924,[11] with a quasi-British model featuring appointed judges, complete with wigs. The government had already sent in the National Army to attack a postal workers' strike in 1922, a marker of O'Higgins's antipathy to organized labour, and he now made clear that strikers and pickets in any public sector workplaces could expect similar treatment.[12] He cut pensions[13] and teachers' wages,[14] clamping down on talk of the state providing free secondary education or other social benefits, suppressed movements for land redistribution by giving extra powers to bailiffs,[15] and imposed extreme fiscal austerity.[16]

Like other counter-revolutions before and since, this one was accompanied by a comprehensive assault on the rights of women. The state's biggest ally in this respect was the Catholic Church, which provided schools, hospitals and what passed for social care. The government targeted unwed mothers, who were often made to enter the now notorious

Swift Blaze of Fire

Mother and Baby Homes, for example the one at Tuam, where 796 babies are known to have died since its establishment in 1925.[17] Many of these women were made to give their babies up for adoption through the Church; others sought adoptions in England; some resorted to illegal abortion or infanticide. New laws and state propaganda also harassed politically active women and those working outside the home. Church opposition to divorce and contraception would lead to bans of both in the 1930s. Censorship curtailed artistic expression,[18] with an emphasis on 'purity' and 'modesty'.

It's not clear how much of this Robert was aware of in 1925, but having long opposed conservatism and supported press freedom,[19] he shared the 'sour disillusionment of the time', in which 'the buoyant optimism of the pre-[civil] war years had disappeared'.[20] One thing he knew was that national identity was becoming ever more closely tied to a sectarian form of Catholicism.

This was to last many years. My mother recalls staying in Killarney in 1930, aged two, with Alice and old Robert. A big procession for the feast of Corpus Christi[21] took place while she was there. The house curtains were drawn shut and she was whisked upstairs for 'a picnic in the attic'[22] lasting the whole day, during which she had to keep very quiet. That the family felt they must hide in their own home during this celebration reflects the entrenched anti-Protestant sentiment that followed independence. Identifying Irishness with Catholicism served a political purpose: 'In post-independence Ireland, Catholicism became a spiritual compensation for the failure to achieve the real improvements many had hoped for during the revolution. The more Catholic and respectful you were of the priests, the more you asserted your victory over the Brits.'[23] Such rejection cut deep for Robert and he struggled with it.[24] Rosemary seemed to offer light, love, hope and sanity. Nothing mattered more to him at this time than his longing to be with her.

Robert loved his parents and knew they had made sacrifices for his education, but he had meant what he said when two years earlier he supported a motion that Ireland offered 'no prospects for a man with a university education'.[25] It's probable that other emotions were also flooding through him which were beyond his rational control. He had spent his

'My friend'

teenage years in an atmosphere of chronic tension, unable to confide in anyone. Having at last poured out these confidences to Rosemary, he might well have found it unbearable to bottle them up again.

Ultimately Robert failed to attend enough Senior Sophister lectures between the autumn of 1924 and the summer of 1925 to qualify as a Candidate Bachelor. Without this qualification he would not be permitted to take his degree. He would get two more chances to become a Candidate Bachelor, in January and April 1926.[26] Trinity left his options open, continuing to list him as a Senior Sophister in January 1926, but by then he had moved to England. The die had probably been cast in May 1925. At a time when he urgently needed to add to his tally of lectures, he had instead spent eight nights at Kingswood Hanger, his longest stay yet.

Robert boxed at Trinity until the summer of 1925, always at featherweight. Three further bouts were reported, all unsuccessful. On 18 February he lost on points to a much larger opponent in the DUBC Tournament, after four rounds in which there was 'a good deal of holding'.[27] On 13 June he lost to F Russell in the Intervarsity draw, taking 'much punishment' in an 'exceptionally fast' match.[28] The two met again three days later and again Robert fought hard but lost.[29] After that his name disappears from boxing reports. He stayed at Kingswood Hanger from 28 August to 10 September 1925, and thereafter visited so often that Rose's Visitors' Book simply notes 'several weekends and Christmas'. For the whole of 1926 it reads 'R M Hilliard – Various weekends.' He must have been living within easy reach, probably in London.

One account of his final departure from Trinity is exceptionally unlikely. It claims he fought a duel in front of the College and was sent down for good as a result. His last words to the College authorities are said to have been 'I'll be back! – and next time you'll ask me to stay!' It's a little too *Terminator* to be true. The documented facts are that even in early 1926, when Rose's Visitors' Book shows he had definitely moved to England, he was still listed as a Senior Sophister on the roll at Trinity and therefore had not been sent down. Trinity College must have quietly given up on him later that year, when his prolonged absence could no longer be ignored.

Swift Blaze of Fire

This new phase of Robert's courtship of Rosemary was marked by gifts of books: *Electra*, by Euripides and *The Choephoroe*, by Aeschylus, both translated by Gilbert Murray. She pencilled 'Rosemary Robins' on each flyleaf, with dates. Within a few years her handwriting would become almost illegibly chaotic, as if her personal alphabet had been sent flying by the impact of a fast-moving object, but in these books her signature is composed and childlike. After their marriage Robert would give her more Gilbert Murray translations. The flyleaves show her tentatively trying out her new identity: 'Rosemary (Robins) Hilliard', and finally 'Rosemary Hilliard'.

How did Robert support himself in England? During 1926 he worked as a copywriter. Family reports suggest this was with Basil Clarke's pioneering PR agency, Editorial Services.[30] He later claimed to have coined the advertising slogan '*Great Stuff This Bass!*' – and indeed 1926 was the year in which the Bass company started using it. A durable and catchy slogan, it lasted on and off until the 1950s, accompanied by a cartoon character by the name of Bill Sticker. Sticker wore overalls and an insouciant smirk, carried a ladder and paste-pot, and stuck posters declaring '*Great Stuff This Bass!*' wherever he went. The joke was that he stuck them in the wrong places: the flanks of a hippo in a jungle pool, the white cliffs of Dover or one of the Pyramids.[31] Sadly, if Robert did invent this slogan he earned nothing from it. Rosemary later lamented that he passed his idea on to someone else and never got paid for dreaming it up.

My mother believes Robert also submitted press articles on a freelance basis, but if printed they are untraceable, since most journalism was published pseudonymously or simply without a name. Robert was sure he would break through one day, but for now had more pressing concerns. He and Rosemary had a disastrous secret. They could not keep it for long.

On 25 September 1926 the Kingswood Hanger Visitors' Book records a surprising arrival under Rose's roof: '*Alice E Hilliard*'. Robert's mother had braved the journey from Killarney to England, possibly for the first time in her life, to help Rose deal with an emergency. Rosemary was pregnant.

'My friend'

As an old woman, Rosemary once told me childbirth had nearly killed her. Her words were, 'The wages of sin are death – and I almost died!' For her the sexual act was a sin. All her lifelong feelings of guilt rose to the surface and she felt humiliated and mortified. How she must have dreaded meeting Alice – and how she must have resented Robert for leading her astray.

She need not have worried about Alice Hilliard, who despite her own strict moral principles was determined to help rescue the young couple from their predicament. The two mothers hastily arranged a 'quiet' wedding on 21 October 1926, well away from Gomshall, in Poplar Registry Office. It was witnessed by Rosemary's friends Gertrude Leventhal and Kit Laidley.[32] While Alice helped Rose, she rehearsed the story she would take back to Killarney, one designed to soothe Robert's father and lift the shadows over the two youngsters by providing a face-saving version of the facts to relatives and friends: Robert had married a lovely English girl from a particularly good background (Alice cannily dropped hints that he was marrying up) who bred Samoyed dogs. Rosemary would be the making of Robert, setting him on track as a respectable, hard-working husband. I know that's what she told them because, seventy-eight years later, that's what old Robin Hilliard, Robert's Lake Hotel cousin and long-ago playmate, told me. 'We had high hopes of him,' he said. 'We heard she was a decent girl, a very decent girl, from a very good family. She bred dogs, those big, white dogs. She was going to be the making of Robert.'

PART V — MARRIED LOVE

11

'I WISH I WERE A QUARTER GOOD ENOUGH FOR YOU'

In 1983, when Rosemary was too old to take care of herself, she moved into a house in Oxford to live with her elder daughter Deirdre (my mother), who looked after her until she died in 1994. One day Deirdre found her loading wadded fragments of paper into plastic bags. Rosemary explained that for several weeks she had been tearing up Robert's papers and throwing them away. Most of his letters and many other personal documents were gone. Deirdre persuaded her mother not to destroy any more but was desolated to see how much was lost. Her own memories and those Rosemary had shared over the years became especially precious.

Apart from two postcards sent from Spain, only one of Robert's letters to Rosemary survives, written from Ireland on New Year's Eve, 1926:

> This is far more a sermon to myself than a letter to you. Darling one, tomorrow night, the first in 1927, I shall sleep with you. Let us think of all the fine things we can think of to each other and to it [the unborn baby]. We must do it together.
>
> I suppose every man puts the woman he wants to marry on a pedestal. I do not think it is possible for him to do otherwise. But some pedestals

Swift Blaze of Fire

are jerry built and fall. The pedestal that I have put you on or rather found you on is not. It is solid.

There is no one I believe who could be a better mother than you, nor a better wife … The baby will have a better mother than any other baby in the world.

There is nothing that I can wish for in you that I have not got. I have an Idealist, a fine woman, a loving and fine thinking wife. I wish I were quarter good enough for you. When I see other men, men whom I admire, I think of how much more worthy of you they would be …

It is striking. There, the last peal has gone. God bless you. God bless us both and It. I shall try to be better. Your loving husband Robert.

The lack of spontaneity in this letter makes it an uneasy read. Its handwriting looks like a neat copy from a previous draft and its wording is stilted and overthought. Robert's longing to sleep with Rosemary again is immediately followed by strained efforts to sound positive. As he says, he had put his wife on a pedestal – his single-sex boarding-school education had left him unversed in any other way of falling in love – but idealizing someone is no substitute for mutual understanding. This reads as if they hardly knew each other. It's also ominously contrite. He feels he's not good enough, and though he will 'try to be better' doesn't trust himself to succeed.

In every courtship lovers present their best selves to each other, often adopting a misleading air of confidence. These very young lovers had been no exception. Now Rosemary's shamed panic at her pregnancy had shown Robert her vulnerability. The letter suggests this fed self-doubt as well as tenderness. That New Year's Eve began three dark years for both of them.

The Irish family generously put together £400 to buy a home for the young couple. Early in 1927 Rosemary and Robert moved into Kingswood Ruffs, Grayshott, near Hindhead in Surrey, a small, pretty house, twenty-six miles from Gomshall, with a big enough garden for Rosemary's dogs.

Robert was twenty-two and Rosemary twenty-one. As they started living together each made unwelcome discoveries. Rosemary found Robert more

'I wish I were a quarter good enough for you'

alarming than she expected. He drank, sometimes a lot. He earned little, and in his line of work was unlikely to earn more any time soon. He did not seem to understand how ill she felt, and he kept wanting sex – too often, in Rosemary's opinion; she once told my mother, with disapproval, that he seemed to want 'a woman every night'. She had fallen romantically in love, but the intimacy of married life had been tainted with shame from the start by her unmarried pregnancy. Now fatigue and nausea made her recoil from it further. Like most young men Robert enjoyed sex, but his physical passion was not returned. According to her, he soon started having affairs. The remorseful tone of his New Year letter suggests they may already have begun.

As Robert built new networks in London, Rosemary's life narrowed. Pregnancy pulled her away from the political activism of her Poplar friends. East End Labour Party members were in any case having a heartbreaking time. Labour had been ousted from government in November 1924, derailed in part by the Daily Mail's fraudulent Zinoviev letter.[1] Mass unemployment and the catastrophic TUC betrayal of the General Strike in May 1926 marked a downturn in working-class confidence and a depth of social hardship far beyond the understanding of Rosemary's well-to-do Surrey neighbours. Robert's fellow journalists were generally hostile to the General Strike, or thought it a game: Graham Greene, working for *The Times*, wrote that 'the atmosphere was that of a rugger match played against a team from a rather rough council school which didn't stick to the conventional rules.'[2] It was hard to hold onto the hopeful ideas that had drawn the couple together. Even Rosemary's unsinkable friend Muriel Lester felt her morale shaken when meeting families whose unemployed older children contemplated suicide as a means of making food available for younger ones.[3] She felt 'an embitterment of spirit' at the betrayal of the General Strike which she later said 'years have not been able to heal'.[4]

Like Orwell's Gordon Comstock in *Keep the Aspidistra Flying*, Robert soon found out that the precarious income of an aspiring writer or journalist did not fit well with unplanned parenthood. Rosemary expected security, but with so many unemployed he was unlikely to find anything more lucrative or reliable. He sold articles where he could; those published

Swift Blaze of Fire

almost always appeared anonymously. The only example of his journalism kept by Rosemary is entitled *In Praise of Baldness*, sold to an Irish newspaper in May 1927. This exercise in cod-learning, which – unusually – carries his name, bemoans his own receding hairline while claiming that baldness is good and hairiness bad:

> Synesius, a Bishop of the early Church … wrote in praise of baldness, demonstrating its close relationship with intelligence in a marvellously clear manner … Consider the stars. They are heavenly bodies and they have no hair. By night they delight the traveller and guide the mariner tossed by the sea. Comets are hairy bodies, and bring in their train plagues and pestilences and famine.[5]

The rueful jokes about thinning hair masked a miserable sense that life was passing him by. The couple only stayed afloat with help from their families. He carried on, dogged as ever, dulling his fear of failure in a haze of alcohol. The atmosphere soon soured inside the pretty house.

Their son Tim was born at home on 1 May 1927. It was a breech birth, and the hired midwife could not save Rosemary from serious tissue damage and blood loss, followed by infection. Postnatal infections were common in the days before antibiotics, and recovery was a long, uncertain process. The shock of the painful labour and the injuries it inflicted were hard to bear. Slowly the exhausting weeks of Rosemary's early motherhood went by. She briefly stayed with her mother when Tim was two months old. In August she and Robert took him to meet the Hilliards in Killarney. Their journey was delayed by a collision while still in port between their ferry and another ship, and they suffered a gruelling journey to Waterford on an overcrowded replacement boat. The upside of this ordeal was that Robert was able to wire out a news story about it.[6]

There's no mistaking the happiness and pride on old Robert's face in the pictures of him and his first grandchild. Unfortunately Rosemary was less happy with the Hilliards. Her own family's fortunes, though continuing to diminish, were linked on both sides to old money, whereas the prosperity

'I wish I were a quarter good enough for you'

of Robert's family was relatively new. When she had first met Robert he appeared perfectly at home among the glitterati at her Aunt Frances's dinner-party. Only with this visit did she fully absorb that his relatives were factory owners and tradespeople. In a surprising train of thought for a socialist, she decided that the upwardly mobile Hilliards, though kind, were vulgar, tasteless and provincial, a view she never lost.

A photo taken during the visit shows Robert looking peaky and strained. His flyaway hair is slicked flat, always a sign that he was trying to please. He badly wanted his parents' approval. His wife's opinion of them, if he sensed it, must have dented his enjoyment of the reunion.

Back in Surrey, Rosemary was alone at home with the baby most of the time. She found comfort in taking photos of him, often in the garden, looking almost overwhelmed by large dogs. She stuck these in an album, giving Tim's and the dogs' names equal billing in her captions. She also snapped him in Marianne's arms at his christening, carefully noting whose family owned his christening robe and that it was antique: 'Robe belonging to the Robins family, 18th century'.

Rosemary and Robert inhabited different worlds. Each day he drove off in their Austin 7 to Alton Station, commuting to and from his work in London by train. On one occasion he paused in his journey to register Tim's birth at Alton registry office. Sometimes he stayed in London overnight. She distrusted his accounts of who he stayed with, aware he was making new friends as well as meeting old Trinity acquaintances. One old face, now a close friend, was Lionel Fleming, working unhappily in a railway company advertising department. Both men felt their lives were on the wrong path but found it hard to admit. As Fleming said, London 'swallowed everyone, reducing them to a collection of faceless and anonymous figures'.[7]

Being a jobbing journalist[8] meant long days trying to get stories and market his talents. The largely male newspaper world was notorious for heavy drinking and treating women as sex objects. Graham Greene records that drinking 'pint for pint with any man'[9] was the route to acceptance. If Robert worked late it was tempting to retreat to a pub, get too drunk to go home and stay with a colleague or friend. Some journalists went to brothels;

Robert may sometimes have joined them or taken opportunities for casual sex. Rosemary found him ever more coarse and unpleasant. She withdrew into her love of dogs and a deepening preoccupation with religion.

Rose, Rosemary' mother, could see all was not well. A believer in birth control, and hoping to relieve her daughter's fear of another pregnancy, she took her to be fitted with one of the new contraceptive caps at the central London clinic recently opened by Marie Stopes, author of the pioneering *Married Love*. Rose told Deirdre all about this expedition twenty or so years later, adding that Rosemary almost certainly never used the device. Rosemary believed sexual abstinence to be the only Christian method of contraception and probably acquiesced to the clinic visit solely to keep Rose happy. It didn't matter, she would have told herself. Sex was out of the question after the pain and injury caused by Tim's birth. Or so she imagined.

The next part of the story is grim for both my mother and Rosemary. As a child, Deirdre noticed Rosemary never showed her the love she sometimes showed her other children: 'I do not remember having a goodnight kiss from her, though I do remember Tim and Davnet [her sister] getting one and me not. I do not remember ever being the one to sit on her knee for a story.'[10]

This implacable coldness continued into Deirdre's adult life. At last, in middle age, she blurted out 'Why have you never loved me?' She wrote an account of Rosemary's answer in 2005: 'When Tim was about five months old my father had come home drunk and insisted on his "conjugals" when my mother was not in a fit state for another pregnancy, [and] that was the result, me. This, she told me … was why she could not love me like she did the others!'

I asked my mother how she felt about this bombshell. Surely 'insisted on his conjugals' was a euphemism for rape?' Things were different in those days,' she said, 'a man couldn't rape his wife.' It's true that marital rape was unrecognized by English law,[11] but Robert knew that what he had done was non-consensual, a violation. His wife's wretchedness shamed him.

'I wish I were a quarter good enough for you'

They kept up appearances with their families[12] but he had torn a gaping hole in their relationship. His drinking accelerated. Sometimes he gambled as well, betting money he could not spare, perhaps hoping to please Rosemary with an immense sum of winnings. No winnings materialized, but the adrenalin-fuelled release of gambling gained a hold.

Rosemary's waters broke without warning on 30 June 1928. Robert ran to fetch the midwife, who found Rosemary lying fully dilated on a sofa used as the dogs' bed. She coaxed her off it just in time to catch the baby. As Rosemary recovered, she recalled the Dublin dinner party where she had first met Robert. James Stephens had joked that she would name a daughter Deirdre after the heroine of one of his books. She decided to follow his suggestion. Lionel Fleming stood as baby Deirdre's godfather.

Tim wasn't there to meet his new sister: he had been sent to stay with Rose because Rosemary felt unable to cope. It was two months before he was brought home. A photo shows him on his return, staring at the new arrival with a baffled expression. This was the first of many occasions when Rosemary gained respite by parking Tim or Deirdre with a grandmother, or even a stranger, for long periods. She would never tell the children she was leaving them; instead they would suddenly find her gone. By 1929 she often left both children with Rose. To her this was normal – much of her own childhood had been spent with servants or relatives – but the children found the unpredictability of these separations hard to bear.[13]

By April Rosemary felt well enough to have both children at home. She photographed them sitting in the garden: Deirdre, ten months old, smiling and creasing her eyes against the spring sunshine, Tim looking downwards, preoccupied. Behind this garden idyll, the marriage was approaching its inevitable crisis.

Terry Trench, brother of Robert's Trinity friend Paddy,[14] remembered Robert in 1929 'as a tough, hard-drinking, hard-swearing Fleet Street journalist'.[15] Such behaviour repelled Rosemary, provoking frequent rows. The children sensed huge threats under the surface of their lives. My mother recalls a swimming trip to Grayshott some time before she was two. When her father swam past the drainage vents in the swimming pool she screamed hysterically, fearing he would be sucked in and lost forever.

In December 1929, while Robert was at work, Rosemary opened the door to a party of bailiffs, who told her they were homeless: Robert had parted with the deeds of the house. She had no choice but to give them the keys. She must have begged a lift to the station with the children and taken the train to Gomshall, where the family stayed with Rose until after Christmas. A rented place was found, so small that Rosemary called it 'the chicken house'. They were allowed to collect the dogs but could keep only one. According to Rosemary, Robert had pledged the deeds of the Grayshott house as security on a gambling debt which he could not pay.[16] All her worst fears about him were realized. Profoundly depressed, she considered separation.

Robert knew he had driven Rosemary to the point of mental collapse. He poured out his remorse and self-disgust (with more than a hint of self-pity) to a Trinity friend: 'I said to him – "You remember when I was at College I had in me the power to do good work . . . I don't mean just good writing and that sort of thing . . . I mean that I had in me the power to be a force for good in the world. Well that has gone from me. I have no power at all."'[17]

At this low point, early in 1930, an old school friend of Rosemary's visited, full of excitement about a Christian movement called the Oxford Group. Founded by Frank Buchman, an American Lutheran priest, the movement advocated complete personal surrender to God. Believers dedicated a daily 'Quiet Time' to receiving God's guidance and confessed their sins to each other at open meetings. Robert's attention was caught. At first he declared he was only interested 'from the psychological point of view'. On hearing similar praise for Buchman from a second friend, he asked for his address and arranged to meet him in London.

Buchman said little when they met, but Robert talked for three hours, quoting the Sermon on the Mount and expounding his own, humanist belief that Christ was merely a teacher of ethics. Buchman let Robert talk himself out before suggesting they take a quiet moment to ask God into their hearts. Robert agreed, 'willing to try anything once'. Then, exhausted, he left to catch a bus.

'I wish I were a quarter good enough for you'

He later wrote a letter describing the experience that overwhelmed him on the way home:

> Going down Haymarket on top of the bus, the miracle that happened to Saint Paul on the road to Damascus happened to me. There was a bright light on everybody's face – I was extremely happy all of a sudden – I was exhilarated – I knew that God was with me and that Jesus of Nazareth, whom I had persecuted and belittled as an ethical teacher, had come into my heart. Everything was certain. I got home and told Rosemary and by the following afternoon she was certain too. Since then we have been so happy, so tremendously happy, that it is almost unbelievable.

The deeply religious Rosemary was as convinced as Robert that his revelation came from God. Like him, she swiftly embraced the Oxford Group. Within days they were gloriously back in love. He swiftly decided he had been blessed with more than a personal call to self-amendment: this was a vocation. He would become a Church of Ireland priest. Through the priesthood he could work to alleviate the hardships suffered by the poor and the alienation suffered by the working men and women he saw around him every day. God had called him to do work which would satisfy both his political idealism and his long-suppressed spiritual yearnings.

One can only imagine his parents' joy at hearing he wanted to return to Ireland, graduate at last, and take orders. He made a successful case to Trinity College for re-enrolling, this time in the Divinity School. His Sizarship had long ended, so his parents must have paid for his course, a tall order with five other children to provide for. Together in Dublin, he and Rosemary looked for somewhere to live. They left Deirdre with Robert's parents in Killarney until the autumn of 1930, by which time she had learned to talk, with a strong Killarney accent. Tim spent two weeks with Rose, who described him as 'a charming little visitor and happy with his grannie and g'grannie and Aunt Madeleine'[18] – but was then sent to a children's home for six months. It seems unbelievable today that loving parents could fail to understand how traumatic this would be. He was distraught when they collected him, and never forgot his months of believing himself abandoned for good.

Swift Blaze of Fire

During this period Robert wrote the letter to Rosemary's Uncle Louis already quoted. In it he owned up to the things he had long felt most guilty about, albeit in the pious language of the recent convert. He knew he had caused terrible damage to Rosemary: 'I had committed, I think, the worst sin in the world … it was Rosemary's Belief … that caused me to love her. It is dreadful to think it but I had nearly destroyed it.'

He had rediscovered his sense of himself as a potential force for good and now planned to serve 'the men and the women, the hundreds of them working in offices as I was, who plod along from day to day, trying to manufacture excitement and fun out of things which are empty and useless. It is a wonderful message I have to give.'

Full of joy and relief, and dashed onto the page complete with crossings out, this candid outpouring could hardly be more unlike the New Year letter to Rosemary at the end of 1926. A tremendous tension had gone out of him. Ever since boarding school, his life had been a journey away from his parents' values. Now he was not only racing back to readopt a great many of them, resolving a guilt that had gnawed at him for years, but also healing the wounds he had inflicted on Rosemary. At last he could please all the people he loved.

Rosemary and Robert found a flat at 5 Herbert Street in Dublin. The plan was for Rosemary and the children to stay with Rose before joining him there in the New Year. Before they parted Robert made a handwritten will, leaving everything to Rosemary to administer in 'the best joint interests of herself and her children by me'. It's a poignant document: Robert's estate can have amounted to little more than books, some well-worn clothes and perhaps some boxing gloves.

Robert wrote to his children while he waited for them to join him, and one letter survives:

> DEAR TIM + DEIRDRE, HERE IS THE SHIP I SAILED TO IRELAND IN and this is the captain of the ship, with a beard and a stick in his hand and this is the train that took me to the ship and here is the house I am living in, marked with a cross. There are lots of houses beside it + here is the hen that laid the egg I had for breakfast. Love from Daddy.

'I wish I were a quarter good enough for you'

After each 'here is' or 'this is' comes a pen and ink picture, ending with a minuscule sketch of 'Daddy': round face, round glasses, wavy blond hair parted on the side.

At Trinity he eagerly returned to debating and boxing as well as study. At Christmas he rejoined the family at Kingswood Hanger and at New Year there was a party. The trouble Rosemary took dressing up for it reflected her delight at being with him again. Deirdre, though only two-and-a-half, never forgot how she looked:

> Mum came up to say goodnight to us … she was all ready to go to the party. She was wearing a beautiful silk dress, with embroidery and lacing at the neck and she wore elegant brown glacé leather shoes with two button straps, and they even had some heel. (I found these shoes with her things when she died, in her ninetieth year, hardly worn …) She had her hair done up with beads, and she had lovely necklaces. She looked beautiful. I never saw her dressed up like that again in all her life.

Robert returned to Dublin early in 1931, joined soon afterwards by Rosemary and the children. Deirdre's account of their arrival captures the joy of the occasion.

> Daddy was waiting with copies of the stories we both loved … he read them to us before we went to bed … I remember having a bath with Tim to wash off the travel dirt, and Dad washed Tim's hair … Tim rushed round, still wet from his bath and stark naked …

Profoundly relieved at the lifting of family tension, the children rejoiced in the news that their lives were going to change for the better. 'We were told everything was going to be different, Daddy was studying, and we would all be together for always now. It was a happy time.'

12

ONWARD CHRISTIAN SOLDIERS

Overjoyed to be back at Trinity, Robert was determined that this time round he would do his best at everything he undertook. He threw himself into public speaking, engaging with theological topics such as Christian missionaries abroad[1] and Zoroastrianism[2] and earning plaudits from *The Irish Times* for his eagerness to share the story of his own religious conversion.[3] *TCD* praised his paper on *Work and Progress in the Oxford Group*, sounding more deferential than it had during his undergraduate career: 'Mr Hilliard is to be congratulated on a fine paper.'[4] Robert's debating positions show him embracing Buchman's teachings with all the ardour of a new proselyte, turning away from the classical ideal of truth reached through logic and towards guidance through divine revelation; for example he called for 'the negation of self'[5] in a debate on 'Religion and Conduct' and spoke up for revelation as the path to truth at a meeting on 'Faith and Reason'.[6] As he prepared himself each day to receive divine guidance during the 'Quiet Times' advocated by the Oxford Group, he may have reflected that at last he was following the Bible text his mother had flagged up to him long ago: 'Trust in the LORD with all thine heart, and lean not upon thine own understanding'.[7]

Onward Christian soldiers

In London he had been a heavy smoker and shown signs of succumbing to alcoholism; he now renounced alcohol and cigarettes. He returned to his boxing training and quickly regained form. In November, in a 'hurricane finish with rights and lefts', he won the quarter-finals of the Dublin Universities' and Hospitals' Championships, but lost the semi-final when his opponent knocked him 'clean off his legs.'[8] Undeterred, he carried on training, and by May 1931 had regained the Trinity featherweight title. *The Irish Independent* described him as 'an old champion'.[9] It delighted him that he could still box as well as a young one.[10]

This was the season of happiness for Robert and Rosemary. Rosemary welcomed the start of a third pregnancy, unlike her earlier ones, but again felt tired and ill. In April she decided she could no longer look after the two older children. Robert had to keep studying, so his sister Phyllis ('Auntie Phyl') conveyed Tim and Deirdre, aged four and three, to England to stay with Rose. The promise that they would not be sent away again had swiftly been broken.

Tim's exile when Deirdre was born had unsurprisingly made him resent her very existence. They could not be left together unsupervized. By the time she was three he had poisoned her once by forcing paraffin down her throat and wound a car window so tightly against her neck that she had to be resuscitated. On their last visit he'd tipped a potty full of urine over her head while she sat in her cot. Rose felt anxious about hosting both children at once, but there was no alternative and the visit went ahead.

Robert and Rosemary came to see their children in June 1931. The family picnicked together on the Surrey Downs, joined by Bob Lund, a family friend. Robert challenged Lund to a tree-climbing contest and they both climbed to the top of some tall beech trees. 'Every now and then Dad would call out, "Look at us, cooee, up here!" getting ever higher ... they came back full of laughter and Dad with a rip in his trousers.'[11] Two photos by Bob Lund preserve this fleeting moment of contented family togetherness. In one, Robert sits in the grass with Tim nearby; in another Rosemary bends over him to mend his trousers as Deirdre looks on.

Rose did her best to cheer the children up when their parents returned to Ireland. Tim's birthday had gone unmarked during their journey to England so she made Deirdre's third birthday on 30 June a joint celebration, with new toys and garlands of flowers for their heads. This time Rosemary did not leave them long: in July she returned from Ireland to Kingswood Hanger so that Rose could look after her for the remainder of her pregnancy. Robert visited when he could, and they both attended Buchman-led house parties in Oxford. The Killarney Hilliards, keen to maintain a friendship, sent Robert's brother Geoff over to Kingswood Hanger for a four-day visit from his school in Ellesmere Port. His sister Phyl came for two days soon afterwards. That autumn, Rose treated her daughter and grandchildren to a holiday in Hayling Island, where Tim and Deirdre both fell in love with the seaside.

Robert gained his BA on 3 July 1931. The course had left an unpleasant taste in his mouth. Many fellow students planned to work in England, but Robert wanted to work in Ireland. He explained his reasons in another letter to Uncle Louis, written after his graduation:

> As there is but one source, the Divinity School, Trinity College, from which almost all Irish [Church of Ireland] Clergy are drawn, they are all very much of a muchness. The Divinity School encourages a kind of colourless individualism while it severely represses personality.
> The result is that those who have come through the Divinity School with some personality left invariably seek refuge in England, where they do very well. If the Church in Ireland is to become a living force again instead of being as it has been at times the catspaw of a Westminster government, somebody will have to begin and be the first to stay there.

There's a flash in this letter of the iconoclastic Robert of old. In his view, the Church establishment had a habit of putting political expediency before Christ's message, and it had to stop. He wrote that unless the Church of Ireland 'awakes from its slovenly attitude of spectator,' religion in Ireland would dwindle away. Foreseeing, correctly, that the Catholic Church would one day lose its grip on Irish thinking, he prematurely expected this within his lifetime, believing there was 'material for an awakening in Ireland now.' With characteristic ebullience, he had dedicated himself to a Herculean project: the radical reinvigoration of the Church of Ireland. The irony was that while Robert wanted to be an inspiring new voice, Buchmanism was every bit as conservative as the orthodoxy he had scorned at Divinity School. He had yet to reject its reactionary ideas, or to recognize that ultimately the Oxford Group would be no help in furthering his radical ambitions.

On 21 September 1931, Robert was ordained as a deacon in a ceremony in St Peter's Parish Church, Belfast, by Charles Thornton Primrose Grierson, the Bishop of Down.[12] The certificate stated that Robert's 'probity of life' was 'sufficiently certified' for the Bishop to grant him a deaconship in the Parish of Derriaghy, on the edge of Belfast and Lisburn. Robert's flock would be small and close-knit, making his 'probity of life' all the more important. He would be expected to conduct himself impeccably; if he slipped up word would soon get round.

The post was only half-time. Robert had to divide his energies between Derriaghy and Dublin, with a further year at Trinity College in order to qualify as a curate. Half pay meant continuing to depend on his father, who was nothing like as well off as most of his peers' fathers, but who would make any sacrifice to see his son established. The whole Hilliard family would later pay a price for the financial support old Robert gave his son's household at this time.

That autumn, again as part of his project of making the best of all his talents, Robert took up an editorship at *TCD*. Editors served in threes, each taking one term. Robert was so stringent with himself and others that in October the magazine printed some verse lampooning the contrast between his rigorous attitude and the torpor of Alcorn, a fellow editor: 'Tis the voice of the Alc-rn, I heard him complain/'You have waked me too soon, I must slumber again.' So he to the H-ll-ard; the cleric severe/Tossing blankets aside, hauled him out by the ear.'[13]

He loved the company of other journalists, and on his return to Dublin had quickly resumed old friendships with Alec Newman and Bert Smyllie, both now working at *The Irish Times*. Lionel Fleming had by now come to Dublin and worked at the same newspaper. Smyllie was a popular assistant editor (and future editor), at the centre of a lively group of newsmen and writers frequenting the Palace Bar in central Dublin. Samuel Beckett later recalled how Smyllie 'ran his newspapers from the pubs'[14] and Fleming affectionately described him as having 'no sense of dignity whatever'.[15] Beckett was another old acquaintance of Robert's, back at Trinity as a lecturer after working in Paris, where he'd been introduced to James Joyce by Irish poet and critic Thomas McGreevy, whom Robert also knew.[16] New friends included future politician Owen Sheehy-Skeffington, who admired him for his idealism.[17] Robert enjoyed the wit and wordplay that flowed around these men, but if he spent any time at the Palace Bar with them it seems unlikely that he always kept his promises to God and to Rosemary to abstain from alcohol.

In November 1931 he lost his Dublin University featherweight title,[18] putting up 'a good display' but 'well-beaten at the finish'.[19] It was the last championship title he would ever hold. He was by now juggling a great many commitments – composing and preaching sermons in Derriaghy, studying, *TCD* editorship – and was still a regular at Theological Society debates. His zeal as a new convert could at times make him sound censorious or pedantic, as some of his debating contributions show. For example, fellow debaters were surprised by the solemnity of his call for a 'serious and sensible' approach to gambling (comments no doubt partly explained by his self-reproach for gambling away his family home). He also made an obscure-sounding speech about 'The Church and her heresies', in which he '... stressed the wickedness of the Monothelites in attempting to re-introduce Eutychianism in a more subtle form, and proved that this heresy was much nearer to us than the seventh century. He shared also the dangerous spiritual pride that engenders Pelagianism.'[20]

These 'isms' related to the relationship between the human and the divine. Eutychians argued against the dual (human and divine) nature of

Jesus, Monothelites that Jesus had two natures but one will, and Pelagians that human beings can gain salvation by their own efforts and without God. Robert evidently believed that variants of these ideas existed in the present day, and perhaps thought he had been something of a Pelagian himself earlier in his marriage. This focus on dusty, ancient heresies points to the pull that Buchmanism and the Church of Ireland were exerting, away from his youthful radicalism and towards a new conformism.

And yet Robert was still Robert. Denis Carroll refers to his liveliness and frequent air of dishevelment: 'Evidence of non-conventionality is given by the student journal's allusions to his "wearing strange suits" and being "a cross between a hornpipe and a fugue, often of a wild nature."'[21] Robert's failure to wear smart suits like his better-off peers was no doubt due to lack of money as much as non-conventionality. But the comparison to a dance 'of a wild nature' also recalls the Dionysian Robert of ten years earlier, and suggests he was forcing himself into a mould which could not always contain him.

On 16 December 1931 Rosemary gave birth to her third child. Baby Davnet arrived at a maternity home in Reading owned and staffed by a Mrs Halliday, a cousin of Rosemary's. The newborn Davnet failed to breathe. Terrified, Rosemary started to pray as Mrs Halliday made frantic efforts to get respiration started. When all else failed, she tried to startle a breath into the little body by dipping her in cold water. At last they heard a cry and realized the child's lungs had begun working. Deirdre has written of the conclusions Rosemary drew from this perilous start: 'She always felt that God had answered her prayers ... As I was growing up I was told that Davnet was special and that God must have a special purpose for her life.'

What Rose thought of her daughter's theory can only be guessed. Divinely ordained special purpose or not, she arranged a speedy bedside christening in case the baby died. She was now caring for two elderly sisters, her frail mother, two young children who could not be left alone together, a convalescent daughter and a newborn baby who was soon diagnosed as

Swift Blaze of Fire

having a weak heart. Foreseeing stretching times ahead, she arranged for a nanny to visit for six weeks.

Robert made sure Tim and Deirdre knew he was thinking of them at Christmas. On Christmas Day they were thrilled at the arrival of two giant parcels containing toy pedal cars. Robert had announced that he was sending these in a telegram to Rosemary. It scandalized the postmistress, who thought he was referring to full-sized vehicles: 'Have bought two cars, arrive on Friday'. It also contained sad news, which the children were not told until Christmas was over: 'Father died yesterday'.

13

A LIVING FORCE?

Old Robert had died on 20 December 1931. Tributes appeared in the local press and Killarney's council passed a motion of condolence to Alice, adjourning its next meeting out of respect. The funeral was packed. *The Liberator* reported 'in addition to ... family and relatives ... an exceedingly large attendance of the general public'.[1] By the time Tim and Deirdre were told of his death, their grandfather was already buried in Killegy graveyard, the hilltop site overlooking Lough Leane where his own parents, Ellen and Richard, also lay.

The old man had been a towering presence in Robert's life. Robert knew he had shamed and disappointed his father by his shotgun wedding and flunking his earlier degree. Since then, old Robert had seen his son graduate to become a deacon and had held two grandchildren in his arms. Had Robert done enough to redeem himself? Standing by the grave, he must have hoped he had justified his father's faith and unstinting support.

Now the towering presence was gone. We can know an old landmark building must one day be demolished, but everything around it looks different when it's finally gone. Robert returned to his life in Dublin and Derriaghy after the funeral; the disorientation of the old man's death lasted longer.

The gap between the Church of Ireland as it was and the kind of 'living force' that Robert wanted it to be was wide. Long the voice of the Anglo-Irish squirearchy at prayer, it was fundamentally at odds with the ideas expressed in his letter to Uncle Louis. Robert had yet to recognize that change would only come on the Church's terms. In a Theological Society discussion about 'Ireland in the Purpose of God' in February 1932 he 'complained that the Church of Ireland tended to look to Imperialism rather than to God for her safety and welfare.'[2] He wanted it to engage with the social and political facts of Irish life, particularly the effects of the Depression. These were brought home to him forcefully as he went about his duties in and near Derriaghy.

The Wall Street Crash of 1929 had plunged the US, German and British economies into a recession which spread round the world, including Ireland. Global industrial output fell by a third; banks and businesses went under; blue- and white-collar unemployment veered out of control. When the free market could not rescue capitalists' profits, they demanded protectionist measures, such as tariffs and import restrictions. Governments worldwide responded with interventionist policies aimed at national self-sufficiency and funded by state investment.

National self-sufficiency was the watchword of Éamon de Valera's new Fianna Fáil party, formed in 1926 out of remnants of the anti-Treatyite republican current which had opposed partition during the Civil War. Fianna Fáil advocated state spending on public works to ease unemployment, redistribution of land, the redirection of farming towards feeding the Irish rather than exports, assistance to home-grown industry, protectionist tariff controls and an end to the land annuities paid to Britain. The ruling party, Cumann na nGaedheal (which largely represented those supporting the Treaty in the Civil War), denounced Fianna Fáil as 'a front for the IRA and communism.'[3] The reality was that Fianna Fáil had no intention of challenging capitalism; on the contrary, its policies aimed to build it, but the capitalists were to be Irish ones.

The new party nevertheless used a radical left republican language. Ignoring the revolutionary essence of James Connolly's socialism, De Valera had quoted Connolly at Fianna Fáil's inaugural meeting in 1926[4] and afterwards continued to make rhetorical links between his party and Connolly's legacy. The party's founding documents declared that 'the resources and wealth of Ireland are subservient to the needs and welfare of all the people.'[5] Fianna Fáil supported many trade union demands as well as certain selected strikes (those against traditional Unionist or British employers[6]), at least while it was in opposition, eroding the electoral strength of the left by attracting organized workers and small farmers away from the Labour Party and other left groups. Like many, Robert found Fianna Fáil's radical gloss very persuasive. The accusations of communism did not deter him but were likely to have gained credence with more conservative members of his family: Robert's liking for Fianna Fáil fed some of the Hilliards' fears that he was a communist.

Robert had already indicated his support for Irish nation-building by rejoining the recently revived Trinity Hurling Club, playing against Queen's University Belfast at Phoenix Park on 14 February.[7] He signalled his approval of Fianna Fáil when he opened a debate in February on the motion 'That this house approves of the policies of Rehoboam' (an Old Testament King of Judah, or Southern Israel), implying parallels between ancient Israel and modern Ireland: 'Mr Hilliard pointed out how it was that Rehoboam's policy ... made the South strong and self-reliant, that it had the best possible economic foundation and that its concentration on culture and education drew the best elements in the North into the vigorous Southern state ....'[8]

Although he had framed his views within an Old Testament analogy, his audience would not have missed these thinly veiled allusions to Fianna Fáil. *TCD* commented archly that 'Rehoboam and his friends seemed almost our contemporaries.' Robert's support for Fianna Fáil became more open after they won an election in February 1932, and in May he supported a motion of confidence in the new government.[9] He also commented in a *TCD* editorial that 'the Protestant layman in the south of Ireland no longer feels a stranger' but was 'becoming nationally conscious.'[10]

The same editorial attacked the Divinity School, claiming its curriculum needed firmer spiritual direction, a longer theological course and an update

Swift Blaze of Fire

on psychology, all this topped off with an elitist-sounding remark that 'a small bit of Greek gives even a third-class man superiority in the pulpit'. It provoked a flurry of critical letters. The Editorial Sub Committee later pronounced his editorship 'reasonable and well-informed, with the strange exception of an editorial on the Divinity School.'[11]

For all his criticisms of the Divinity course, Robert stuck with it, and on 18 June 1932 gained his Divinity Testimonial. In a surprising move that same month, he also joined the Trinity-based Lodge 357 of the Freemasons, probably persuaded to do so by the father of Moll's fiancé, who was the lodge's Grand Master.[12] The explanation may lie in his urgent need of a job, which he could only gain with a bishop's approval: he may have thought membership would help.

Despite his hopes of working full-time in the South he was given a half-time curacy in Derriaghy, in the North, where he had already been deacon for a year. He was obliged to soldier on and trust that a full-time post would come up soon. On 29 June he was ordained by the Right Reverend Dr Grierson, Bishop of Down, at St Patrick's, Ballymacarrett, Belfast.

Given the affluent backgrounds of many of its new clergy, the Church could assume their families would support them while they settled into their careers. But Alice, still waiting for old Robert Hilliard's estate to be valued, was desperately economising. This had unfairly harsh results for Geoff, who was removed from his school in Wales and sent to one in Ireland, with no prospect of going to university like his siblings. Handouts to Robert had stopped. In a wealthier parish he might have received help from well-off parishioners, but Derriaghy wasn't wealthy. With no hope of supporting his family on a half-time stipend, he and Rosemary had to run up debt, rely on future earnings to repay it, and make the best of anything Rose gave them.

Robert collected Rosemary and the children from Kingswood Hanger and the whole family moved into a new built, semi-detached house in Knocknadona, near Lisburn. Other houses in the same development were still being built. Tim and Deirdre's first game on arrival was to scrape all the putty out of the freshly installed window frames in the half-built houses

A living force?

and use it as modelling clay. Rosemary had to placate a furious builder, who wanted his putty back.

Deirdre remembers the daily rituals of a family trying to live by the ethos of the Oxford Group:

> Tim and I were expected to take part in daily "Quiet Times". These were
> when we had a Bible reading and then a time of silence when we opened
> our minds to God and then were supposed to write down our guidance
> from God in our "Quiet Time" guidance diaries.[13]

Neither Tim nor Deirdre could yet read or write so to please their parents they produced a kind of scribble. They had to own up to bad behaviour and make plans for atoning and doing better.

> God was a sort of Big Brother always watching and always seeing; nothing
> was secret from him we were told. The adults shared too and the pressure
> was terrible. I never knew what to own up to or what I could do about it.
> I used to quite often invent bad things I had done so that I could get the
> glory of penitence and atonement.[14]

Not many parents make daily disclosures to their young children, and to each other, of their every sin of thought and deed. This regime required an almost childlike purity of mind and must have been as much of a strain for the adults as the children. As well as daily Quiet Times there were Oxford Group meetings in the evenings, and they all went to church on Sundays.

Knocknadona, where they lived, is a three-and-a-half mile walk from Derryiaghy along a country road. Rosemary felt socially isolated. She had longed to be back with Robert, but coming to Ireland meant she now had three children under six to care for. At Kingswood Hanger, Rose had kept her company, seen to the children, paid the bills and dealt with the housework. Rosemary badly missed her. Robert hired a Mrs Mulligan to help with cleaning and laundry, but paying her pushed them further into debt. Lack of money posed never-ending challenges. A pastor must wear a suit, and

Swift Blaze of Fire

shoes without holes; his wife and children cannot look like ragamuffins; refreshments must be offered if people call. The humiliations of genteel poverty had to be concealed, but the bar set for luxury was miserably low. It was very different from a vicar's life in Surrey, and not at all what Rosemary had expected.

Robert tried to face things down with a Micawber-ish bonhomie: something would turn up. At some point after his ordination he dashed off three limerick verses whose thrust was that things could only get better. Rosemary's social standing would rise with his promotions. The first verse dwells on the future novelty of being a curate's wife, the second on how popular she would be when he became a rector, and the last invokes all the grandeur of being a bishop's wife: 'But I won't have to wash up or dish up/ When in silk and fine raiment I'll swish up/Episcopal stairs/And Diocesan Lairs/As the wife of his Lordship the Bishop.'[15]

Beneath the rough and ready lines, with their reference to not having to 'wash up or dish up', lies Robert's awareness that Rosemary hated housework and resented her slide down the social ladder in marrying him. He wanted to comfort her and make her laugh. Or was he trying to comfort himself? It can't have been pleasant to reflect that, despite his best efforts, he might never be able to keep his wife in the style to which she was accustomed.

Robert's approachability made him well-liked in the parish, however. He rode around on a bicycle, and one story tells of him cycling through Ballymacash, an area hit hard by the Depression, where men stood idle on street corners. One of them, Bryson Close, greeted him:

> 'Your reverence, your reverence, there's a man dying.'
> 'A man dying? Tell me who is it Mr. Close?'
> 'Me, your reverence, dying for a smoke!'

The story ends with Robert handing over tuppence for a packet of Woodbine, describing him as 'a popular figure amongst the youth of the area' who 'would have given you a lift on the bar of his bicycle at any time.'[16] This image of Robert carrying people on his crossbar, bantering with parishioners and generous with money he didn't have, is engaging and believable.

A living force?

Though strapped for money, Robert knew that the poverty created by the Depression in Belfast was of a different order from his own. Up to 73 per cent of Belfast's workers in the city's key industry, the shipyards, were laid off. Catholics had always found it harder to get work; now thousands of Protestants joined them on the dole queues. People from both communities sought 'exceptional distress relief' from the Board of Guardians. This was given to married men only, often taking the form of cash payments for 'outdoor relief schemes', such as road-building or other hard labour. In July an Outdoor Relief Workers' Committee was set up, led by members of the Revolutionary Workers' Groups, a small communist organization. This Committee demanded an increase in the rates paid and an end to payments in kind and piecework. It held its first rally on 8 August. A second rally on 18 August was larger than even its most optimistic supporters had predicted[17] and a third on 31 August was twenty thousand strong.[18] By 3 October outdoor relief workers were beginning a solid, determined strike,[19] with pickets mounted all over the city. A huge demonstration gathered, defying a ban, and marched round the Catholic Falls Road and the Protestant Shankill district.

Remarkably, the outdoor relief movement united Catholic and Protestant unemployed. One participant later said that 'people were beginning to have sympathy for each other rather than bringing the religious question to the forefront.'[20] This demonstration wound through different districts, bringing Protestant and Catholic marchers together. By evening a peaceful crowd of sixty thousand, led by torchbearers, had rallied at the Custom House, paralysing central Belfast by sheer force of numbers.[21] The next day thousands marched on the workhouse, demanding to be admitted. The political establishment was appalled – cross-sectarian workers' unity was the stuff of nightmare for Orangeism – and so were the Churches. The Pope urged vigilance against communism on Irish bishops. Trade was being disrupted. The authorities made a plan to use force.[22]

On 11 October an even larger march was accompanied by a rent strike, a school strike and a hire purchase strike. Police, including B Specials, attacked the marchers. Catholic and Protestant workers fought them side by side, digging trenches across roads and erecting barricades. The police retreated, but opened fire as they went. Two workers were killed, one Protestant and one Catholic, and hundreds were wounded. When police began a house-to-house search of the Falls Road and other Catholic areas, Protestants came out of Protestant areas such as the Shankill to help fight them off. There followed Belfast's biggest riot for years.

In another moving display of cross-sectarian solidarity, 100,000 people from both communities attended the murdered workers' funerals. Veteran English communist, Tom Mann, came for one funeral and was immediately detained by the police and 'deported' back to England.[23] But violent suppression merely strengthened the two communities' fellow feeling.

The city authorities saw no way out except by making concessions. On 15 October the strikers agreed to accept an effective doubling of the outdoor relief rates, to be paid in cash rather than kind, and improvements to the means test. Suspended strikers would have their entitlement to relief reinstated. Unmarried men still received no relief at all, a divisive factor among the strikers, but despite this real shortcoming the deal was a major achievement for the protests.[24]

It was now brought home to Robert where the Church stood when the chips were down. Church of Ireland leaders had not hesitated. For them, protecting the status quo had come before easing the starvation of Belfast's poor. There were pulpit denunciations of the 'communist menace' and several clerics had actively worked with the police to help suppress the protests.

As bullets flew and doors opened in one community to shelter members of another, of what relevance was Robert's quest for personal redemption or the Oxford Group's preoccupation with individual sin? There can be no doubt where his sympathies lay. The fellowship and solidarity he was witnessing had much in common with what he'd heard from Rosemary and Muriel Lester about the Poplar struggles. Unlike the General Strike, Belfast's outdoor relief protests had been successful. The last time he himself had seen people win results by striking and standing together against the state and its repressive measures had been the general strikes of his Cork schooldays. Potent memories and impulses stirred after years of lying dormant. What could he do? As a pastor he was barred from participating.[25]

A living force?

This was not his first experience of having to remain a bystander to an inspiring social upheaval, but it would be his last.

A fresh challenge faced Rosemary and Robert after these protests: Rosemary was pregnant again. Her body was exhausted from three previous pregnancies and the couple could not afford a fourth child. As ever, she turned to Rose for help with childcare. Deirdre was too young for school, so Rose paid for an Austrian governess to come to Derriaghy.

Unfortunately this governess found the children so unmanageable that she left after a month and Rosemary had to look after them again. Robert took turns when he could, often carrying one or other of them with him on his bicycle to see parishioners. On one trip with Deirdre he made a stop as he pedalled back:

> On the way home he propped the bike against the kerb and a lamppost and left me perched there on the luggage rack for a long time while he went into a 'shop' that had a dark brown tiled wall below a smoky looking window. After a while people came and asked why I was sitting there, and I said I was waiting for my daddy ... They tut-tutted and ... fetched him out. Looking back I know it was a pub; also he told me not to tell Mother.

This pub visit was an early sign of a slow backsliding from Buchman's regime. Robert did not own up to it at the next family Quiet Time and Deirdre kept quiet, worrying because God was all-seeing, and because she wanted her parents to tell each other everything.

Robert's reserves of fortitude and self-belief were ebbing away. He regularly witnessed harrowing scenes among his parishioners. Hard-working days ended in homecomings to a wife who was once again deeply disappointed in him. Rosemary's burdens were too heavy for her to bear. After all the joy and optimism following his conversion, there were ominous hints of the resentful accusations of their early marriage. If only he'd been able to abstain from sex, she would not be pregnant again. If only he were wealthier, she would not have to live like this.

141

Swift Blaze of Fire

Just before Christmas, the estate of Robert's father was finally valued at £18,180, chiefly comprising the house at Moyeightragh and its contents. The Killarney family were now in an unexpectedly fragile financial position. The modest interest from this estate must support Alice, Robert's sisters and Geoff for the foreseeable future. Handouts to Robert had severely depleted the old man's assets. They included the purchase of the house in Surrey which Robert had gambled away. Robert inherited (and treasured) his father's gold watch – the one the old man used to take out of his pocket to amuse Deirdre – but could have no further expectations.

Robert tried to keep his family's spirits up as they celebrated a very frugal Christmas. Tim and Deirdre's present from their parents was a block of Plasticene, to make up for giving the builder his putty back. On Christmas Eve they foraged for holly but were disappointed to find none with berries. As if by magic, they woke next morning to find berry-covered holly pinned to the walls. Robert had gone out at night to gather hawthorn berries, tied them to the holly boughs and decorated the house.

Tim shared his father's determination to make everyone laugh. One prank was to pour a complete jar of Eno's Fruit Salts into his father's chamber pot. Robert, relieving himself in the dark that night, was astonished to hear his urine frothing over the edge of the pot and onto the floor. He played along, and to Tim's delight there was much talk next morning about Robert having a mysterious disease. But Tim's mischief could backfire. Fascinated by anything mechanical, he dismantled old Robert's gold watch and hid the wreckage under his mattress. When it was found, he refused to apologize. Robert had never yet hit his children but was so upset at losing this last memento of his father that he decided to give Tim a formal beating with his belt. He told Rosemary to take Deirdre and Davnet for a long walk. As they set off Deirdre heard Tim's anguished shrieks. Afterwards Robert told his children he would never strike any of them again, and he never did.

Towards the end of 1932 Robert at last managed to gain a full-time post at a mission attached to St Anne's Cathedral, in central Belfast.[26] It was very good news – but almost at once a new blow fell. Early in 1933, weeks before her due date, Rosemary's waters broke and she started to bleed. She was taken to hospital and told she must remain. Yet again Robert took the

A living force?

children to Kingswood Hanger. Anxious about Rosemary, and wondering how to pay the hospital bills,[27] Robert organized the house move required by his new job while they were all away, to 9 Ravenhill Park Gardens, a semi-detached house in a middle-class Belfast suburb.

The couple's fourth child Christopher (always called Kit) was born on 2 March 1933. Rosemary haemorrhaged severely during delivery. She left hospital acutely anaemic and very weak. One thing was certain, the doctors said, there must be no more pregnancies.

The Pope had ruled in 1930 that contraception was 'an offence against the law of God and of nature.'[28] Protestant opinion both North and South was in broad agreement with this view. Even if Rosemary wished to use contraceptives, which she did not, they were stigmatized and hard to obtain. Her Marie Stopes cap was past its use-by date and in any case no barrier contraceptive is 100 per cent effective. Abortion was illegal and she would never have considered it. She was twenty-six and Robert twenty-seven. From now on their marriage must be celibate.

At this low point, there were some cheering developments. As was standard practice at that time, a monthly nurse had visited Rosemary for the first month after Kit's birth. When she left, an Oxford Group member called Grace Maundrell joined the household. Grace asked only her bed and board, staying because they needed help, which she felt it her Christian duty to provide. A few weeks after her arrival she helped Robert collect Tim, Deirdre and Davnet from Kingswood Hanger.

Grace was an austere young woman and there was little warmth between her and the children, but her hard work meant they were better looked after, with more regular mealtimes and less household chaos than they had known for a long time. Rosemary was still too ill to leave her bed, but a photo from this period shows her wearing an uncharacteristically broad smile. At last there were chinks of light. She liked their new, larger house in Ravenhill Park far more than Knocknadona. Grace's presence made everything easier. Robert was preaching full time in St Anne's Cathedral rather than part-time in a small-town church. Was their luck changing?

143

14

BREAKDOWN

Rosemary's anaemia lingered for weeks. Eventually Rose came to nurse her until she was able to get out of bed. Rose was appalled to discover that Tim and Deirdre were both illiterate and had never been to school. Before returning to Surrey, she arranged places at a nearby private school and paid the fees.

The children could see their parents were happier. Robert was doing well. He initially preached at the second evensong but was soon promoted to the first, a more elaborate service featuring choral works by well-known composers.[1] He worked hard, and his 'enthusiastic personality and down to earth preaching'[2] drew large congregations.

He joined the local rugby team and the children proudly watched him play in the park close to their house. When the family moved again, to an even larger house in Knock, near Upper Newtownards Road, the children left their school and Rose sent another governess. Like the last one, this hapless woman found Tim and Deirdre uncontrollable. As each day's lessons began, they climbed out of the window and sat outside in a bush, leaving her talking to an empty room. Rosemary was reassured by her voice when she passed the door and everyone was happy until the deception was discovered. The governess left, and Rose paid for a new private school.

Breakdown

Deirdre would later look back with longing on their father's hands-on parenting at this time. It was always Robert who got up to comfort her if she cried at night, who mopped her clean when she vomited after eating flyblown blackberries, who took her on his knee and told her stories. His storytelling wove a contented, secure atmosphere around the children's bedtimes. Tales of Brer Rabbit were among his favourites, and he made up his own stories too: strange yarns, like the one in which two children blow a giant bubble, a magic crow casts a spell and they float away in it. A protective father, he once leapt out of an upstairs window at the new house and sprinted to a nearby field, where he had spotted a local youth harassing Tim and Deirdre. Robert gave a scorching impromptu sermon and the boy promised to be the children's friend from then on.

He was also a dutiful son-in-law. He conducted 'a beautiful service … filled with friends … rich and poor, high and low'[3] for the funeral of Rose's mother Marianne, who died (or went 'to our real Home', as the devout Rose phrased it) in August 1933, aged 101. Rose sometimes found an ally in Robert as she tried to compensate for the ailing Rosemary's incapacity as a caregiver. When, that autumn, someone at the new school at last noticed that Deirdre could barely focus her eyes, it was Robert who brought her to England to see a Moorfields oculist at his London practice. She was prescribed new glasses, which improved her distance vision, though she remained unable to see print. Rose had moved with her sisters to a more affordable house in Shere, Surrey. Robert brought Deirdre down to stay there and Rose took her back to Belfast six weeks later.

Robert's own mother, Alice, had taken the life-changing decision to leave Killarney. Early in 1934 she sold Moyeightragh and bought an interest in the lease of a house at 203 Upper Rathmines Road, Dublin.[4] From now on Alice, Phyl, Marjorie and Geoff would be based there. Robert went to Dublin to help his mother settle in and choose furnishings. Rosemary visited soon afterwards. She had always considered all the Hilliards except Robert to be vulgar, but believed herself to have recently received divine guidance in her Quiet Time to think more kindly of Alice. She approved Robert's choice of furniture and wrote to Rose that 'he really has excellent taste.'

145

Swift Blaze of Fire

Robert still often carried Tim or Deirdre on his bicycle for his parish visits, as he had at Knocknadona. Young though they were, the children were struck by the extreme poverty of those they visited. As an adult, Tim would recall Robert lugging sacks of coal to people who were too poor to keep a fire in the grate. Deirdre remembers groups of 'men in raincoats standing on the corner of the street doing nothing.'[5] Parishioners who could barely feed themselves would serve her and Robert tea and cake in damp front parlours, on tea sets kept specially for visits from the parson. This hardship was evident on Church days out, like the charabanc trips to the sea: 'There were lots of elderly ladies ... in black, button-strap shoes with the straps sunk in tired, swollen flesh ... even as a five-year old I was aware of an overall atmosphere of depression.'

Such grinding poverty continued to cause unrest in Belfast and across Ireland after the Outdoor Relief Protests, and Robert again found himself confronted with political dilemmas that he could not resolve. The lull in his personal troubles was also proving short-lived. During the two years that followed those protests his personal and financial difficulties, combined with political and religious pressures, would intensify until they impelled him out of Ireland like a cork from a shaken bottle.

Early in 1933 the mostly Protestant workers of the Great Northern Railway (GNR) company went on strike against a 10 per cent pay cut. The strike spread to other rail companies, North and South. When companies recruited Southern strikebreakers to carry passengers in buses and trucks, it spread to Southern bus workers. Armed soldiers forced strikebreaking buses through pickets on both sides of the border, sparking retaliation in the North: rail infrastructure was bombed, strikebreakers were attacked, and a train derailed, killing two men; a policeman was also shot dead. In a potential game-changer in February, Belfast dockers struck unofficially in sympathy, but dockers' leaders undermined this by withholding official backing. Eventually the rail union settled for a pay cut, albeit of 7 rather than 10 per cent. Like the Outdoor Relief unrest, these strikes were marked by cross-sectarian solidarity.[6] Sadly it began to fracture into renewed sectarianism after this unsatisfactory settlement.[7]

At baby Kit's christening ceremony, Robert found himself and his family at the wrong end of anger against his Church, prompted either by Church leaders' active opposition to workers' struggles or perhaps by this sectarian feeling. Kit's ceremony was shared by Davnet, her original baptism having been a hasty affair following her initial failure to breathe. Robert baptized the two children himself at the Belfast Mission where he worked. Deirdre describes events: 'During the service, just as my father had my sister in his arms and was putting the mark of the cross on her forehead with holy water, there was a crash, maybe a shot, and then a window splintered and crashed down, and some stones came in, and there was a noise of people shouting outside. My father stopped for a moment, said "Peace be with you" and then carried on as if nothing had happened.' After a while the noise quietened and pulses returned to normal.

Such outbursts made it impossible for Robert to ignore his conflicted position. Here he was, still in Belfast, sympathizing with the struggles of Belfast working people yet part of an institution which colluded in their suppression. All the churches viewed worker militancy as essentially communist and vehemently opposed it. The Catholic Church had issued a pastoral letter in 1931 declaring that one 'cannot be a Catholic and a Communist. One stands for Christ, the other for Anti-Christ,'[8] and since then had stirred up anti-communist hostility by every means at its disposal. This climaxed in March 1933, when crowds led by St Patrick's Anti-Communist League and the Catholic Young Men's Society mounted violent attacks in Dublin on buildings used by the Revolutionary Workers' Groups and the Workers' Union of Ireland. The Church of Ireland loathed communism with equal ferocity and opposed any sign of working-class struggle.

The Communist Party of Ireland (CPI) was set up in Dublin on 3 June 1933, with Betty Sinclair and Tommy Geehan, popular leaders of the Belfast Outdoor Relief campaign, elected to its central committee. In the hostile climate, membership remained small. There's no evidence that Robert joined it.[9] Protestant and Catholic Church leaders alike supported state moves to proscribe the CPI's meetings and get its members fired from their jobs. A CPI-organized march on the anniversary of the Outdoor Relief riots was banned and heavy-handed measures clamped down on the CPI's commemorative meeting. The police seized one of its speakers, Seán Murray from Dublin, despite angry protests from the audience. Another speaker, English communist Harry Pollitt, was arrested before reaching the hall. Both were deported from the North.[10] On the same day the RUC wrecked the CPI's offices and jailed its leaders. It's possible, if unlikely, that Robert went to the meeting. If not, he would have read about these events in the papers or heard of them from parishioners and fellow clergy, whose views often jarred with his own.

Where did he really belong? Little more than a year ago he had set out his stall as a Fianna Fáil supporter who hoped to gain a Church of Ireland post in the South. But looking across the border during 1933 now brought the ominous spectacle of the Blueshirts, Ireland's version of the fascist movements gathering strength across Europe. Originally named the Army Comrades' Association and formed by members of Cumann na nGaedheal, the Blueshirts followed the lead of Continental fascist parties by taking up the 'shirt' uniform, straight-arm salute and violent street behaviour[11] of a fascist corps. They announced plans to march on Dublin, imitating Mussolini's march on Rome.

The Fianna Fáil government had been strengthened in an election in January 1933. Robert, like many on the Irish left, would have supported its efforts to outmanoeuvre the Blueshirts. During the summer of 1933, de Valera invoked the Public Safety Act of 1924, first banning the Blueshirts' march on Dublin[12] and then the Blueshirts themselves. In response Cumann na nGaedheal, with the Blueshirts and another small party, set up a new entity, Fine Gael, in September 1933. It was soon to become Ireland's second major party. In February 1934, in a Dáil debate on banning paramilitary uniforms, Fine Gael politician John A Costello would infamously declare: 'the Blackshirts were victorious in Italy and … the Hitler Shirts were victorious in Germany, as, assuredly … the Blueshirts will be victorious in the Irish Free State.'[13] Antifascists, many

Breakdown

from Fianna Fáil, confronted the Blueshirts at their rallies and on the streets throughout 1933.

Robert may have itched to join these antifascists.[14] Though he had not joined the CPI, Belfast's class conflicts and the spectacle of the Blueshirts' rise must by this time have been exerting a strong pull on his opinions. An incident at Moll's wedding to her long-term fiancé Thomas Shellard in January 1934 suggests he was moving further to the left. The ceremony was held at St Mary's Church, Killarney. The Very Reverend Dean of Ardfert officiated, assisted by Robert.[15] After the service Robert changed into a suit for the reception, putting on a red tie. That red tie at Moll's wedding reception is the most often repeated of the family tales about him.

For the Killarney Hilliards, the tie confirmed their worst suspicions: he must be a communist. Ties were flashier in the twenties and thirties than in earlier years; they came in all colours, red included, so it may have been a random choice – yet he must have known what conclusion his family would draw.[16] His subsequent political trajectory confirms that by this time he either saw himself as a communist or soon would. The tie may indeed have been his characteristically mischievous way of letting them know which way his opinions were moving.

Working in one of the most impoverished places in Western Europe, he now saw how immovably the Church of Ireland had set its face against demands for social justice. Rosemary would maintain in later years that Robert saw communist principles as a logical extension of Christianity (an idea also floated by some within the CPI[17]). The days when Robert believed he would be allowed to make a difference as a priest were slipping behind him. A future existence as a communist activist lay not far ahead, though he was only just starting to glimpse it. Each new political upheaval, each new example of the Church of Ireland hierarchy's hostility to change, pushed him further down the road. There would be no more playful limericks about one day joining the Church hierarchy himself. Any such ambitions were dead.

Robert was also becoming disillusioned with the Oxford Group. Buchman was making repeated attempts to meet and recruit Adolf Hitler, and had

Swift Blaze of Fire

declared in the summer of 1932 that National Socialism 'whether you liked it or not ... was there to stay, and ... it was high time to try and win it for Christ.'[18] During 1933 Hitler had forced anyone with a Jewish parent, grandparent or spouse out of public sector employment, the professions and many German Protestant churches. This was combined with a war of terror on Jews and the left, involving 'brutal beatings, torture and ritual humiliation of prisoners from all walks of life and all shades of political opinion apart from the Nazis,'[19] enabling Hitler to take complete political control of German society. None of this worried Buchman, who would eventually state that human problems 'could be solved through a God-controlled Fascist dictatorship.' His opinions didn't make headlines until a *New York Times* interview in 1936, but Group insiders knew what was afoot. Robert's vocation had rested on twin pillars: a vision of the Church of Ireland as a potentially radical force and the Oxford Group's somewhat militaristic evangelism. As the first of these faded, Buchman's Hitler-courtship made the second look ever more sinister. While still at Trinity Robert's own opinions had at times been pulled rightwards by the Oxford Group; since then the scales had fallen from his eyes.[20]

Quiet Times and Group gatherings were no longer occasions where Robert could confess and feel cleansed. He was smoking cigarettes again, and drinking. His celibate marriage probably led to other 'sins' which he could never own up to. The 'sin' of masturbation was a frequent topic in Oxford Group meetings because Buchman used masturbation guilt to recruit and retain members. One account of a typical men's meeting, for example, describes Buchman asking those 'troubled by that problem' to raise their hands (they all did, eventually) before leading a 'spiritual clinic among fellow sinners.'[21] Such openness was as impossible for Robert as confessing to smoking and drinking: it would cause gossip and might well cost him his job.

As Rosemary's and Robert's beliefs diverged, mutual tolerance fell away. Deirdre had returned from her stay in Shere to find her parents arguing bitterly and often, and Christmas 1933 in Knock was marred by a drearily quarrelsome atmosphere.[22] Rosemary was dismayed at Robert's drift away from Buchmanism. The Oxford Group was still her solace, her refuge from domestic pressures. She loved its house parties, where she immersed herself for days, leaving the children with Robert and Grace. Her musings in a letter to Rose in mid-1934, for example, after a Group house party in Howth, are rhapsodic to the point of incoherence: 'Quiet Time is to meet God. Guidance is a by-product. Like a deaf man at a concert you cannot hear unless surrendered. Christianity as a world force, a quality of life really in touch with God. Something new that the world can't touch. If we keep a proper quiet time we are ready for the day.' And so on, for several pages.

The letter then proceeds to skate quickly over some of the many issues which were pushing the couple apart. There's no mention of the rows with Robert, but Rosemary's distance from his family is clear from the strong hint of disdain in her description of a visit to Moll: 'Moll is living in a huge house with two maids. I don't envy her. It really belongs to Pa-in-law, who lives there too of course. Everything in it huge and awful.'

It would be fair to guess from this letter that Rose had urged Rosemary to pay more attention to her household and budget. Her response is sincere but vague, and very brief: 'I felt that I had been neglecting my home too much and that because there was Robert and Grace here too that it was definitely a strategic position and that it must definitely be run with the maximum efficiency for God. Since getting back I have been getting down to the money side.' Rosemary had good intentions about managing domestic life but little idea how to achieve them. The letter doesn't mention her children until its final sentence, when she remembers Rose will want news of them and briefly tells a story about sending them out to creosote a fence.

There's no good reason why a woman should be judged by her interest in child-rearing or her ability to keep house. Rosemary had come to motherhood very young, and for the most part unwillingly. Now she was trapped inside the oppressive expectations which society imposes on wives and mothers, expectations that ground her down although she never challenged them. It's difficult to read this letter without a pang for her and her children. A pang for Robert too – she was in love, not with him, but with the man she wanted him to be: a well-paid clergyman who would provide her with a comfortable life, a husband who would love and

Swift Blaze of Fire

protect her without being troubled by sexual feelings, a religious soulmate who would share her uncritical approach to Buchmanism. When she felt resentful, it was because he had not yet become these things.

Financially, Robert was trapped and could see no means of escape. He still worked very hard, and at a Vestry meeting in April 1934 the Dean commended the 'gladdening progress' achieved within the Mission district, noting that 'the men's and women's work there is flourishing.'[23] Unfortunately his stipend reflected neither his dedication nor his popularity. He pressed on, hoping for a rise, but it never came. Throughout his time at the Cathedral he was paid a quarterly sum of £6 and five shillings, totalling £25 a year,[24] a drop in the bucket for a man with a sick wife and four children to support. He did his level best to increase his income by officiating at a great many weddings and baptisms, often on dates when fellow pastors were unwilling to do so. In 1933 he officiated at seventy-four weddings, fourteen of them on Boxing Day;[25] in 1934 he officiated at 103, and between May 1933 and September 1934 he carried out 199 baptisms.[26] But however hard he worked, old debts persisted as he ran up new ones. Food and clothing for seven people, medical bills, fares to Oxford Group house parties – the list never ended. Rose did what she could, but he was in more debt than before his conversion. This brought an agonizing sense of futility.

His financial problems were intertwined with the deterioration in his relationship with Rosemary. He'd spent years trying to bend himself into a shape that would please her, but had instead impoverished her and damaged her health. They were drowning in worry about money and barred from refreshing their bond through sexual intimacy. No act of will would allow him to earn enough for them to live on or turn him into the person his wife wanted him to be.

During 1934 this sense of futility became too much to bear. Why should their lives be overshadowed by perpetual debt? Why should his children go without things most families of his class could afford? Tim and Deirdre noticed he had begun acting as if he had all the money in the world. Suddenly they were allowed new toys. New furniture arrived. As the year wore on, Robert's behaviour became unpredictable, in ways that frightened them all. He bought a large motorbike, on credit, which he rode into Belfast for work. The children loved going for pillion rides, but their fear mounted when he started staying away for longer periods. Where was he going? Rosemary didn't know, and he wasn't going to tell her. Her reproaches became distraught as his spending on the children rose further: a rocking horse, a trapeze, a climbing frame, a bicycle, a scooter. Then he left for London, by plane, far costlier than by boat. 'When he came back things were very wrong. He smelled of drink and he did not always get up in the mornings and he and Mother were always quarrelling.'

He refused to say why he had gone to London. Quiet Times had become a miserable farce: 'Nobody said what was really wrong, and it was all a pretence that even a child could see through. I would wake up in the night and be so frightened'.

In mid-September someone suggested a holiday at Brown's Bay, on Ireland's north coast. Few things are more bleak for children than a family holiday when the love affair between their parents has fallen apart. Robert borrowed a car but asked a friend to take his family, promising to join them later. There's a picture of Tim and Deirdre, barefoot and with sun-bleached hair, keeping a daily vigil in the doorway of their rented cabin, hoping to hear the motorbike. Their faces are miserable because Robert hardly ever came and never stayed for long: '… my Father … never came properly at all. He visited us on the motorbike and did not stay. In the end the friend who took us there … took us home'. Rosemary believed he had been kept away by an affair with a neighbour. All trust was gone.[27]

Late in 1934 Robert made one more attempt to deal with his debts by appealing to the Dean of St Anne's Cathedral. No-one, however frugal, could keep a wife and four children on his meagre income. The Church of Ireland was not an impoverished institution. Could it help him with a loan? His request was refused.[28] Robert was humiliated. He came home and told Rosemary, and they talked of bankruptcy. His creditors were closing in. Should he return to journalism? – he had earned little then, but it was more than he earned now.

Swift Blaze of Fire

He was deeply despondent in the weeks that followed. Somehow they carried on until Christmas. Robert worked flat out on Christmas Eve, officiating at eleven weddings. Christmas Day was strained and grim. Tim and Deirdre spent most of it in bed with glandular fever, an illness often associated with emotional stress. Rosemary's present from her mother was a tea set with a hand-embroidered tablecloth. She loved the pretty china and after admiring it stacked it in its box under the tree. When she next picked up the box, the bottom fell out and the whole set was smashed except for one jug. It's understandable that Rosemary was upset, but to Tim and Deirdre the event seems to have been more than just a china breakage. It imprinted itself on their memories as a terrible disaster.

Early in 1935[29] Robert left for London. Rosemary told the children he would be back, but this time he was gone for good.

PART VI — ANTI-FASCIST

15

'WHY DON'T YOU KUM BACK?'

In 1935 Robert's old Trinity acquaintance Samuel Beckett was living in Chelsea, south-west-central London, and writing *Murphy*, his first novel. That book's description of the street scene on Chelsea Embankment captures the area's bohemian exuberance: 'Artists of every kind, writers, underwriters, devils, ghosts, columnists, musicians, lyricists, organists, painters and decorators, sculptors and statuaries, critics and reviewers, major and minor, drunk and sober, laughing and crying, in schools and singly, passed up and down.'[1]

Chelsea's dilapidated flats and low rents provided a haven for writers, artists and poorly paid professionals. Now Robert found a haven there too.

His absences from his Belfast home had allowed him to reconnect with old friends, like fellow Trinity republican Paddy Trench.[2] His plane visit to London may have taken him to stay with Trench, then living in West Kensington with his second wife Eve Hayden.[3] Rosemary loathed Paddy Trench,[4] which would partly explain Robert's secretiveness on his return. The two men had evidently begun a new phase of their friendship, helped along by politics: Robert was moving rapidly leftwards and Trench was already a radical socialist. Subsidized as he was by his father,[5] Trench

Swift Blaze of Fire

had the means to help Robert as he resettled. At any rate, they were close enough for Samuel Beckett, on spotting Robert in London later in 1935, to assume 'no doubt [Hilliard] is staying with Paddy Trench, whom I see flying about on an old motor bike'.[6]

If Robert did stay with Trench it was not for long. The 1935 electoral register records him living in a flat in Beaufort Street, a wide road running through the middle of Chelsea. Number 104 housed three other men and nine women, mostly professional people.[7] Robert lived in its basement for a while; by 1936 he had passed the flat over to Trench.[8]

Paddy Trench's brother Terry later wrote of this time that Robert and Rosemary's marriage had gone 'badly wrong'.[9] Lack of money and debt were the marriage's most pressing difficulties. Robert may have hoped his escape to England would provoke a bankruptcy petition, staving off his creditors at least for a while. After the Dean's refusal to help, this probably seemed his only option. If that was the plan, it failed. Rosemary apparently believed him to be bankrupt, and often spoke of him as such, but no bankruptcy order was ever issued by a Belfast court.[10]

He tried to re-enter London journalism, this being his only work experience outside the Church. But Britain was still gripped by the Depression and he remained unemployed, month after month, barely able to keep body and soul together. He had no money to send Rosemary but sent his new address.[11] They kept up a regular correspondence. Rosemary's surviving letters are loving and devoid of reproach. Robert valued them and took several to Spain, where they were found on him when he died. If his last postcards to her are any indication, his letters were affectionate and friendly, though not romantic. As we have seen, she later destroyed them all.[12]

Rosemary wrote a harrowing letter to Robert soon after his departure. She had left the children in Belfast with Grace and was staying with Robert's mother in Dublin. Robert had brought her to that city during the joyful time following his conversion and the sight of it now was almost unbearable. 'Everything here is so filled with yourself,' she wrote, 'all Dublin shouts aloud of you and my heart is aching, aching' – then in almost the same breath rebuked herself for being 'mawkish'. Having looked down on the Hilliards for years she now felt glad of their warm hearts. 'I have come much nearer your family', she writes, 'I love your mother.'

Moll showed Rosemary a letter from a mutual friend who had visited Robert in Beaufort Street, which was painful for Rosemary to read, as she yearned to visit him herself. Robert had called in to see Moll on his way to England,[13] but nothing he had said during his visit could exonerate him in her eyes. He would never be able to explain to any of his siblings, or his mother, the sequence of events which had caused the failure of his ministry and his marriage. He had abandoned the world they inhabited, inflicting a degree of pain he could do nothing to relieve, and they viewed his flight with uncomprehending horror.

As they cast about for ways to make sense of it, all the past sins he'd tried to live down were recalled. His character was set in stone as a womanizer, a gambler, a black sheep who would always stray, and they would forever see his departure as unforgivable. Rosemary reports that Robert's mother Alice was like a 'tiring swimmer', drowning in sorrow and shame: 'her prayers for you are becoming too fast and strained and I am sure you are seldom from her thoughts.' Rosemary's raw nerves were further stung by hearing from Alice's mother ('dear Grannie Martin'), who was up from Killarney to comfort Alice, that Robert's flight was 'common knowledge in Killarney.'

Rosemary coped with her misery by refusing to accept their split as final. Her letter angles for an invitation to visit his new flat, saying she 'long[s] to come to you and put the basement shipshape.' Signing off with 'Good night. Always my love,' she encloses a desolate note from Tim:

> Dear Daddy
> Why dont you hav kwat tim [Quiet Time]. You ot [ought] to kum back to us so why dont you kum back? And why dont you kum and hav fun with us.
> Love
> From Timothy Hilliard.

Swift Blaze of Fire

Tim's laboriously neat handwriting shows how hard he was trying to bring his father home.

Rosemary knew they must leave Belfast. Tradesmen needed the money Robert owed them and they tore at her conscience. Deirdre remembers 'the milkman coming for payment and saying, when he turned away in deep distress, that he had thought the money would be safe seeing as it was to a "Man of the Cloth". I was only six and a half, but I felt most ashamed and guilty and what my mother felt I can only imagine.'[14]

The family had to do a moonlight flit. Friends in the Oxford Group collected them one night and drove them forty odd miles through lashing rain to Annalong, a seaside village at the foot of the Mourne Mountains. The journey was made wretched by Deirdre's violent car-sickness. Baby Kit wailed because she vomited into his only spare nappy and he could not be changed. They arrived in the dark, unloading by candlelight. A small truck brought Rosemary's belongings, beds and cots, and some clothes. Most of their furniture and the presents Robert had splashed out on were abandoned, along with the children's toys. Tim was so upset without his teddy that the friend driving the car went back to collect it and brought it the next day.

Johnny Rice's Cottage in Heathery Hill Road was made of asbestos and had four rooms. There was no electricity, bathroom, toilet, or mains drainage, but it was cheap – five shillings a week – and a long way from Robert's creditors. The family lived on porridge, potatoes, herrings at a penny each and mackerel at twopence. Sometimes there were eggs, which Rosemary soft-boiled and thriftily sliced in two, shell and all, giving each child half. Robert's sister Marjorie visited and gave Rosemary five pounds; she eked this out as long as she could. Some friends stayed in touch. Deirdre's godfather Lionel Fleming sent a present, a clock with a Mickey Mouse face, which she loved during the short interval before Tim destroyed it.

During their time at this cottage Robert's mother Alice set up a trust fund which paid out two pounds interest a week. The family lived on this money. Tim and Deirdre went to the local Catholic school but were hopeless at their lessons. Their daily walks to and from the school sound like a bad dream. They had to ford a river in a deep gully, using stepping stones: 'Sometimes the river was very full and then the stones were mostly under water … The other children started to follow us to the gully, and when we were … near the river they would start throwing stones and shouting "Prods, Prods!" and other things at us.'

But the nearby sea was lovely. On the first morning after their arrival Tim and Deirdre set off to walk there. Tim ran ahead and reached the harbour while Deirdre, whose close-range vision was still very poor, lost both her shoes and her way. A local resident found her and took her to rejoin Tim. As they looked for him, Deirdre gazed round at this wonderful new place.

> The harbour was magical. It was full of little fishing boats and several larger boats with masts and furled-up sails and figureheads on the front of them. They looked as if they belonged in the pictures of a fairy story. They were not like any boats I have seen before, or since for that matter. There were baskets full of gleaming herrings and mackerel being pulled along the quay, an amazing smell of fish, seagulls swooping and crying and busy people everywhere.

Then an irate Grace arrived on her bicycle to take them back to their new home.

Tim and Deirdre remained unhappy at school and were learning almost nothing, so within a few months Rosemary decided they must move again. With the help of friends, she found places for them at a Quaker School near Lisburn. The fees were low and Rose agreed to pay them. Off they went again, this time to Weir Cottage in Ballinderry, about eight miles from Lisburn. The small truck which was to transport them arrived late, so again they travelled at night. They tumbled out at the other end into the darkness and the 'fusty, mouldy smell' of their new home. Their few belongings were hastily stacked in one room as Grace tried to make cocoa for everyone. When she lit a fire in the grate the chimney caught fire and the flames rapidly spread to the beam over the

Swift Blaze of Fire

fireplace. Adults and children rushed around, frantic to find water before the cottage burned down. At last they found the water-butt, under the eaves, and quenched the fire. Amid pools of water and a stench of soot, the four children piled into one bed and slept.

Rosemary later wrote an account of the move called *The Midnight Flitting*. It's a poignant tale, full of descriptions of the sea and mountains at their old cottage and punctuated by the melancholy cries of curlews flying overhead. In it she reflects on how much she will miss living by the sea: 'It would be strange without the sound of the waves, to sleep again in silence.'[15] Annalong had been Rosemary's first experience for years of living independently from Robert. This piece reads as if it had freed her to rediscover a long-ago self, the pensive, solitary girl who revelled in beautiful landscapes and loved to write.

Weir Cottage was damp, even in summer, and had no lavatory, bathroom, or piped water supply. Cooking was done on a paraffin stove or using a hook hung over the fire. Catching their mother's mood of making the best of things, the children enjoyed the garden, with its roses and orchard, and got to know old Miss McCord, who lived at the other end of the cottage. Even the noise of rats partying in the thatch at night entertained them. Each day they donned their new green uniforms and took the bus to school in Lisburn. They still learned little but the teachers were kind. They were often hungry at home, so the large school dinners were very welcome.

Some say Robert had lost his Christian faith. It's more likely he'd lost faith in the Oxford Group, the Church of Ireland hierarchy, the pietism which meant that though Rosemary loved him she could only ever be disappointed in him – and above all in himself, for failing to live up to his own promises. There's no evidence he lost faith in Christianity itself. He never renounced or hid his clerical title. Future comrades in Spain would write of him as a 'Reverend' and Rosemary's surviving letters are, on the face of it, letters to a fellow Christian. She would always maintain that Robert saw communism as an extension of Christian principles.

'*Why don't you kum back?*'

According to sculptor Jason Gurney, who later got to know Robert in Spain, Chelsea's bohemians spent their time either 'roaring around the clubs and parties in a welter of drink, sex and nonsense' or deep in an 'intensely serious atmosphere of politics and philosophy.'[16] Robert liked a drink, though he could ill afford to pay for it, and this mix of uproarious socializing and committed discussion would have appealed to him, but it quickly led to a new, serious purpose. He had spent much of his life trying to 'be better' and feeling guilty at his own failures. It's fair to guess that his guilt at abandoning Rosemary and the children made him want to redeem himself now. The speed with which he joined the Communist Party of Great Britain makes clear how strongly he was influenced by the communist-led activism he had witnessed in Belfast. Within only a few weeks of his arrival in London he was a signed-up communist himself.

His membership card was a folded rectangle of blue cardboard with his name on. Inside he stuck rows of stamps to show his paid subs, starting in April 1935. The Communist Party offered him both theory and practice. The theory was an explanation of why capitalism always makes workers pay for its crises and why social justice therefore has to come through a revolutionary end to capitalism, rather than reforming it through parliament. The practice comprised campaigns and direct action for material improvements to workers' lives in the here and now. It was all a far cry from the Church of Ireland's collusion with the cruelly unequal status quo in Belfast, and he was more than ready to be part of it.

Chelsea presented a microcosm of the English class system. Beyond the World's End pub, at its western edge, was 'a slum area where the working class lived in … great poverty and despair'. At the other end, around Sloane Square, 'the very rich … lived a life of great elegance, with large houses, staffs of servants and magnificent cars.'[17] This inequality was reflected in its political geography. Communists and Labour supporters lived in the impoverished western part, whereas Oswald Mosley had set up a barracks and HQ for his Blackshirts near Sloane Square, an appropriate location, since his funds came from wealthy UK supporters as well as Mussolini's regime in Italy.

The Labour Party, in which Rosemary and Robert had once placed so much trust, was in tatters. Labour Prime Minister Ramsey MacDonald had entered a National Government with Conservatives and Liberals in 1931. This government's harsh austerity measures had led to even worse hardships than those endured in the 1920s. MacDonald and his supporters, expelled from Labour, were reviled as class traitors. Soon after Robert arrived in London MacDonald stood down as prime minister in favour of Conservative Stanley Baldwin.

The Independent Labour Party had disaffiliated from Labour in 1932. Paddy Trench, a revolutionary socialist and Trotskyist, had joined the ILP and may have tried to persuade Robert to join as well.[18] The two men must have had lively debates, but found enough in common to stay friends despite their differing party allegiances.

The Communist Party, at a local level, looked far more principled than Labour. Even a non-member like Jason Gurney could comment that 'We all had a tremendous admiration for the energy and initiative of the Communist Party.'[19] Party pamphlets in early 1935 outlined a clear class position, such as this one demanding an end to casual dock labour: 'At present the big employers and the landlords get the best of everything – all at the expense of working people. That is why Communists stand up against the rich.'[20] Such language was music to Robert's ears. The party also organized lectures on history, economics and international events. Robert told Rosemary how illuminating he found them; she later wrote back 'Are you still going to communist lectures on history and things?'[21]

Communist Party members were central to the struggle to keep Mosley's Blackshirts from dominating London's streets. There were terrible lessons to be learned from Germany. The German Communist Party (KPD) had followed the Comintern's 'class against class' policy of avoiding cooperation with the German Social Democratic Party, whom they branded 'social fascists'. This fatal self-isolation had undermined the KPD's attempts to work with others to stop Hitler. During 1933, tens of thousands of German communists were imprisoned in concentration camps and thousands killed. Hitler had then skewed the economy

'Why don't you kum back?'

towards a new war drive, threatening to march east, towards Russia. Faced with this monstrous threat, the Comintern had changed tactics, trying to build links with other workers' organizations to develop anti-fascist 'united fronts'. United front mobilization would be crucial in opposing the Blackshirts in Britain.

Another focus for Communist Party members was their support for strikes. For example, when Robert joined, they were supporting the long-running – and ultimately successful – official strike at East London clothing manufacturer L Coleman and Company, against sackings and union victimizations.[22] Party members were also at the heart of the National Unemployed Workers' Movement, which organized 'demonstrations, hunger marches, protest meetings against the Government's policy, and propaganda for the introduction of public works and higher benefits'.[23] Besides campaigns there were stunts, such as hoisting a red flag over the German Embassy, or dropping a banner, proclaiming 'Workers of all lands unite!' on one side and '25 years of hunger and war' on the other, across Fleet Street during the procession for George V's Silver Jubilee in May 1935.[24] A constant and necessary activity was the defence of working-class families from eviction: 'When the bailiff arrived, doors and windows would be barred and the house packed out with unemployed people, while in the street outside a crowd would be gathered ... Often the public response ... was enough to quash or delay the eviction.'[25]

The party was led by Harry Pollitt, its General Secretary since 1929. Pollitt, a boilermaker and political organizer from Droylsden, Manchester, had come to London in 1918, where he led a fight in Poplar to black ships carrying munitions for use against the Russian Bolshevik government (a parallel blacking campaign in Dublin had raised uproar while Robert was at school there). Pollitt kept in close contact with the Comintern and generally adhered to its line. Self-educated, with an impressive intellect and an engaging manner, he was physically small but had a powerful impact on the audiences he addressed. He would play a key role in recruiting members for the International Brigades, including Robert, and in liaising with their relatives.

Swift Blaze of Fire

Robert would meet many of the party members he met or heard of in London again in Spain. Several of them would become leaders in the British Battalion of the XV International Brigade. The party's London District Secretary was Dave Springhall, a long-standing party cadre who had spent three years at Moscow's International Lenin School. Described by Jason Gurney as 'hopelessly obtuse and humourless,'[26] he adhered to every shift and turn of Stalin's party line and would later become the Battalion's political commissar. Some of the party figures in London had notably mutinous pasts. Tom Wintringham, imprisoned in 1925 for seditious libel and incitement to mutiny and a co-founder of the *Daily Worker*, would later be Robert's commanding officer. Jock Cunningham, imprisoned in 1929 for leading a mutiny in the Argyle and Sutherland Highlanders, led the NUWM Hunger March to Brighton in 1933. He would take command of the Battalion at a crucial moment during Robert's last battle. Fred Copeman, another NUWM activist, was a hefty, bellicose ex-prizefighter who had taken part in the Invergordon Mutiny. He would later join the Communist Party in Spain and go on, briefly, to hold a commanding rank in the British Battalion.

None of these figures yet knew such responsibilities would fall to them. The International Brigades still lay ahead.

16

'PROMINENT CP MEMBER'

Robert and his comrades anxiously watched developments in Spain, where impoverished, landless peasants were agitating for their own land against a deeply conservative landowning ruling elite, traditionally kept in place by rigged elections, and an organized, militant working class wanted fundamental change. Spanish landowners relied on the support of the Catholic Church and a bloated, semi-autonomous army. After years of unrest the 1931 election had brought in a republican government and King Alfonso XIII had fled the country. Republican reforms promised improvements for Spanish workers and peasants, but the uneasy republican coalition collapsed in November 1933 and a right-wing government succeeded it in a low turnout election. Since then employers and landowners had attacked workers' and peasants' conditions and workers had fought back with strikes and swiftly suppressed unrest.[1]

In summer 1934, less than a year after the election, Largo Caballero, leader of the PSOE (Spanish Party of Socialist Workers) and of the UGT (General Workers' Union) had called for insurrection. This insufficiently prepared uprising was brutally crushed. It was limited to Catalonia, the Basque country and Asturias, where miners and other workers held off the

Swift Blaze of Fire

Army for two weeks. General Franco then unleashed his Army of Africa, Moroccan troops under his personal control, on the Asturian miners, murdering and torturing hundreds of them. After this savagery, division between the 'two Spains' was irretrievably entrenched. Many on the Spanish left believed there was no alternative to a successful insurrection. The right's determination to block all avenues to social and liberal reform was clear: they wanted workers and peasants curbed conclusively by force. By autumn 1935 Spain was on the edge of civil war.

There were major shifts in the Communist Party line that autumn for Robert and his comrades to absorb. A new 'popular front' doctrine had been launched in Moscow during August 1935 by Dimitrov, head of the Comintern, in a speech at the Comintern's Seventh World Congress. It called for the creation of 'a wide anti-fascist People's [or Popular] Front on the basis of the proletarian united front'.[2] Dimitrov was picking his words carefully here, blurring the 'united front' towards a 'popular front'. There was a fundamental difference. A united front[3] meant organizing in a common cause with other workers' parties or groups and non-aligned workers. The popular front, by contrast, extended these alliances to include groupings within the capitalist class, hitherto seen as the enemy.

This new doctrine arose from Stalin's wish to form pacts against Hitler with non-fascist Western governments. Communist parties across Europe, including Britain, were now told to establish anti-fascist fronts with any organizations, regardless of their class nature, that might help draw the British and French ruling class towards allying with Russia. Any idea that Russia sought to foment revolution in Western countries must be avoided, as it might alienate their governments.

This profound shift posed a dilemma: was the Communist Party in favour of workers' revolution or wasn't it? The dilemma was resolved by tacitly postponing the revolution to a distant future: 'What was not said was that the new course implied the postponement of the pursuit of proletarian revolution in favour of … the defeat of Fascism.'[4] Revolution was henceforth to be seen as unattainable for the present, a distraction from the task of building a Popular Front of cross-class alliances. For Robert and his

'Prominent CP member'

comrades involved in supporting workplace struggles, the emphasis became less about supporting rank-and-file activism and more about channelling workers' demands upwards for trade union officials to deal with. This prompted heart-searching and debate for some members,[5] but most were persuaded that the shift was necessary to defend the Russian state and fend off further fascist expansion. Robert believed in democracy from the bottom up, made by the rank and file, as he would indicate in a letter he later wrote from Spain, but he stayed loyal to the Communist Party.

Party members had to make another shift with the launch of a huge propaganda offensive to increase Russian workers' productivity, built around Stakhanov, a Russian miner hailed as a hero for supposedly achieving miraculous feats of coal production. An article by Stalin announced this in the *Daily Worker* of 26 November 1935 and much was made of Stakhanovism in Britain. But intensifying workers' labour to produce an increased surplus sounded rather like capitalism to some of Robert's fellow party members, running directly counter to what communists had fought for since Marx's day, namely less exploitation and shorter hours.[6] Like the popular front doctrine, Stakhanovism postponed the end of workers' exploitation to an ever-receding future date. Joe Jacobs, a London Communist Party member, acidly commented 'This kind of appeal had a familiar ring ... we often referred to it as "pie in the sky".'[7] Despite these flashes of scepticism, it was unthinkable for most members to acknowledge that Stalin was engaged in a programme of counter-revolution. Robert and his comrades saw the Russian state as the bulwark against fascism. Anything necessary to defend it must be accepted.

At the end of October, after twenty-seven weeks of party membership, Robert started using different stamps in his party card. Evidently he was at last finding enough journalistic work, probably freelance, to consider himself employed and pay the full rate.[8]

He wasn't the only one finding it easier to get work. The Depression was bottoming out in southern England, with the advent of new manufacturing industries (cars, electrical goods, chemicals). Rapid British rearmament also brought more jobs. It reflected government alarm that fascist expansionism was now much more than sabre-rattling. The Japanese had occupied Manchuria for four years. On 3 October 1935 news came of Mussolini's invasion of Abyssinia. In a brutal campaign there, Italian forces would use mustard gas, bomb hospitals and kill tens of thousands of civilians, annexing much of the Horn of Africa. Not content with annexing the Saarland after a plebiscite, Hitler was demanding the reinstatement of pre-Versailles German borders, 'Anschluss' with Austria, the expansion of German influence into eastern Europe and the return of Germany's African colonies.[9]

Europe had become the most unstable zone in the world order. Governments nervously cast around for new alliances. In June 1935 the UK had signed an Anglo-German Naval Alliance, allowing German naval capacity to rise to 35 per cent of Britain's and breaking the Versailles Treaty. Perceived in Germany and elsewhere as a possible step towards a British-German alliance against France and Russia, it caused yet more anxiety to Stalin.

Concern about the spread of fascism pushed up Communist Party membership. About 6,000 strong when Robert joined, it would nearly double by May 1937. Robert and his fellow party members campaigned hard for a Labour victory in the General Election of November 1935 but without success,[10] though Willie Gallagher won West Fife for the Communist Party, its first seat for a decade. The popular front policy meant that party members now prioritized electioneering. Debate about Dimitrov's policy shift continued privately, with some members continuing to focus on workers' struggles and confrontations with the Blackshirts.

British intelligence sent agents to Communist Party meetings and noted the members who stood out in them. When they later compiled a list of British volunteers to the International Brigades, they referred to Robert as a 'Prominent CP member'.[11] Since he appears to have held no formal position, he can only have earned this description by his contributions to meetings and general activism. No doubt he was as voluble and energetic

'Prominent CP member'

in his Communist Party branch as he had been in everything else he ever undertook.

Samuel Beckett, then living at 34 Gertrude Street, had run into Robert in July 1935: 'Hilliard has been discerned on the Embankment, between the Institute of Preventive Medicine and Don Saltero's Coffee House.'[12] They had met again one Sunday in September: 'Hilliard is still about. I walked out the door one morning and there he was playing cricket with the street urchins.'[13] Robert playing with children in the street is a pleasant picture with a sad side to it: his own children would have loved to play cricket with him that autumn. As the weather worsened their lives were becoming harder.

The walls of Weir Cottage had become so damp that the wallpaper slithered off them overnight. Every morning Grace, Rosemary and the children gathered it up and slapped it back in place. It was a struggle to mop the pools of water out of the house. Beds were damp and so was everyone's clothing, but the family battled on. Robert's sister Phyl came for Halloween and bobbed apples with the children. Alice sent Halloween barmbrack. Then winter grew harsher, with high winds and lots of snow. At first the children enjoyed making snowballs and sliding on ice. What kept their spirits up was that Robert was coming to stay for Christmas. He couldn't afford the fare but Alice had bought his ticket. They were filled with hope. Was he coming back?

The children's delight when they at last saw Robert was tempered by shock at his appearance. If Rosemary had entertained any illusions that he could have sent money from London, they ended when she saw his weight loss and worn-out clothing. Unemployment had damaged his health. Deirdre wrote later, 'He was not himself, all his underclothes were ragged and he had lumbago and a dreadful cough. He was thinner and balder ...'[14]

Determined to avoid another pregnancy, Rosemary had made up a bed for him in the children's room and told Tim and Deirdre they must sleep with her. She need not have worried. The children were soon painfully aware of an extreme awkwardness between their parents. Robert 'did

Swift Blaze of Fire

not seem to know what to do, and neither did [their] mother'. He and Rosemary could pen each other affectionate letters from a distance, but it was quite another thing to meet in person, surrounded by the upturned faces of anxious children. The feeling grew in the cottage that everything was wrong. As the days of Christmas went by, filled with disappointment, a series of disasters struck: 'The beautiful Samoyed dog got distemper and died of pneumonia, and the angora rabbit, Fluff Bun, was found dead in her hutch. The pump froze and my father went back to London.'

That Christmas was the last they would ever see of him.

It had taken a while for the cold and damp to make the children ill but now their health gave way with a vengeance. Deirdre went down with rheumatic fever and spent weeks in bed in great pain. Tim was hospitalized by a chest infection, at first wrongly diagnosed as tuberculosis. Davnet and Kit had tonsillitis. Then they all caught threadworms, for which Rosemary gave them enemas, using a rubber tube, funnel and jug. Returning from hospital, Tim declared he wanted to be a doctor and set about finding ways to practise his medical skills. Rosemary found him standing one day over a prone, intubated Davnet, a large, water-filled jug in one hand, the funnel in the other. She was just in time to stop him decanting a gigantic enema into his sister.

It was Rosemary's old friend Muriel Lester who rescued them. She came to stay in the spring and was horrified at what she found. Grace was battling to keep things going but Rosemary was too deeply depressed to function properly, all the children were ill and the family was overwhelmed by damp and misery. She summoned Alice, and the two women agreed the family must move, but where? Someone in the Oxford Group knew a cottage for rent in Falmouth, Cornwall, and they set off again, this time on the Liverpool ferry.

Rosemary could only afford to take the minimum luggage, so the children had to leave behind the last of their toys and most of their clothes. In a private ritual of farewell, Tim and Deirdre made primrose garlands to wear, before vowing to each other to return to Ballinderry. 'We held hands and cried and rocked about in the grass, saying we never wanted to move again. We comforted each other with the thought that Daddy was in London and we were going to go through London on the way to Falmouth. Perhaps he would come back.'[15]

Rosemary had no money for a cabin, so the family spent the ferry journey huddled on deck. Then came two long train rides, with no chance to meet their father in London, a sickening disappointment for the children. They reached 10 Hillside Road, Swanvale, Falmouth on 1 May 1936, Tim's ninth birthday.

The new house had toilet, bathroom and cooking facilities but no furniture. Over the next few weeks Rosemary picked up bits and pieces second-hand and even got hold of some of the belongings left behind on previous moves, kept safe and brought over by friends, such as the wireless Rose had given them. The children were given Great Western Railway posters for their rooms. They loved one poster, which showed purple, heathery mountains like those at Annalong, and a cottage like the one at Ballinderry. Tim and Deirdre began school, yet again paid for by Rose, where it was at last noticed that Deirdre's glasses did not enable her to see print. After a row with the optician, who said Deirdre had been neglected, Rosemary bought another pair. Deirdre learned to read at once and delightedly read one book after another. The weather warmed up and the children learned to swim in the sea. At last they recovered their health.

One cause of Robert's awkwardness in Ballinderry may have been that he had formed a new relationship. In late 1935 or early 1936 he handed over the Beaufort Street flat to Paddy Trench and moved in with a new partner.[16] He did not conceal this relationship from Rosemary and it came as a blow to her, though they continued to write to each other, reverting to the friendly style of their correspondence before the unhappy Christmas visit.

Like his comrades, Robert remained preoccupied with the ever-widening shadow of fascism. The shadow spread further when Hitler invaded the Rhineland in March 1936. But in Spain something different was happening. Crisis-ridden since the 1934 uprising, the right-wing

Swift Blaze of Fire

government called new elections early in 1936. It mounted a stridently anti-Marxist campaign with an authoritarian agenda, but had overplayed its hand. In February 1936, to the joy of Europe's left, these elections brought a Popular Front government into office.

This new government comprised a fractious coalition[17] between socialists (whose main party, the PSOE, or Spanish Party of Socialist Workers, was itself split into two factions), republicans, the relatively small Communist Party (PCE[18]) and a group of breakaway communists called the POUM, the Marxist Workers' Unity Party.[19] It was supported by the millions-strong anarchist CNT[20] union and the smaller[21] but still strong socialist UGT[22] union. The Spanish right had lost the election but increased its vote, so that in 1936 'a fragmented Left confronted a determined and increasingly desperate Right.'[23]

The Popular Front government took steps towards reinstating the earlier republican government's reforms, but they were tentative, partial steps. Spanish workers, seeing they must rely on their own strength if they were to gain more, joined the CNT and UGT in droves. Thousands stormed jails and freed political prisoners. Land occupations by peasants began in the south; mass strikes and demonstrations demanded a faster reversal of the earlier conservative offensive. Appalled, the right, which included the fascist Falange, monarchists, conservative Catholics and other traditionalist elements,[24] demanded the forcible overthrow of the new government. Practically everyone in Spain knew there was a military conspiracy to mount a coup.[25]

17

CIVIL WAR IN SPAIN

On 17–18 July 1936 it began. News burst across Europe that a group of Spanish army officers had launched a rebellion. On 17 July the rebels seized control of Spanish Morocco, and with it Spain's Army of Africa.[1] On 18 July rebel forces attempted to take power across Spain. In these crucial first two days prime minister Santiago Casares y Quiroga refused to issue arms to the workers' militias, who were clamouring for them. The generals expected to succeed within hours but met unexpected resistance. A determined, if insufficiently armed, mobilization of workers in major cities and peasants in much of the countryside brought the offensive to a halt in many parts of the country. Hugh Thomas describes how in one Spanish town after another, after the local rebel leader had read out his declaration of war and proclaimed military law from the town hall, local socialist, communist and anarchist militias would begin to resist. As they fought back in the streets, the civil governor would 'vacillate in his office' trying to phone Madrid.

> The officers loyal to the republic, and, in most cases the assault guards, would resist the rising and attempt to rally both the civil government and the working-class organisations. A general strike would be called by

Swift Blaze of Fire

> both UGT and CNT, and barricades ... would immediately be erected. Fighting would follow, with both sides showing disregard of personal safety.[2]

Where workers mobilized, armed themselves and fought, particularly where the workers' movement was strong, the rebels were defeated. On the night of 18–19 July Quiroga resigned and his successor José Giral at last gave the order to issue arms. A bloody battle took place in Barcelona on 19 July; another followed in Madrid. In both, the Assault Guards and even some of the traditionally anti-working-class Civil Guards stayed loyal, kept so by the thousands of workers on the streets. But where workers waited for the Republican government to act, or dispersed after accepting assurances of loyalty, the military were successful. Thomas comments, 'had the government distributed arms, and ordered the civil governors to do so too, thus using[3] the working class to defend the republic at the earliest opportunity, the rising might have been crushed.'[4] Unfortunately that didn't happen.

By 20 July Spain was divided into two territories, about 60 per cent in the hands of the Republic. The rebels controlled the north, apart from a strip covering Bilbao and other industrial cities, plus the south tip of Andalusia and the Balearic Islands. The government controlled the centre, south and east. The Spanish Navy stayed loyal; the Army was split. The future of Spain hung in the balance.

For many workers and peasants, pushing back the rebellion was part and parcel of overturning the oppressive dominance of the big land-owners, the Church and the army which had for so long borne down on the people of Spain. An inspiring mood of revolution gripped those who had stopped the generals. Portraits of Lenin appeared in the Plaza del Sol in the centre of Madrid. In Barcelona, where anarchists had played a major role in the resistance, Lluís Companys, president of Catalonia, offered his resignation to anarchist leaders. They declined his offer and left him in post, ostensibly to preserve unity with other workers' forces in the rest of Spain, a decision they would later have cause to regret.

The rebel generals, with all the advantages of a centralized command, a great many highly-trained professional officers and – within the first

Civil war in Spain

two weeks – arms and assistance from fascist Germany and Italy, were pressing ahead to invade the rest of Spain. Workers' initiative and courage had accomplished much, but unless they quickly took control of the state and its decision-making, that control would revert to the dithering, divided leadership that had failed to prevent the generals' rising, or to arm the workers as soon as it began.

Bits and pieces of news filtered back to London from members of the British left in Spain. Barcelona, where the right were swept from the streets after heavy fighting, was soon a focus for Britons volunteering to help fight the generals. Some had originally come to watch the Barcelona People's Olympiad, planned as a protest against the Olympic Games in Hitler's Berlin and now impossible to hold. One such was the first British volunteer to die, sculptor and Communist Party member Felicia Browne.[5] Others included East London garment workers Nat Cohen and Sam Masters, and the Communist poet John Cornford, who wrote a description of Barcelona's heady atmosphere: 'It's as if in London the armed workers were dominating the streets – it's obvious they wouldn't tolerate Mosley ... And that wouldn't mean the town wasn't free in the real sense. It is genuinely a dictatorship of the majority, supported by the overwhelming majority.'[6]

Paddy Trench, who suffered from tuberculosis and was unable to fight, went to Barcelona as a journalist attached to the POUM, which had links to the ILP.[7] Bert Smyllie at *The Irish Times* sent Lionel Fleming to report on Spain. Fleming had maintained his friendship with Robert,[8] and his opinions may have been influenced by correspondence with him. The paper took the position that the Spanish Republican government was legitimate because it had been democratically elected. Fleming's own view was that Republicans were fighting a 'legitimate struggle, both against the evils of Nazism and Fascism ... and the claim of the Catholic Church ... to control almost every aspect of Spanish life.'[9] His series of ten articles enraged those in Ireland who saw Franco as a defender of the Catholic faith. Some threatened to withdraw advertising, and Fleming was recalled to Dublin.[10]

Swift Blaze of Fire

For the left in Britain and the rest of Europe, the struggle of the Spanish working class was a beacon of light in the encroaching darkness of fascism. It was impossible not to be moved by the heroism which had pitted poorly armed, untrained people against a professional army and carried the day in so much of Spain. As reports rolled in of the advancing Francoists' atrocities, the British Communist Party, its youth wing the Young Communist League, members of other left groups and trade unionists campaigned flat out to raise money for aid to Republican Spain. Literary figures and intellectuals donated work and staged fundraising events. A wide swathe of British public opinion called for the British government to support the Spanish republic.

But the British and French governments had no intention of doing anything of the kind. In August 1936 they organized a Non-Intervention Agreement, pledging to withhold arms and assistance from either side. The Soviet Union, Germany and Italy signed up, as eventually did twenty-four other countries, though in reality Hitler and Mussolini were already sending armaments to assist the Francoists, including tanks and aircraft. Hitler and Mussolini had previously helped Franco land Moroccan troops in Spain, without which the rebel generals would have suffered an early defeat.

Stalin was 'as concerned as policy-makers in Britain to keep the international scene in equilibrium'.[11] Fascist victory in Spain would strengthen Hitler's hand against Russia and he wanted to avoid or at least delay it. At the same time he did not want a successful Spanish working-class revolution. If Russia were accused of aiding such an event he would lose all hope of allying with France or Britain. It would also encourage working-class dissent in Europe and perhaps in Russia too.[12]

In France, Britain and Spain itself, the communist parties therefore followed the Comintern's line: the struggle in Spain must be waged solely as a battle to defend an elected Spanish government and the institutions of bourgeois democracy, not as an opportunity to depose the Spanish ruling class. With the blessing of the Comintern, a new Spanish Popular Front government under Largo Caballero was set up in September. It embarked on a long, futile policy of trying to conciliate the middle classes and gain

17. Robert's father holding Tim, 1927 (Rosemary's photo collection).

18. Robert with Tim at Kingswood Ruffs, circa 1929 (Rosemary's photo collection).

19. Tim and Deirdre in the garden at Kingswood Ruffs, 1929 (Rosemary's photo collection).

20. Deirdre looks on as Rosemary, pregnant with Davnet, mends Robert's torn trousers. Surrey Downs, June 1931 (Rosemary's photo collection).

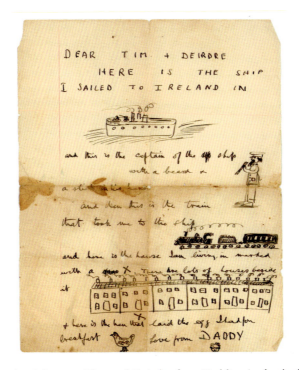

21. Robert's letter to Tim and Deirdre from Dublin. Author's photo.

22. Outdoor Relief workers and supporters, Belfast, 4th October 1932: Chronicle/Alamy Stock Photo.

23. Rosemary recovering from Kit's birth (Rosemary's photo collection).

24. Davnet, Robert and Rosemary walking through Belfast to Kit's christening, Deirdre present but not shown. (Rosemary's photo collection).

25. Deirdre and Tim keeping their daily vigil for Robert at Brown's Bay, September 1934 (Rosemary's photo collection).

26. Weir Cottage, Ballinderry, 1935 (Rosemary's photo collection).

27. Optician's shop in Albacete: photo on reverse of Robert's new spectacles prescription, saved in his wallet in 1936 and sent to Rosemary after his death (Author's photo).

28.1 Robert Hilliard's last postcard to his family, written before the Battalion left Madrigueras for the front at Jarama, 24 January 1937 (Rosemary Hilliard's papers).

28.2 Robert Hilliard's last postcard to his family, written before the Battalion left Madrigueras for the front at Jarama, 24 January 1937 (Rosemary Hilliard's papers).

30. The hospital in Castellón where Robert Hilliard died (Author's photo, 2017).

31. The letter from King Street telling Rosemary of Robert's death, March 1937 (Rosemary Hilliard's papers).

32. Robert and Tim, Surrey, June 1931 (Rosemary's photo collection).

33. Historian Guillem Casañ stands above the mass grave in the Cemetery of San Josep, Castellón, where Hilliard now lies (Author's photo, 2017, reproduced with kind permission of Guillem Casañ).

Civil war in Spain

the support of foreign powers. One example of this conciliation was the government's failure to grant Moroccan independence from Spain. An immediate move to do so might perhaps have undermined the loyalty of at least some of Franco's Moroccan troops. It would however have displeased Britain and France, who also had African colonies, and the idea was rejected.[13]

Meanwhile the Francoist generals gained ground. As General Mola's army took territory in the North, Franco advanced from the south and took Toledo, where Francoist forces had been besieged by Republican militias. If something were not done, the Republic would soon be defeated, releasing Nazi firepower to attack Russia. Stalin began to send military aid to the Republican government, at first without publicity, then more openly as German and Italian breaches of the Non-Intervention Agreement became obvious to all.[14]

A plan was formed in Moscow from August onwards to bring together and add to the numbers of international volunteers who were flocking into Spain, to form International Brigades. Covert assistance deploying volunteers rather than Russian troops could avoid antagonizing the French and British governments, yet hold up Francoist advances and 'crucially, keep Germany embroiled in a costly war, far removed from Russian territory.'[15] Caballero formally agreed the Comintern plan and a coordinated programme of international recruitment began.[16]

At the end of October Franco launched a massive attack on Madrid. Azaña, the president, decamped to Valencia, which became the new seat of government.[17] Spain had one of the largest gold reserves in the world, of which a significant fraction had been used in purchasing arms from France; the remainder was now sent from Madrid to Russia.[18] After days of heroically hard fighting by workers in the street, and following the arrival of the first International Brigade, made up of German, French and Polish battalions, the Francoists' Madrid offensive was halted.

It was at this point that Russian tanks and planes first had an impact on the balance of forces, though at no stage would they ever be a match, quantitatively or qualitatively, for the armaments and materiel supplied to

Swift Blaze of Fire

the Francoists by fascist powers. Stalin's plan was to supply just enough arms 'to keep the Republic alive, while instructing his agents in Spain to make every effort to ensure that the revolutionary aspects of the struggle were silenced'.[19]

The inevitable effect of military aid arriving from Russia was that 'Soviet advisers penetrated many institutions of the Spanish government'.[20] Moscow's directives acquired a dominant influence over government policy. The Spanish Communist Party made big gains in support and prestige. It did all it could to persuade workers' and peasants' representatives to surrender control of the factories and estates they had seized, dismantle their collective structures and fall in behind a government coalition that could supposedly win the support of the middle classes: 'The most outspoken champions of private property were ... the Communist party and its Catalan subsidiary, the PSUC.'[21] Disastrously, workers in some places went along with this; where they didn't they could expect, over time, to be forced to do so. In the process of standing down the Spanish revolution, the PCE and the government weakened the only forces that could defeat the generals' rebellion. As Jason Gurney puts it: 'It was the revolutionary elements in Spain that had gone out on the streets in the early days of the revolt to defend the republic. They had defeated the regular Army in pitched battles all over the peninsula in every major city bar five, in spite of their lack of arms or organisation ... it was no more than a dream that the petty bourgeois clerks and shopkeepers would join them to fight against the Army and the Church.'[22]

It was even more of a dream that the bourgeoisie, either in Spain or abroad, would act against their own class interests and take this stand. If Republicans relied on that dream, or on foreign governments who were never going to help them, they would lose.

If Robert was considering joining others going to Spain that summer or autumn, Rosemary was unaware of it. On 16 August 1936 she wrote a newsy letter, addressing him as 'Dearest One,' asking if he had received some seashells she had sent and describing a Church outing to North Cornwall.

Civil war in Spain

The outing had ended badly for Rosemary, with a High Church service on the beach in which 'the rich red robes of the clergy, the lace and incense, the plainsong and all' had made her long for 'the Carpenter ... to come striding over the grass with John and James and Andrew and Peter, laughing and talking'. This letter, evoking an egalitarian People's Christ, shows Rosemary straining every nerve to bring Robert back. Apparently fearing that he sees her as lacking courage or a sense of humour, she describes her own valiant rescue of a dog from a quicksand, and a visit to see Chaplin's *Modern Times*: 'I wept with laughter, which was good for me – I don't seem to laugh enough.' The letter ends in a flurry of whimsy: 'Did you know earwigs are very old. Way back before there was colour or birds in the world there were earwigs – they are of the scorpion family and lay eggs and hatch them like pelicans.'

She wrote another bustling letter in September, about an upcoming Oxford Group house party in London. Before signing off – 'Love always, your wife Rosemary' – she hinted that this could include a visit to Robert, ending with a final question: 'What do you think of the Soviet Trial?'[23]

She was referring to the USSR's first big public show trial, which had begun in August. The two most eminent defendants were Zinoviev and Kamenev, who had been Stalin's closest allies in taking power after Lenin's incapacitating stroke in 1923. These two men had since then publicly challenged Stalin's theory of socialism in one country. Though later forced to make grovelling apologies,[24] they and other older revolutionaries were now on trial. Stalin wanted to eradicate any possible challenges to his leadership that might garner support from Russian working-class discontent at the brutal enforcement of his Five-Year Plan. Zinoviev, Kamenev and fourteen other leading figures were charged with all manner of treacheries and crimes and executed as soon as their trial ended, in the basement of Moscow's Lubyanka Prison.

Well might Rosemary ask what Robert thought. Had he lived to see one show trial after another, each with its implausible charges, who knows what conclusions he might have reached. Some party members left during the show trials, but most believed the old Bolsheviks really had plotted against

Stalin and therefore against the workers' state. Unfavourable reports were 'put down ... to Tory misrepresentation',[25] even by non-communists like Gurney. Robert's reply to Rosemary is lost, but his party loyalty in other respects suggests he was loyal in this too.

Rosemary might want to visit him in London, but Robert could hardly invite her if he was living with someone else. He gave no invitation, and he did not visit Falmouth. A decisive separation, explained to the children, might perhaps have allowed him to visit them without raising false hopes. But that didn't happen, and his absence lengthened.

Robert had grown up as a republican in Ireland, a country familiar with the ruthlessness of big landowners, the land-hunger of small farmers and the oppressive conservatism of traditional Catholicism. In his teens he had been inspired by the heroic resistance of civilians against a well-equipped army and the sight of striking workers in the streets. The parallels with Spain were obvious and the call to join the International Brigades would have held immense appeal. What finally made him volunteer? For many British volunteers, a tipping point came with the Battle of Cable Street. Perhaps more than anything else, this extraordinary event brought home both the urgency of the fascist threat and the potential for defeating it by united working-class action.

The British Union of Fascists was supported by loud voices in the British establishment and press and had gained a measure of support in some working-class areas. Public life was ever more tainted with anti-Semitism. Jews were being scapegoated for poverty, bad housing and all Britain's economic ills. Blackshirt attacks on Britain's Jews were frequent and confident. In East London, where the working-class Jewish community was most concentrated, the Blackshirts whitewashed the words 'Perish Juda' onto walls wherever they could, sometimes abbreviated to PJ because everyone knew what it meant.[26] Jewish people lived in fear of assaults and beatings. Many Jews joined the Communist Party, drawn by its members' readiness to confront the Blackshirts and its principle that Jews and non-Jews should unite.

Civil war in Spain

With funding from British industrialists, wealthy individuals and European fascist leaders as well as considerable personal wealth, Mosley could afford a large team of full-time staff. Hitler had taken control of the German state after his forces had used sheer thuggery to gain control of the streets. Mosley was trying to tread a similar path. Blackshirt marches, on the streets of London and many other cities, were an exercise in terror. Their black uniforms were designed to instil fear, and they used their boots, together with the heavy, sharp buckles on their belts, as weapons. A number of accounts show just how intimidating they had become:

> The marches followed the pattern of the Nazi Party with the Leader in an open car escorted by a dozen uniformed outriders on motor cycles. Next came ... the strong-arm section – in black uniforms with breeches and jackboots ... followed by the band and ordinary members in black shirts and black trousers, while the 'armoured car squad' brought up the rear.[27]

This account stresses that 'one of the alarming aspects of the marches was that they were able to demonstrate that they had the support of the police'. In theory anyone had the right to march on Britain's streets; in practice police repeatedly joined with the Blackshirts in physically assaulting the left.

When Robert had first arrived in London people were still talking about a Hyde Park rally Mosley had organized in September 1934, which had been successfully swamped by a demonstration of 150,000 anti-fascists.[28] Since then there had been innumerable clashes between fascists and the anti-fascists who understood the need to contain them. Now Mosley wanted to stage a big set piece. On 4 October 1936 he planned to lead the Blackshirts into Whitechapel. The prospect of this march was terrifying for Whitechapel's large Jewish population. The British government refused to ban it and instead mobilized over 6,000 police to escort it into the heart of the area. The Communist Party leadership initially urged its members to attend a rally for Spain in Trafalgar Square, only going to the East End later, but had to change their minds when it was clear that members were going straight to Whitechapel.[29] The few thousand Fascists who marched that day were met by 20,000 or more members of Jewish organizations,

183

Swift Blaze of Fire

communists, trade unionists and local people, both Jewish and non-Jewish, determined that the BUF should not pass.

The centre of antifascist opposition was Gardiner's Corner and Cable Street, off the Whitechapel Road. A barricade was built in Cable Street. As the police tried to clear the way, attacking protesters with baton charges, they were met with sticks and stones. A violent battle between police and anti-fascists ensued. Eventually the police had to divert the Blackshirts away from the East End, but continued to attack protesters and residents. A total of 150 people were arrested; many were beaten by police. About 170 were injured, including police, women and children.[30]

The significance of this confrontation can hardly be overstated. It was the beginning of the decline of the British Union of Fascists. One result was the 1936 Public Order Act: from 1 January 1937, advance permission had to be obtained for any march and uniformed marches were banned. Far more importantly, Cable Street showed that even with police support the Blackshirts could not control the East End. Their standing suffered a heavy blow. Instead of parading through the area as the master-race, they had been sent packing. Mosley continued to organize, holding a massive indoor rally as late as 1939, but his credibility at home and overseas, and in due course his funding, took a big hit. This battle, with many more on a smaller scale, accounts for the fact that fascist organizations never managed to take street power in Britain, and therefore never achieved the standing during the 1930s that they did in many other countries. Cable Street left a legacy, and a model for anti-fascist organization, which is with us to this day.

It's almost certain that Robert was at Cable Street. In the unlikely event that he was not, it can only have had an enormous influence on him. Unity between Jews and non-Jews, trade unionists and unemployed, communists and non-communists, had won the day. Analogies were freely drawn inside and outside the Communist Party between anti-fascist battles in the streets of London and against the Spanish generals. As a triumphant speech put it that same evening: 'Mosley has sustained a crushing defeat today, and

Civil war in Spain

something he will remember for a long time, and in addition to this, great encouragement has been given to the comrades in Spain.'[31]

Great encouragement, too, to volunteer for the International Brigades. By December 1936 a gathering stream of men and some women were on their way to Spain.

Robert's British passport had expired on 8 October 1933. On 16 December 1936 he took it to the Foreign Office for renewal. Perhaps the only surprise is that he had waited so long. Possibly thoughts of his family had contributed to his delay. But in a postcard he later sent from Spain he explained that the idea of his children had in the end been a spur to volunteer: 'I still hate fighting but this time it has got to be done. Unless we end fascism in Spain and in the world it will be war and hell for our kids.'

Once he had renewed his passport, Robert made his way through the barrows, lorries and stands of fruit and vegetables at the back of Covent Garden market to the wooden staircase leading up to the Communist Party offices in King Street. From there he would be sent to a nearby office in Litchfield Street, where a Communist Party official called Robson processed volunteers' applications[32] and did his best to dispel romantic illusions:

> It was a bastard of a war, we would be short of food, medical services and even arms and ammunition ... He could promise us nothing but the opportunity to fight Fascism, on the evils of which he enlarged at great length ... Robson asked us if we were fit and healthy and took our word for it. We were given twenty-four hours to make our personal arrangements and told to report back at the same time on the following day.[33]

None of Robson's warnings put Robert off. On 20 December 1936 he took the ferry to France and disembarked at Dunkirk, on his way to Spain.[34]

18

MADRIGUERAS

Robert's journey from Dunkirk to Paris must have brought back memories. Only twelve years earlier he had travelled in the opposite direction, bruised from his defeat at the Olympics but hurrying with the *Rubaiyat* in his pocket towards Rosemary and the hope of love. Now he had a different kind of hope, one shared with other volunteers on the Paris train. Mostly working-class men, often in Sunday best and with little luggage, they stood out from the ordinary tourists. A name and West London address jotted in Robert's passport – 'Jack, 8 Torrington Sq' – suggests he made a friend on this journey and planned to look him up when they all got home. In Paris he made his way to the Maison des Syndicats at 33 Rue de la Grange-aux-Belles,[1] where France's main trade union confederation, the CGT,[2] organized volunteers from different countries onto the next stage of the journey. They were told to find their own lodgings for the night and stay inconspicuous.

The next day, 21 December, Robert took the famous 'Red Train' to Perpignan. 'The departure of the 'Red Train' ... had become one of the sights of Paris ... crowds with banners came to wave us off. I suppose there must have been all sorts of people travelling on the Perpignan train but

Madrigueras

the crowd had no difficulty in picking out the ... volunteers of different nationalities who were on their way to Spain.'[3]

These trains were overcrowded and the first part of the long journey was cold. In Perpignan volunteers were taken to a ruined chateau used as a barracks. Robert found time to buy a postcard of Perpignan's Palmarium and dash off an upbeat message to Rosemary:'Dear Mummy, This is where I am today. Tomorrow elsewhere. Quite safe and well. See you in a month or two. Love Robert.'[4]

His cheerfulness seems intended to reassure her, perhaps hoping with the promise of a visit to placate her for not having paid one before he left. He doesn't mention his destination, since the less the English and French authorities knew about the volunteers' route the better.

From Perpignan, volunteers travelled into Spain on lorries and buses. These slow, winding journeys into the Pyrenees were made under cover of darkness, as Gurney reports: 'The buses arrived at midnight and the whole affair was supposed to be carried out in total secrecy ... Things were completely uneventful until we reached the French border post. We were stopped at the barrier and I could see various officials moving about with lanterns.'[5]

Volunteer Tony Hyndman describes how they were instructed to stay silent at the frontier post as the driver handed over a passenger list of Spanish names. Once waved through they could relax, talk and smoke.[6] Robert later wrote a long letter comprising an account of some of his Spanish experiences, in the style of an article intended for publication rather than a personal message, which eventually reached Rosemary, probably after his death. She did not keep it, instead passing it on to Owen Sheehy Skeffington, who managed to get a substantial extract from it published in TCD.[7] It begins with an account of this journey, describing the high spirits on the lorries as they arrived in Spain. Men joked that Franco had heard they were coming and was already on the run. 'In the morning,' Robert writes, 'we were in the barracks at Figueras,' an impressive medieval castle. They were there only a few hours when '... we were given the choice of a day's rest or of moving on. Unanimously we voted to move. Four hours sleep and breakfast. Then the train to Barcelona.'[8]

Swift Blaze of Fire

Barcelona was in the grip of revolution. The Communist Party talked of a war aimed only at defending a Popular Front government, postponing a revolution for another day, but in Barcelona Communist Party members were a minority. For anarchists, revolutionary syndicalists, POUM members and much of the city's working-class, the revolution was already underway. Conscious that nothing less would be enough to repel the generals, they were in a fight to take charge of the economy and political life. George Orwell reports businesses collectivized under workers' control, buildings taken over by workers' militias and covered in banners and posters, public transport commandeered for the common good – 'the working class were in the saddle'.[9]

Jason Gurney describes the remarkable social energy this workers' takeover unleashed: '... everything was going flat out ... there were processions, with or without military bands, flags everywhere, the singing of all kinds of revolutionary songs, and the chanting of slogans ... the whole city was a riot of colour and sound.'[10] People in the streets dressed without marking social distinction or wealth in their clothing, looked each other in the eye without deference and addressed each other as equals. For Gurney, '... what was exciting was the glorious feeling of optimism; the conviction that anything that was not right with society would assuredly be put right in the new world of universal equality and freedom which lay ahead ...'[11] The air vibrated with an extraordinary sense of solidarity and creativity.

In Cork and Dublin as a boy, Robert had experienced the heady periods during 1919–21 when the Irish working class had challenged the power of the state. Barcelona was a compelling experience for him. New volunteers were given an ecstatic reception by chanting, banner-waving crowds. 'We marched through Barcelona,' his letter reports, 'What a march!' – and he describes a woman who moved him deeply, not least because she reminded him of Ireland:

> Everywhere the people were out to salute – the clenched fist anti-fascist
> salute. But in particular I remember one woman. She was about four
> foot in height. She wore a brown shawl with a design on the border – a
> shawl very like what an Irish woman from the country wears in town

on market days. She carried a basket on her left arm, but her right arm was raised and her hand was clenched in the anti-fascist salute. Her face, though, was what mattered. Her hair was black, her forehead wrinkled and heavy lines marked the sides of her mouth. She stood to attention as we passed, nearly 200 of us marching in fours, and her mouth was moving rapidly up and down, holding back the tears … Who knows whom she had lost in the fight against fascism?[12]

International Brigade volunteers in Barcelona were housed in an army barracks, where the commanding officer had originally declared support for Franco, triggering a weeks-long siege of the garrison by local people. Miners from Asturias had eventually enabled a successful storming of the building by laying explosives to blow a hole in the walls.[13] These quarters were dirty and chaotic, but volunteers were fed and made welcome.[14] Their next journey was by train to Albacete, via Valencia. Robert soon got talking with another passenger: '… in my carriage was [a] woman … In her arms was a baby. She showed us her Communist Party card and a document to say that she had certain rights and privileges with regard to transport and food … She had been a Commandant in the Women's Militia in Madrid. She was sent back because of her baby, still at her breast, but fighting in the capital were her husband and two sons. The older son was 18.'[15]

Behind this woman's account lay the story of the Francoists' first attacks on Madrid, which Robert would have read about while still in England. Francoist forces had first arrived at the suburbs of Madrid on 7 November. One eye-witness, *Daily Telegraph* correspondent Henry Buckley, describes how they had been held at bay:

> … down by Toledo Bridge … I saw a sight which made me very ashamed of my petty worries … Going up into line were long files of civilians. They had no uniforms. Just ordinary suits and a rifle slung anyhow over the shoulder … They were just men [sic] called up by the trade unions and the political organisations to fight for Madrid … Believe me, those were the men who saved Madrid … [in the] two critical days of November 7 and 8 when the situation hung in the balance. It was the courage and sacrifice of the Madrid people which alone held the feeble lines which separated Franco from the city.[16]

Swift Blaze of Fire

Buckley goes on to describe how Franco's advance was stalled by the 80,000 or so civilians who 'just stayed doggedly in the positions in which they were put and fired blindly at the foe'. From 8 November several thousand men from the International Brigades began to arrive, bolstering the Republican side in a series of counter-attacks. Madrid had been under attack ever since, pounded by shelling and bombing. The Francoists had lined up a convoy of lorries to bring food into Madrid after it fell. When it didn't fall as expected, the lorries' cargoes sat and rotted, while Madrileños suffered ever greater food shortages.[17] The reports Robert had read in England were brought to life by this woman. She must have been heavily pregnant when she fought.

The town of Albacete was the organizing centre for the International Brigades. Volunteers slept in the Guardia Civil barracks and paraded in the town's bullring. New arrivals had to pick out 'uniforms' from heaps of miscellaneous brown clothing, and hand over their civilian clothes and effects.[18] The blankets, capes and leather equipment issued to volunteers were cumbersome, the helmets outdated,[19] and there would later be complaints that neither the treasured Sunday suits nor the personal possessions were returned.[20] Some men surrendered their passports but Robert hung on to his, keeping it carefully alongside a precious selection of letters from Rosemary and Tim that he would carry with him until his death.

Robert had broken his spectacles during the journey and visited an optician to buy new ones, folding the Spanish prescription into his wallet in case they broke again. He was no Spanish speaker, but his habit of striking up a rapport makes it easy to imagine him trying out a few words in the shop, his eyes squinting wildly as they always did with no glasses on.

The town boasted an International Brigades Club, though Robert doesn't mention it. According to Gurney's rather stereotyped description, the Club's Germans kept singing the same few songs, the French argued and smoked, while the English drank and complained about Albacete.[21] They didn't complain long. More trucks came to carry English-speaking volunteers the thirty-two kilometres to Madrigueras, a town on the dusty La Mancha plain, where a new British battalion was forming. Robert discreetly refers to it as 'somewhere in Spain'.

In Falmouth the children had enjoyed the summer. Tim and Deirdre were happy in their school (as usual, Rose paid the fees). Later came another crop of winter illnesses. Kit and Davnet had to have their tonsils out and as winter advanced all the children caught whooping cough. Deirdre developed brucellosis, an acute bacterial infection caught from drinking unpasteurized goats' milk, which gave her fevers and joint pains and kept her off school. She filled her time at home with books. They reminded her of her father's bedtime stories and she found in them a comforting refuge. At eight-and-a-half years old she read everything she could get her hands on.

Just before Christmas Rosemary learned Robert had gone to Spain. His postcard from Perpignan did nothing to ease her anxiety. She listened intently to radio news bulletins and subscribed to both the *Daily Worker* and the *News Chronicle*, combing through them for articles about the war in Spain. Deirdre sat with her, poring over the reports in these papers. 'I started to listen to the news on the wireless too; there was often news of Spain that winter, and I used to wonder what was happening to Daddy.'[22] It would be a long, tense wait before they had any news of him.

The British battalion of the XV International Brigade was formed in Madrigueras on 27 December 1936, just after Robert arrived.[23] Although it included seasoned volunteers who had fought with Spanish militias or other Brigades, most were recent arrivals. The battalion was mainly British and Irish, with a sprinkling of other nationalities.[24] Many were Jewish; some were refugees from fascism. Despite the mythmaking, only a minority were middle-class poets or professional intellectuals; the majority were working-class people. Eventually they would total about 600 men, forming four companies. Other XV Brigade battalions trained in other towns: the

Swift Blaze of Fire

Balkan nationals' Dimitrov battalion, the Franco-Belgian battalion and the US Abraham Lincoln battalion, in which, unlike the US Army, black and white were treated as equals.

Each company within the battalion had a political commissar, whose job was to build political loyalty, and team spirit – and to 'maintain constant vigilance towards defeatist elements, Trotskyists and deserters.'[25] Robert already knew, or knew of, some of these commissars. Glaswegian Peter Kerrigan was a senior figure in the British Communist Party who had studied at Moscow's Lenin School and it was no surprise to find him a political commissar in Spain. Dave Springhall, also a political commissar, was seen by Gurney as a humourless apparatchik but Wintringham called him 'Springie' and thought him an excellent judge of men.[26] Commanders, too, were well-known figures. Jock Cunningham, who led No. 1 Company, was an activist in the NUWM[27] in London who had already fought in Lopera and Madrid. Tom Wintringham led No. 2 company (the machine-gun company), and Bill Briskey No. 3. Robert would have heard of Briskey, a Hackney bus driver and prominent activist in the Transport and General Workers' Union. No. 4 company was headed by Bert Overton, who had been in the British Army.

Madrigueras was a small, impoverished town which depended on the growing of saffron.[28] Its unpaved streets had been reduced to mud by the rain which continued throughout nearly the entire period the battalion spent there. The 'potholes a yard across or more – and nearly as deep' and the ruts worn by mule-carts made these streets difficult for marching.[29] The modest houses were 'mostly one-storeyed, with narrow windows prison-like even to the bars, and shuttered, the shutters nearly always closed'.[30] Although Gurney described the inhabitants of Madrigueras as 'silent and taciturn'[31] other volunteers were more positive; Fred Thomas, for example, thought them 'pleasant, friendly and courteous,'[32] and John Lochore writes of children being sent out to invite groups of men back to people's homes for meals.[33]

Battalion commander Wilfred Macartney was billeted with his team in the grandest house, taken over from a wealthy local. A number of men

Madrigueras

were billeted in the cinema, which was more like a garage but had been used as a cinema while the 12th Battalion was stationed at Madrigueras.[34] This building's cement floor at first housed twenty men, later a hundred or so, by which time the latrines and washing facilities were completely inadequate.[35] The impossibility of staying clean and keeping clothing dry was an unpleasant side of Madrigueras life. Men had not been there long before they suffered from lice in their clothing and the never-ending damp. Besides the cinema, volunteers were put up in villagers' houses and one slept in a hay loft.

The church, by far the largest town building, was gutted and daubed with slogans, a common fate for churches during the Spanish Civil War. Priests had sided with local landlords and the conservative cause for as long as anyone could remember and now supported the Francoists. Madrigueras's priest was said to have barricaded himself in the church tower when the generals' uprising began, taking potshots at anyone fetching water from the stone trough and well which provided the villagers' water supply. Ultimately, it was said, two villagers scaled the tower to capture and hang him.[36] Now the church was used as a mess hall for the International Brigaders. The food served there was monotonous and unappetizing: vegetables stewed in oil with occasional low quality meat, widely thought to be donkey, or a form of tinned meat known to the French volunteers as 'singe' (monkey). The water was undrinkable unless made into coffee and the coffee was widely disliked, so the three cafés selling wine and other alcohol plied a profitable trade. Thirsty volunteers used to drinking pints of British beer found it hard to adjust the volume down when the drink was stronger so drunkenness was frequent. It was punishable by being locked in the guardroom, or later in a 'draughty place ... under the leaking roof of an abandoned building'.[37]

Robert was one of many likeable characters who emerge from volunteers' reminiscences. One hero for Gurney was Jack Lemaans, a member of the US Industrial Workers of the World, or Wobblies, who loved to quote US socialist leader Eugene Debs: 'While there is a working class, I am of it. While there is a revolutionary party, I belong to it, and

Swift Blaze of Fire

while there is one man in jail, I am not free.'[38] Christopher Caudwell, known as Christopher St John Sprigg or Spriggy, was 'an exceedingly modest, pleasant man'[39] who had been an active socialist and anti-fascist in Poplar, East London. Only thirty years old, he had published six books of criticism and philosophy, nine novels and a great many poems and short stories, but kept his fame to himself. His close friend in Madrigueras was Clem Beckett, a professional speedway and wall-of-death motorcyclist from Oldham.

Robert Hilliard is affectionately described by battalion members who knew him. His work as a pastor had often entailed offering fellowship in a lonely hour, something he still did, for example keeping John Lochore company during night-time guard duty:

> It was on the occasion of those long, black, bleak watches I made the acquaintance of an Irish minister of religion. The Reverend R M Hilliard hailed from Killarney and embraced the Protestant faith. He was known as 'the boxing parson', and with his short-cropped hair and broken nose he certainly fitted his nickname. Beneath that outward appearance he was a very kind, sincere person with a fine sense of humour and no task was too big or too small for him. He would come during my watches and chat for hours on end and relieve the boredom of the night.[40]

Jason Gurney also pays tribute to Robert's open-hearted comradeship: 'his friends were of all classes' – as well as recording that he was '[o]ne of the most amusing characters in Madrigueras', and 'a great drinker', liked for 'his sense of humour and his consistently cheerful attitude'.[41]

Opinions differed about battalion commander Wilfred Macartney. Robert praised him highly:

> We were fortunate. The commander of our battalion had the experience of an imperialist army behind him. He also had advantages unknown to any imperialist army in the world – he knew and knows the worst in men, also the best. He fought for us, he secured English food for us, he determined we should not go into the line untrained.[42]

Wintringham also respected Macartney, seeing him as 'sensitive and friendly ... downright and far-seeing and therefore socialist', and calls him 'the man who mattered more than any other in the shaping of the battalion that held the Jarama ridge'.[43] He also praised Macartney's attempts to improve the food,[44] despite his limited success, and the 'realism' he brought to training manoeuvres. Macartney used rattles to imitate the sound of machine-guns and taught men to spread out and take cover while advancing, so as not to present too easy a target for enemy fire.[45]

As time passed, however (and probably after Robert wrote his letter), criticisms of Macartney increased. Gurney described him as 'a strange man' with 'very little idea of the duties of a Battalion Commander'.[46] More influentially, Peter Kerrigan relayed grave doubts to Harry Pollitt in London in late January, describing him as 'a problem and a worry'.[47] Early in February Macartney had to make a quick visit to England.[48] Kerrigan accompanied him and during a discussion in which they showed each other their guns he shot Macartney, non-fatally but disabling him from his role. Kerrigan resigned his post, and debate has continued ever since as to whether the shot was deliberate. The well-liked Wintringham took over Macartney's command.

Prior to this there had been a major upheaval in the ranks. Many of the battalion's Irish members had fought with the IRA for Irish independence. On 12 January a simmering disagreement boiled over. Wilfred Macartney and George Nathan, the XV Brigade staff officer, had served in the notorious Auxiliary Division,[49] which had played a murderous role in British attempts to suppress the Irish independence struggle. Some of the Irish volunteers could no longer endure obeying orders from these men. After a furious debate, a contingent of Irish volunteers voted to leave the British battalion and join the US Abraham Lincoln battalion.

Their military experience would be much missed. A fair proportion of them had fought at Lopera, Cordoba or Madrid and the *Daily Worker's* failure to acknowledge the Irish contribution at those battles had fuelled the anger they now expressed.[50]

Not all the Irish departed; for example seasoned IRA fighter Frank Ryan stayed, having stated his opinion in a letter to Irish volunteers: 'in

Swift Blaze of Fire

the International Brigades … there are no national differences. We are all comrades.'[51] Another veteran of the Irish independence war who stayed was Kit Conway, who would later be given the command of company No. 1, in which Robert served.

Robert stayed too. A month later all four companies of the British battalion would be sent to the frontline. The effects of the Non-Intervention Agreement meant there were formidable hurdles to surmount before they went.

19

'TEACH THE KIDS TO STAND FOR DEMOCRACY'

Robert hardly ever fired a weapon while in Madrigueras. The Non-Intervention Agreement severely hampered training by preventing supplies of weapons and ammunition from reaching the Republican side. Volunteer Fred Copeman's figures are not exact but give the general picture: 'six weapons between seven hundred men gives some idea of the amount of practice possible.'

The weapons which at last arrived, weeks after training began, were nearly all defective: the useless Chauchats or 'shossers' which always jammed, the American Colts with perished unusable ammunition belts, the Russian rifles with badly designed bayonets that many of the men simply discarded. Only the ancient Maxim guns were much use. Despite all this even the sceptical Gurney could say 'everybody did their best and remained fairly cheerful.'[1] An expanse of red earth outside town served as a shooting range, though they still had almost no ammunition.[2]

The detail Robert went into about the political commissar regime in his letter to England shows how important the issue of battalion democracy was for him. As he explained,

> … political commissars were appointed to each company. To each section, 40 men approx.. and to each group 12 men approx. political delegates were elected. In some cases the delegates were communists and in some cases members of the Labour Party. Communist cells, Labour Party and Trade Union sections met, with the result that political lectures were arranged and the conscious understanding of the anti-fascist war brought new life to the battalion.

But this was not the democratic accountability of a revolutionary army. Electing delegates with no power was a far cry from electing officers, which some battalion members had come to Spain expecting to do. Wintringham cites a 'Young Communist League member from the East End' who 'laid it down that in a "revolutionary army like ours" discipline must be by agreement … [and] wanted to know why there had been "no proper election of officers"'.[3]

Robert again: 'Many of us had come out here thinking we were joining a "Red Army", a "Workers' Army" or a "People's Army" … It was thought that we could elect our own officers, or alternatively, depose them at will. In fact our officers are appointed by the Government of Spain, and short of proven incompetence remain as such. The practice of electing officers had been tried out in anarchist battalions in the early stages of the war with results that compelled all parties to agree to permanent appointments.'

Here Robert was repeating what he'd been told by political commissars like Springhall and Kerrigan. In reality the appointment of officers was a political decision. The Comintern wanted to limit this war to defending the Popular Front government. The Communist Party therefore had no intention of allowing the International Brigades to become a revolutionary 'People's Army'. The plan (though never carried out) was to integrate the Brigades, like the militias, into the government army,[4] which did not elect its officers. Maintaining conventional army hierarchies accorded with keeping social revolution off the menu. It's no surprise that commissars were emphatic in saying the election of officers did not work.

Macartney saw no problem with these hierarchies while he was battalion commander, disdainfully dismissing the political discussion cells which

'*Teach the kids to stand for democracy*'

Robert felt were so important: 'Harry's anarchists! That's my name for this battalion! All deputations and opinions and little Soviets discussing each order before they obey it, or don't obey it.'[5]

Wintringham, too, took for granted many of the mores of the British Army, where he and Macartney had both learnt their soldiering. For him, discipline came from the top. Despite all his admiration for those he led 'as men and as friends,'[6] he fretted over petty infringements and the limits of his authority like a housemaster fussing about school uniform: 'Some men ... would turn out on parade of a morning in their overcoats, because they felt cold ... An outbreak of red scarves had to be repressed ... A green beret and some green scarves among the Irish of course had to be winked at.'[7]

In his letter to England Robert carefully differentiated between different kinds of democracy. This was a 'Democratic, though not a "RED" nor a Workers' army', he explained; that is to say, its *raison d'être* was the defence of bourgeois democracy from fascism, but it was not under the democratic control of its members. Was its discipline, then, any different from that enforced in the army of a country like Britain or France? Robert argued that it was, because 'in contra-distinction to an imperialist army, political thought and activity were encouraged', and 'the greater the political activity the stronger and more effective would be the fight against fascism'.

He was thus one of many in the ranks who viewed the conflict with a kind of double vision. On one hand, most were inspired by the idea of a democratic army, where discipline was all the more effective for coming from within and below, informed by debate and collective political understanding. On the other, they all had to go along with the political commissars, who did their utmost to lower revolutionary expectations and justify discipline from the top down. Robert was clear that fascism threatened even the most limited forms of bourgeois democracy. He was prepared to be persuaded by the political commissars' case. But as a logician he must have known the position he loyally advanced held logical gaps. In particular, what would happen if or when collective 'political thought and activity' strayed beyond commissar-approved limits?

Swift Blaze of Fire

His friend Jason Gurney referred to this double vision as 'the command's ambivalent attitude towards discipline', adding:

> This was a people's army and everybody was addressed as Comrade and referred to by function – Comrade Battalion Command, Comrade Political Commissar, down to just Comrade. We were all supposed to be equal in some respects but not in others and just where the division lay was always obscure. The confusion between political and military functions or responsibilities was never entirely resolved throughout the history of the International Brigades.[8]

Some months after Robert's death this ambivalence would become glaring, as conflict escalated in Barcelona between the Communist Party on the one hand and the CNT and the POUM (who did elect their officers and decided strategic questions in conference) on the other.[9] Gurney describes how events in Barcelona '... were reflected in the situation within the Brigade. Rumours of men disappearing, of trials and executions, increased more than ever before. People started to guard their tongues and to look over their shoulders when they spoke in any critical way of authority.'[10]

Robert had thought long and hard about the issue; he would not otherwise have dwelt on it at such length. When he says that many of 'us' (rather than 'many of the men') thought they were joining a People's Army, the implication is that this had included him. Is there a whiff in this letter of suppressed disappointment? Wary of his own rebelliousness, Robert had always tried to conform wholeheartedly with any institution whose ideas he decided to adopt, but could never maintain this conformity all the time. Just as while training for the priesthood at Trinity he sometimes appeared as 'a cross between a hornpipe and a fugue, often of a wild nature',[11] he sometimes dropped his guard in Madrigueras, especially when he'd taken a drink. Gurney writes that Robert had 'developed the most startlingly irreverent manner by the time I knew him. When in wine he would put on his parsonical voice and make a benediction – "In the name of Marx," – and with two fingers raised he drew the curve of the sickle. "Engels" – he drew the handle. "Lenin, Stalin, Stakinov [sic], Dimitrov" – the points of the hammerhead; "the Party line" – its handle. All delivered with extreme unction.'[12]

'Teach the kids to stand for democracy'

Just who or what was Robert making fun of here? Was it the rituals of Christianity? Or was it rather the transmogrification of these political figures – including Dimitrov and Stakhanov, identified with some of the most controversial aspects of Comintern policy – into revered icons? Did his jokey benediction suggest that the Party line had become quasi-religious dogma? Was he feeling under pressure, yet again, to suspend his powers of reasoning in favour of blind faith?

Rosemary was desperate to find out whether Robert was safe. In December she wrote to the Communist Party in London, sending five shillings for the Special Spanish Fund and begging for news. Harry Pollitt wrote personally to thank her for the money, and a week later she heard from The Secretariat, saying they had no news: 'we receive very little indeed and apparently there is no official casualty list published ... As soon as we receive any information it is published in the *Daily Worker*'. The letter invited Rosemary to send them a letter 'with a view to its being delivered to your husband'. She probably did, though it's not clear that it ever reached him.[13]

She had also written to the Transport and General Workers' Union, hoping they might help her, and at last received a belated reply. It was reassuring, though its information was out of date: 'I can assure you your husband is OK. He was at the base in Albacete when I left and was likely to be there some time.' In fact, as we have seen, he was in Madrigueras. The letter provided her with an address in Albacete and recommended sending 'English cigarettes, tobacco, chocolate, spearmint ... The lads have a method of swopping one thing for another, they are very clanish [sic] and share many of their comforts. Hope this letter will ease the tension in your mind ... With working class greetings, yours in the struggle, A F Papworth.'

Rosemary wrote to Robert at this address, with parcels of the items suggested. The parcels never reached him, but her letter was delivered to him on 24 January by a trade union delegation. It gave him the chance to send back a postcard by the same means.

Swift Blaze of Fire

The battalion expected to be moved up to the Front shortly. Robert's card is written in the knowledge that he will soon be in active combat. It's sober in tone and he makes every word count. He has only minutes in which to write it before the delegation leaves, but in these few words, pencilled hurriedly in a muddy square in Spain, he must say everything that will be needed if he's killed. He wants Rosemary and his children to understand that if that happens his death won't be wasted, that in fighting fascism he's fighting for them. He wants the ideal of democracy to be something his children will stand up for. He must avoid striking too sombre a tone, because he's also trying to reassure them. Above all he wants to send his love, not just to Rosemary but to his children, individually naming them, so that if he doesn't survive each one of them will know they were loved.

> My dear, Five minutes ago I got your letter. There is a T.U. [Trade Union] delegation here that will take this back. They leave in ten minutes so I have time for no more than a card which will have an English post mark. Teach the kids to stand for democracy. Thanks for the parcels, I expect they have been forwarded to me but posts are held up very long & specially parcels. Do not worry too much about me I expect I shall be quite safe. I think I am going to make quite a good soldier. It was good to contribute to the Harry Pollitt fund. You'll get news in the *Daily Worker* from time to time. I still hate fighting but this time it has got to be done, unless fascism is beaten in Spain and in the world it means war and hell for our kids. All the time when I am thinking of you & the children I am glad I have come. Give my love to Tim, Deirdre, Davnet and Kit. Write when you can, it will help. Love to you.

By the time the battalion's stay in Madrigueras ended, early in February, Harry Fry commanded the Maxim machine gun company and Bert Overton an infantry company which (according to Gurney) included Colt machine-gunners. Jock Cunningham had taken over No. 1 Company – probably the company Robert was in[14] – but was hospitalized with flu. Irishman Kit Conway, an IRA veteran who had fought in Madrid and Cordoba, replaced him. Briskey commanded the remaining infantry company. Springhall and Kerrigan had left Madrigueras and the new political commissar was Scottish Communist George Aitken.[15]

'Teach the kids to stand for democracy'

Rifles and ammunition were issued before the men left for the front. The atmosphere as they waited by torch and candlelight in the darkness and rain was 'like that of the crowd that collects at a pit-head after news of a mine disaster – a compound of hope, fear and awe.'[16] Each of them received a rifle, ammunition and a bayonet. The next day brought a brief opportunity to fire their newly-issued weapons, before climbing on board a convoy of trucks. A crowd of townspeople came out to give them an emotional farewell as they left Madrigueras.[17]

20

JARAMA

The Battle of Jarama was fought to stop Franco seizing the Madrid-Valencia road. It had already begun when Robert left Madrigueras, and the British Battalion were on their way to join it.

Against all odds, Republican Madrid had continued to resist Franco's forces since their first attack in early November 1936. The government had however moved its administrative seat to Valencia, on the east coast of Spain. Now Franco decided to sever Madrid from the government and the rest of the Republican zone by seizing control of the road linking it to Valencia. This battle therefore had immense strategic significance. A Francoist success would cut off this vital supply line, making it impossible to move troop reinforcements, war materiel or food and medical supplies to the Madrid front and spelling inevitable defeat for the Republic.

General Varela commanded the Francoist drive to capture this road. At his disposal were 'five brigades of six battalions each, [and] a further eleven battalions in reserve, totalling some 25,000 men,'[1] mostly North African soldiers, backed by German tanks, artillery and machine guns. Republican forces, under General Miaja, comprised about fifty battalions with Russian air support. The two sides were evenly matched in infantry numbers but in all else they were far from equal. Varela

Jarama

was commanding perhaps the best-trained, best-armed ground force in Europe at that time.

By the end of 6 February the Francoists had pushed the Republican side back to the Jarama river, despite fierce resistance, and by the morning of 8 February they controlled most of its west bank. The river was too swollen to ford, but in the early hours of 11 February North African soldiers knifed the sentries on the Pindoque railway bridge and the Francoists began to cross there. Next morning they captured another bridge. Part of their forces then swung away, with the aim of taking the Pingarron Heights before advancing to the Madrid-Valencia road.

On the night of 11 February three battalions of the newly formed XV Brigade arrived to defend the Pingarron Heights. The 600-strong British Battalion was to be on the left of the line, to their right would be the Franco-Belge Battalion and further to the right the Dimitrov Battalion.[2] Further north, to the right of the whole XV Brigade, was the XI Brigade.[3]

The English Battalion's journey from Madrigueras had allowed little chance of rest. Their lorries had brought them to a train, which took all night to get to Chinchón, about forty miles from Madrid. Its unheated third class carriages were too crowded for much sleep.[4] The next day they had a chance to do some training with their new weapons: 'More than eighty percent of the men had never held a loaded weapon in their hands before. They had been shown roughly how to aim a rifle while in Madrigueras and now their total experience was to be the firing of ten rounds on an improvised range laid out on the hillside. Naturally enough it was not a very impressive performance.'[5]

That night they marched six miles to the new English Battalion base, on the road from Chinchón to San Martin de la Vega, carrying blankets, packs, rifles, ammunition and any other luggage they still had with them. Most of the men fell asleep on arrival, too exhausted to eat, some lying under the olive trees without taking their gear off.[6]

Early the next morning, on 12 February, they began the climb into the hills, to the plateau overlooking the Jarama River. Many of those still

205

carrying personal belongings dumped them at this point. Jason Gurney describes the sea of possessions he found a few days later, spread across the hillside, in particular books, which ranged from Marxist textbooks to pornography to 'the works of Nietzsche, and Spinoza, Spanish language textbooks, Rhys David's *Early Buddhism* and every … taste in poetry.' Not only books but clothing, blankets, overcoats and much else had been left in bundles by men who, naïvely optimistic, thought they would achieve their military objective in a few hours and be back to collect them.[7]

The countryside that morning was empty of people, clean and sparkling, with a light frost on the ground.[8] Wild thyme and other aromatics grew underfoot. The hills were clad with olive groves and the olives were ripe for harvest; where they fell and lay crushed they gave out bursts of scarlet juice, like blood.[9] The men crossed a ridge and a narrow sunken road and began to descend into the Jarama valley, towards another ridge topped by a small white house. This was the 'Casa Blanca', standing on what would soon be known as 'Suicide Hill'. As they passed these landmarks the Battalion came under sporadic fire and were told to pull back and dig in.

Companies 1 and 3 were sent to the Casa Blanca on the hill, Number 4 Company took a position on the right-hand slope with the San Martin-Morata road on their right, and the machine gun company was told to give cover. Robert, almost certainly in Number 1 Company, went to Suicide Hill. The ground ahead ran downhill to the Jarama river, about two miles away. They could see fighting on their side of it as Spanish units tried to hold back the Francoist advance,[10] but it seemed a long way off. Wintringham set up his HQ on the narrow track behind the ridge, called the 'sunken road' because its surface was four feet below ground level.[11]

What had been almost a holiday mood ended without warning as the Battalion suddenly came under saturation-level machine gun and artillery fire. At first the fire focused on the Casa Blanca and Suicide Hill. The volume of noise was ear-splitting and unnerving. Soon all positions were under heavy bombardment and shrouded in smoke. Most of these men had never until this moment heard the sound of 'metal tearing through the air'[12] as shells approached, or felt the blast of deafening explosions as they

Jarama

landed, or been targeted, unremittingly, by machine-guns. The effect was of physical shock and sheer terror. It went on, without letting up, for hour after hour.

As if this wasn't enough, many found that their weapons jammed or failed to work; the 'shossers' in particular proved almost useless. Soon injured men were walking or being carried from the lines. The battalion was being cut to pieces. As the barrage at last died down, three hours later, those who had survived it saw, to their horror, North African soldiers advancing towards them, 'bobbing up and down, running and disappearing again, while all the time maintaining a continuous and accurate fire.'[13] Their speed and skill at finding cover inspired dread:[14] '[their] uncanny ability .... to exploit the slightest fold in the ground ... to make themselves invisible ... is an art which only comes to a man after a lifetime spent with a rifle in his hand ... [t]he effect ... was utterly demoralising.'[15]

The machine gun company could not fire at the advance. They had waited some time for their ammunition to arrive, only to discover it was the wrong kind. Worse still, the Franco-Belge Battalion was now driven back, leaving the British Battalion exposed on the right flank. The line began breaking as men retreated, carrying the wounded and horribly aware of how far their numbers had shrunk. As they went, North African soldiers rushed forwards across Suicide Hill to occupy their positions. But – with time running out – the machine gunners were at last brought the right ammunition. Waiting for their moment, they opened fire. 'The result was like mowing down wheat. As the bullets struck home, a still, thick black line appeared on the ground ... No cover was possible ... the slaughter was almost complete.'[16]

This long fusillade halted the Francoist advance. The day was ending. The few survivors in the attacking party withdrew as darkness fell. Astonishingly, the Francoists had been held at bay.

In seven hours the Battalion had lost over half its men. Among the dead were Christopher St John Sprigg and his close friend Clem Beckett. Bill Briskey and Kit Conway were also dead. Robert Hilliard was alive but one of only 125 riflemen to survive; 275 were dead or wounded. Many survivors

Swift Blaze of Fire

now had no weapons. Those who could gathered at the HQ in the sunken road, dazed and desperate for food and water. Others had wandered away to the cookhouse behind the lines, or elsewhere. George Aitken spent the night rounding them up, forcing those who would not return voluntarily to do so at pistol point.[17] One group was found hiding in the cookhouse wine vaults; they, too were forced back.[18]

The days were hot but nights were bitterly cold and that night was no exception. The men mostly slept in the sunken road, hungry and thirsty, some without blankets. George Aitken arrived at dawn, with his truckload of rounded-up men as well as coffee and sandwiches. George Nathan turned up soon after, rallying spirits with his air that everything was under control.

But the Francoist attacks on this second day would be as intense as on the first and all the more terrifying because their own forces were so much thinner. The machine gun company started the day well, driving back Francoist soldiers who had pressed forward during the night. Various unrealistic-sounding orders were issued to Tom Wintringham, who was more than once told to lead a charge down the hill and drive the enemy back across the river. Since in his opinion the best they could hope for was to hold their positions, he disobeyed and stayed put. The Francoists attacked again and again[19] and as the day advanced the battalion was surrounded on three sides. Bert Overton's company, greatly depleted from the day before, retreated without sending any message they were going, leaving Harold Fry's machine gun company unexpectedly exposed. Fry and his men were quickly captured; an appalling blow.

Overton realized too late what the effect of his retreat had been. He and forty or so men charged in an attempt to recapture Fry's trenches, only to be mown down by the battalion's own machine guns, which were now in enemy hands.[20] Wintringham was shot in the leg as he also led a charge, disabling him from further command. He would be replaced that evening by Jock Cunningham, just back from hospital. At the day's end the ground in front of the ridge had been given up. Only 160 men were left.[21] With so few, the companies started to merge.

Jarama

The frontline was now the sunken road. A sense of disarray prevailed as they settled there for the night. Few had much sleep. One volunteer describes how it passed: 'It was a night of alarms: flaring Verey lights, continual bursts of wild firing from both sides. When morning broke we were still holding the sunken road … most comrades had been unable to contact the food wagon. For many it was the third day without food.'[22]

On the third day, in intense heat and with no water, the battalion again came under severe fire. By early afternoon the Francoist attack was supported by tanks. Tank fire decimated the nearby Spanish company: 'The slaughter was terrible. One would see five men running abreast, and four of them suddenly crumple up …'[23]. The Battalion had nothing with which to counter a tank attack: 'In those days we had no anti-tank guns, no grenades, no anti-tank materiel.'[24] Under this onslaught the line broke. The tanks advanced inexorably up the hill, crushing the battalion's remaining machine guns as they reached their positions, and Jock Cunningham was forced to call a retreat. Abandoning the sunken road, those who were left straggled down the hill, completely disorganized. Some way down, towards Chinchón, they met General Gal, the unpopular XV Brigade Commander, who had issued some of the day's more unfeasible orders. He told them they were the only ground force between the Francoists and the Madrid-Valencia road and must go back. Jock Cunningham somehow rallied the men around him and turned them round. As they marched back up the hill they fell into step, and other stragglers joined them, stray Spanish soldiers as well as International Brigade members. They began to sing the *Internationale*, which raised morale and attracted more stragglers. As they got close to the frontline, Cunningham ordered them to fix bayonets and they charged.

And the Francoist soldiers who had taken their positions fell back. In an extraordinary reverse, they apparently believed a body of reinforcements had arrived. It was an act of bluff, and it succeeded. As Tom Wintringham later pointed out, there was a gap in the Republican line to the south of Suicide Hill, where the Francoists could have advanced without opposition. But the fight to defend Suicide Hill and the nearby positions had obscured

Swift Blaze of Fire

the glaring weak spot, which was never exploited.[25] This was a decisive moment. That night, and subsequently, more units arrived to reinforce the Republican positions, as well as Russian tanks. Both Francoists and Republicans dug in and although the rest of February saw fierce attacks and counter-attacks and great loss of life, Franco's advance on this front became a stalemate. Encirclement of Madrid had been averted. The city's supply lines from Valencia remained open and Madrid would not be taken until the end of the Civil War.[26]

The rally came too late for Robert Hilliard. Hopefully he was told of it, but he had fallen wounded in the Francoist tank advance. It's not clear when or how he fell, though *Daily Worker* correspondent William Rust says he was 'prominent in the fighting'.[27] One account describes how 'here and there, little groups rallied to stem the fascist advance. Five or six times, a little bunch of No.1 Company … held up the Moors. Finally they too had to give up the unequal fight, but not before they had evacuated their wounded.'[28] Another writer tells us that Robert was a member of one of these small groups: '… the Rev. R.M. Hilliard, the "Boxing Parson" from Killarney … was the sole survivor of a party of four who held up the fascist tanks during the retreat on February 14.'[29]

No other known[30] accounts back this up, though Copeman states Robert was 'Hit running back to the line from no-man's land'.[31] Who knows if either recollection can be relied on, but a stubborn determination to fight on, even after the retreat was called, sounds just like Robert Hilliard.

Shot in the neck,[32] he was brought to a medical unit, possibly the one under the medical direction of Len Crome, which was operating '… in the thick of the Battle of Jarama, ferrying the casualties to improvised rearguard hospitals at Chinchon and in the Hotel Palace in Madrid.'[33] From one of these rearguard hospitals, Robert was evacuated by train to Castellón, a town on Spain's east coast, seventy or so kilometres north of Valencia. John Lochore, whom Robert had befriended in Madrigueras, travelled with an arm injury on a similar train. Lochore was clearly in shock and his account is frank about his confusion: 'Where we travelled I'll never know.'[34]

Jarama

He believed he was taken to a hospital in Murcia, but since his journey was the same length as Robert's, and given that he heard news of Robert soon after arriving,[35] they were quite possibly taken to the same place, perhaps on the same train. He describes ambulances ferrying walking wounded to a bomb-scarred railway siding, with stretcher cases brought on open lorries.

> A train with empty carriages stood there and we boarded ... The main bulk of mobile cases sat on the hard seats, the stretcher cases were laid down the passages. Fortunately, because the train was of old vintage, it moved slowly – very slowly – and by virtue of its country route it regularly stopped in orange groves and then there was the exodus of hobbling soldiers on 'make-do' crutches and in blood-stained bandages who climbed from the windows to pay homage to nature. The stretcher cases – poor creatures – had to relieve themselves as best they could lying flat on their backs.[36]

It's unlikely that a man with a neck injury could endure sitting in a jolting train. Robert was probably one of the stretcher cases on the floor.

Robert reached hospital in Castellón on 17 February, three days after his injury. He died on 22 February, perhaps of wounds, perhaps of sepsis, or perhaps, as some accounts state, after a wall collapsed on him during a bombing raid on the hospital.[37] He was thirty-two years old.

The German Thaelmann Battalion administered the hospitalization of injured volunteers in Castellón from the nearby town of Benicasim, where the International Brigades Convalescent Centre was based. On 26 February, in this Benicasim centre, the Thaelmann Battalion's Lieutenant-General Stucker dictated a message in German recording Robert's death at the Castellón hospital and also his burial: 'the interment followed in solemn form in the presence of a delegation from Benicasim'. Having completed it, he had it typed out again on the same page in English, and sent it with Robert's remaining few possessions to 'the Health Office, Albacete'. At the end of the notice Stucker listed the last things Robert still had with him:

Swift Blaze of Fire

passport, Communist Party membership card and a small wallet holding letters. These items would eventually reach Rosemary, but not for many weeks. Tucked into the wallet were a packet of Spanish cigarette papers and the prescription for Robert's glasses. The letters he had kept with him were all from Rosemary, apart from the one from his son Tim asking, 'Why don't you kum back?'[38]

The funeral was indeed 'in solemn form'. Robert was buried on 24 February, the first International Brigade member to be buried in Castellón. The town did him proud. *Heraldo de Castellón*, the local newspaper, describes how his body was first displayed in the hospital chapel, where a queue of townspeople and International Brigade members paid their respects, then carried through the streets in its coffin, on the shoulders of local carabineros.[39] Heading the procession was the banner of the International Brigades and the coffin was draped in the flag of Socorro Rojo Internacional: International Red Aid, a kind of internationalist, communist Red Cross. It was followed by nurses from the hospital, a cohort of wounded and convalescing International Brigade members brought from Benicasim and 'a great number of antifascists', including some who had travelled from Madrid. The procession wound round the town until it came to the Cemetery of Sant Josep, with its imposing arched gateway, and they buried him there, just inside the entrance.[40] John Lochore (soon to be taken to the convalescent centre in nearby Benicasim but still believing himself to be in Murcia[41]) attended the funeral and tells us that Peter Kerrigan gave a graveside address.[42]

The townspeople of Castellón can have known little more about Robert Hilliard than that he had come from another country to join their cause, but that was enough. '*Desde los balcones y en la calle*' – on the balconies and in the streets – '*una verdadera muchedumbre*' – a veritable multitude – gathered to honour and mourn him.

EPILOGUE

A trail of paper tells the story of Rosemary's efforts to get word of Robert. She kept lists of jotted names scoured from the *News Chronicle* or *Daily Worker* of people who might help her – individuals like Wilfred Macartney, Peter Kerrigan and Dave Springhall – and of organizations like Spanish Red Aid, the English Section of the Foreign Service in Barcelona, the Communist Party in London. She wrote to those she had addresses for, with stamped, self-addressed envelopes to encourage them to reply. On 5 March she wrote to a Communist Party-linked Committee in north London which provided support for volunteers' families, asking for news.

The next day she read about the Battle of Jarama in the *Daily Worker*. 'Epic of Anglo-Irish Battalion in Madrid's Greatest Battle' was the headline, 'You have never read, and you never will read, a story greater than this.' The article, by Peter Kerrigan, framed the fighting as a defence of the Arganda bridge over the Jarama. 'I wish I could make the TUC General Council stand by and watch what I saw,' Kerrigan wrote, calling for Labour and the TUC to lobby the government over non-intervention. To add force to his case he emphasized the heavy death and casualty rates, and the injuries he had witnessed after the battle, describing for example 'Jock C ___'s runner with one foot a pulped mass as a result of a shell burst and a hole in the other leg at the same time … his quartermaster with the blood oozing from

Epilogue

his bandages as a result of the same shell burst'. Rosemary must have been beside herself after reading this article.

Three days later Norah C Brown, from the committee helping families, replied to Rosemary's letter, saying she would 'certainly be informed immediately, should any news come through'. She also suggested sending Robert 'a pair of socks or packet of cigarettes'. Her exertions didn't end there; she carried Rosemary's letter down to the Communist Party HQ and asked if anyone had news of this poor woman's husband. The King Street office was flooded with such letters and Harry Pollitt spent much time writing back to relatives, often to explain how hard it was to get reliable information.[1] But as it happened there was news of Robert. On 10 March the Communist Party wrote to Rosemary. It was what she dreaded most.

> Miss Brown has been to see us and has conveyed to us the contents of your letter … We very deeply regret to have to tell you that your husband was one of the casualties during the recent heavy fighting during which the British Battalion played a most heroic and decisive part in preventing Franco's army from breaking through and cutting the road connecting Madrid with Valencia. Unfortunately we have absolutely no details whatever, merely the bear [sic] announcement that he was killed in action.
>
> It is difficult for us to convey to you how deeply we sympathise with you in the loss of your husband, which we as part of the working class movement feel that we share with you. At the same time we can assure you that the … British Battalion … played a major and in fact decisive part in preventing the fascists being victorious in that offensive.

It ends with an offer of any 'necessary and possible' assistance and is signed 'The Secretariat'. MI5 heard the news at around the same time. A handwritten note in Robert's file, dated 'March 1937', reads 'Killed in Spain'.

The letter from King Street left Rosemary, and the children distraught. 'That was a dreadful time, my mother was devastated and so were Tim and I. I think Kit and Davnet did not remember Daddy so well … But for Tim

Epilogue

and me there was an awful finality to everything. Always in our plans he was going to come back, and I think in my mother's too.'[2]

This was when Deirdre began to suffer from terrible dreams, which lasted into adulthood. 'For years we would dream of him, my dreams were of seeing him walking in the road ahead, and I would run and run to catch him up, but ... [h]e would just melt away in the distance. The worst dreams were if I got near to him and he turned and he would look through me or not know me, or turn out not even to be him at all; then I would wake up crying with misery.'[3]

Such dreams have a hellish, unresolved quality. There had never been a chance for the children to grasp that Robert's departure was permanent. Rosemary had always promised he would live with them again. Now he was dead. The nightmare image of emptiness in the eyes of the father who had forgotten the child he should love haunted Deirdre and could not be shaken off.

Using guesswork, since they had not yet seen Lieutenant-General Stucker's notification, the Communist Party at King Street issued a death certificate for Robert, mistakenly giving the date of death as 15 February. As word spread in Falmouth that Rosemary's husband had died fighting for the Spanish Republic, there were unexpected expressions of sympathy and solidarity. She came home with the children one day to find the Co-op grocery store had left a big box of free groceries by the door. Touched to the heart, she sat down on the step and wept.

Having at last heard the worst, Rosemary found the generosity to think of Robert's partner in Chelsea. This woman, too, would be living in suspense, desperate for news, and would hear nothing through official channels. Rosemary took a train up to London to see her at Robert's old address. She never told the children the woman's name, where she lived or what the two of them said to each other, but she did bring back four half-completed wooden toys, which Robert had been making for them before he went to Spain. There was a dog for Deirdre, with a nodding head and wagging tail moved by strings, a doll's bed for Davnet and similar presents for Tim and Kit. The toys had an unhappy effect: as Deirdre later wrote,

Epilogue

'It all made the tears start again.' Years afterwards Rosemary told Deirdre that Robert's new partner looked as if she might be pregnant. My mother has wondered ever since about a possible sibling whom she has never met.

For a long while Rosemary kept the faith with Robert and his cause. She carried on reading the *Daily Worker* and *News Chronicle*, collecting issues with major articles about the Spanish Civil War; she attended memorial events and kept their programmes.[4] At the end of 1938 she read that the International Brigades were leaving Spain, and early in 1939 she carefully laid aside a *News Chronicle* report of a commemoration in Earls Court of the 543 International Brigade members killed in action. Upbeat journalistic rhetoric could not conceal that the Republican side were losing. The litany of defeats at Brunete, Teruel and the Ebro told their own story. Month by month she read about the refugees leaving Spain, the slaughter of civilians as Franco's grisly progress continued, the inexorable shrinkage of the area on the map where the Spanish government[5] still held sway. At last came the conquest of Madrid, the city in whose defence Robert had died. At some point the letter from Lieutenant-General Stucker was forwarded to her, with Robert's personal effects. Robert's final postcard also arrived, with its message of love to each of the children. Perhaps because she remembered the tears when she handed over his toys, she laid these things away without speaking of them.[6]

While all this happened she kept on keeping on, moving the family to Letchworth in the summer of 1937. Rosemary had always found housekeeping difficult and now her grip loosened further. When Grace found a job in Letchworth, Rosemary told the children that she had never been brought up to do housework, and resigned herself to leaving Grace's cleaning workload undone. The result was that when the children made friends at their new school they dared not bring them home because of the squalid state of the house. 'I remember the massive clean-up there would be if we were going to have a visitor,' Deirdre wrote, 'most often just one room, and the problem would then be keeping the visitor in that room only … A great anxiety of my Mother's was that we might get a visit from the "Sanitary Inspector", a fearsome person that other visitors might tell if they saw the dirt in the kitchen.'

Epilogue

In 1939, when Stalin signed his pact with Hitler and it was obvious a war with Germany was on its way, Rose took charge and decided that she and Rosemary, with Edie, Madeline, Grace and the four children, would all move as one household, away from the south-east, to a large house in Tiverton, Devon. They lived there together until a month before D-Day. As the war ended, Rosemary moved back to Surrey with Rose, into a large wooden bungalow near Peaslake. There she bred and showed poodles, with considerable success but little financial return. She still had the interest from the trust that Alice had set up, but school fees, like much else, were paid for by Rose, who drained away the last of her capital, selling off her residual investments to provide money for Rosemary and the children, all the time growing frailer and more dependent on their care herself. The bungalow was soon in a similar state to the house in Letchworth, exacerbated by the presence of a great many unhousetrained poodles. Rosemary's devotion to dogs increased in proportion to her disillusionment with people.

The children grew up and left home. Tim went to art college and became an accomplished painter and ceramicist.[7] He married a beautiful and generous-natured Cornish potter, with whom he had four children of his own.[8] Deirdre[9] married young, and also had four children. Her match was disliked by Rosemary, who made clear (not least to us children) her opinion that our father was not 'out of the top drawer' and was too old to marry her daughter (he was thirty-six). Davnet took a screen test in 1953 and was offered a leading role in the film *A Town like Alice*,[10] but turned it down to train as a nurse. She married soon afterwards, left for Bulawayo (now Harare) with her husband, and died there of polio in 1958, leaving two small sons. Kit joined the Army, married and had three children. He led a soldier's roving life, so that for many years we hardly ever met him, and died in 2015.

Grace left to look after her father during their time in Tiverton. Madeline died in Tiverton in 1941 and Edie in Surrey four years later. Rose knew her daughter loved her, but it can be guessed that after Edie and Madeline died, her life with Rosemary was not an easy one. She became bedbound in 1948 and lived in one room, dependent on whatever food and

Epilogue

drink Rosemary brought in on a tray. Rosemary was used to Rose's support and practical help and found it difficult to adjust to this reversal of roles. One hot, stuffy day in 1950, Rose struggled out of bed to open a window and fell, breaking her hip. She died soon afterwards.

Rosemary never recovered from her sense of betrayal at Robert's departure or her grief at his death. As the years went by she fell into a deep depression, neglecting her own health, rarely washing or brushing her hair and refusing to visit the dentist. One by one, her teeth rotted or fell out until almost none were left. She grew ever more devoutly religious and as conventionally conservative as she had long ago been socialist. Her fidelity to Robert's memory metamorphosed into a profound, slow-burning embitterment. There had been too many separations and bereavements and betrayals in her life, starting at so young an age that she could never unravel them all. Her abiding view of Robert, the view she passed on to her children, was that he had never really loved her or them at all, or at best had not loved them enough.

Eventually she opened her home to a group of women friends, who kept the Peaslake bungalow reasonably clean and lifted her mood, so that when we visited as children there was a sense of good cheer and someone would produce a spread of food. Rosemary had come full circle. In her childhood she had lived in a house in Surrey where no housework was required of her, surrounded by elderly women and engrossed by dogs; she could now do so again. In her final decade she came to live with Deirdre, my father and my stepfather. My mother looked after her and, before she died in 1994, she at last made friends with my father.

The town of Castellón (or Castelló, or Castelló de la Plana) has three cemeteries.[11] A building at the newest houses the cemetery archives and I'm standing in its spacious, air-conditioned foyer, where the archivist has spread three photocopied A4 pages in front of me; they lie in a row on the raised rim of the reception desk.

One is from a ledger of burials, with an entry for Robert Martin Hilliard.[12] The second is a map of the old Cemetery of Sant Josep, with

Epilogue

a hand-drawn X marking his grave by its entrance. The last shows that by a later date someone with a different name occupied that same grave space.

I already know he had been removed from his grave. Earlier in the day the historian Guillem Casañ[13] has shown me two oblong plates in the ground, some distance apart, at the rear of the Cemetery of Sant Josep, and explained that bodies, some from the 1930s or later but many far older, have been added to the communal pit beneath. Their emptied graves were given over to new burials. At an unknown date during Franco's reign one of those two metal plates was lifted – I have no way of knowing which – and Robert's remains were tossed into the mass grave below.[14]

Hundreds of thousands of Republican dead were buried in unmarked mass graves after battles and civilian massacres. Others, like Robert Hilliard, were ejected from their individual, marked graves because Franco's regime demanded their anonymity. By contrast, there are plenty of fascists buried in the same Castellón cemetery. Their graves commemorate their names for posterity, carved into grandiose masonry, sometimes in the shape of the Falange's fascist insignia. While these are allowed to stay, Robert's anti-fascism has ensured his removal.

The ledger entry for his original burial makes me cry, which I didn't expect, though the archivist is already holding out a box of tissues. As she courteously turns her gaze away, I wonder how many conversations like this she must have had. A patient person, she has borne with my halting Spanish, looked up the records, taken these copies and gently explained in English what it all means. The long task of excavating Spain's mass graves has far to go,[15] but she does what she can to excavate buried facts from her record books and files. I grab a handful of tissues, pick up the copied papers, thank her profusely and walk outside, feeling heavy all over, to sit for a while in the heat and glare of the grounds before catching the Madrid train. Only later do I remember that I should have asked the kind, efficient archivist her name.

I wish I had known my grandfather. Had he lived, he would have been forty-seven when I was born. Deirdre's memories of him are the emotional and physical impressions of a small child: '… a shoulder to ride on, a rescuer

Epilogue

of small girls from the usual scrapes, smelling of tobacco and tweed … who read or told grand stories at bedtime.'

What remained of him by the time I and his other grandchildren arrived? His humour lived on in Tim, who inherited his quickness of mind, his delight in the absurd and an unflagging readiness to make jokes in even the grimmest circumstances. Deirdre, too, inherited his love of a good joke or good story, his sharp intelligence and an unsinkable doggedness. But like waves rubbing out footprints, human agency and time have eroded many of the other traces Robert Hilliard left. He's been evicted from his grave, files have been weeded and many of his letters are destroyed. His story has at times been obscured by hagiography and myth, but it remains a story worth telling, because he stood up to fight the battle against fascism, the most urgent danger of his time, risking and losing his life. That anti-fascist tradition lives on and now, again, urgently needs our support.

It's March 2005 and Deirdre, my mother, is at a book launch held by the International Brigades Memorial Trust at the Imperial War Museum. I am with her. The book, *Connolly Column* by Michael O'Riordan, was first published in 1979 and this launch is for its second edition. We have heard one address by the author's son, historian Manus O'Riordan, and another from Spanish Civil War veteran Jack Jones. We're well into the drinks and socializing phase of the event, and my mother is on a mission.

She has made a discovery. Rosemary died ten years ago, and Deirdre had to go through her things. There were a great many papers, and they took a long time to read. Only recently has she found the postcard her father sent from Madrigueras. As its meaning gradually sank in, it has filled her with an extraordinary relief, and tonight she is almost euphoric. She has the postcard with her, and she holds it up, first to Manus O'Riordan and then to other people she meets or is introduced to. 'Look,' she says to each of them, 'look what I found, look at this postcard from my father' – and without waiting for a reply she reads out the parts of it where he writes of his children: 'Teach the kids to stand for democracy,' and 'Unless fascism is beaten in Spain and in the world it means war and hell for our kids.'

Epilogue

The room is full of chatter, and it takes each person that she speaks to a while to grasp what she is telling them, this small woman – my mother is barely five feet tall – hopping from one foot to the other with excitement, waving the scuffed, yellowed postcard that has reached her at last, sixty-eight years after it was sent. One by one, they take notice; wineglasses are put down, spectacles pushed up over foreheads, people take the card from her and read it, and agree it is a wonderful thing. 'Look what he says,' she keeps saying, 'we never knew, all these years, we never knew. He says "Give my love to Tim, Deirdre and Davnet and Kit." He sent us his love, each of us, by name. All this time. He hadn't forgotten us. He loved us. He loved us all the time.'

BIOGRAPHICAL CHRONOLOGY

7 April 1904	Robert Martin Hilliard born in New Street, Killarney.
20 April 1905	Rosemary Robins born in Kasungu, Nyasaland (now Malawi).
1915	Robert enters Midleton College. He leaves after one term and enters Cork Grammar School in January 1916.
1920	Robert enters Mountjoy School, Dublin.
1921	Robert enters Trinity College, Dublin as a Sizar and establishes himself as a frequent speaker in TCD debates.
1922	The anti-Treaty Paddy Trench enters Trinity College and forms a lifelong friendship with Robert, who also opposes the Treaty. Robert takes up boxing and wins the Trinity College Boxing Club Novices' bantamweight medal.
1923	Robert wins the bantamweight All Ireland Amateur championship.
1924	Robert and Rosemary Robins meet in Merrion Square, Dublin.
	Robert wins the Dublin University Boxing Club Championships at both bantam- and featherweight. He travels to the Paris Olympics as a member of the first ever

Biographical chronology

	Irish Olympic boxing team but is eliminated by the Argentine champion. Visits Rosemary in Surrey on the way home from Paris. Joins the staff of Avoca School, Blackrock, Dublin.
1925	Robert abandons his degree, leaves Ireland and starts visiting Rosemary every weekend.
1926	Robert reportedly works as a copywriter in London. Rosemary becomes pregnant and the couple marry in a registry office in Poplar, London.
1927-1928	Rosemary and Robert set up home in Grayshott, Surrey. Robert works as a journalist. Tim is born in May 1926. Rosemary falls ill and the couple's relationship deteriorates. Deirdre is born 30 June 1928.
1929	The family lose their home. Rosemary considers separation.
1930	Robert visits Oxford Group founder Frank Buchman. He and Rosemary embrace the Oxford Group's teachings and Robert decides to become a Church of Ireland priest. He returns to Trinity College.
1931	Robert takes up debating again, regains his Trinity College Boxing Club featherweight title and achieves a BA in Divinity. Ordained as a deacon, he is appointed to a half time post in Derriaghy in the North of Ireland. Becomes editor of TCD magazine. Rosemary gives birth to Davnet. Robert's father dies.
1932	Robert voices support for Fianna Fáil in debates. He is ordained a curate and leaves Trinity for a half-time curacy in Derriaghy. The family moves to Knocknadona. Robert is appointed to a full-time post at St Anne's Cathedral, Belfast.
1933	Rosemary, pregnant once more, becomes ill and is hospitalised. The family moves to Ravenhill Park Gardens in Belfast. Kit is born and Grace Maundrell joins the family. Family debts and tensions mount. Robert moves the family to a house in Knock, Belfast.

Biographical chronology

1934	Robert, deep in debt, is refused a loan from the Church by the Cathedral's Dean.
Spring 1935	Robert leaves Ireland and moves to a basement flat in Chelsea, London. He is unable to find work but becomes an active Communist Party member. Rosemary escapes their creditors by moving to a series of semi-derelict cottages.
Winter 1935	Robert at last finds work in London. He visits Rosemary and the children in Ballinderry but he and Rosemary remain estranged. He begins living with a new partner in London.
1936	Rosemary and the children move to Falmouth, Cornwall. Robert leaves for Spain. The British Battalion is formed in Madrigueras.
January 1937	Many Irish members of British Battalion join the Lincoln Brigade but Robert stays where he is.
February 1937	Francoist forces cross the River Jarama, threatening to cut off Madrid. Three XV Brigade battalions, including the British Battalion, take up positions overlooking the Jarama River. The British Battalion comes under heavy fire for three days.
14 February 1937	A Francoist tank attack forces the decimated British Battalion to retreat. Members of the Battalion rally, recapturing their position and preventing Francoist forces from cutting off the Madrid-Valencia road. Robert is shot in the neck. He is hospitalised in Castellón three days later.
22 February 1937	Robert dies and is buried in Castellón on 24 February.

SELECT BIBLIOGRAPHY

Allen, Kieran. 2016. *1916: The Irish Revolutionary Tradition*. London: Pluto Press.

—. 1997. *Fianna Fáil and Irish Labour: 1925 to the Present*. London: Pluto Press.

Barry, Tom. 1962. *Guerrilla Days in Ireland*. Dublin: Anvil Books.

Baxell, Richard. 2007. *British Volunteers in the Spanish Civil War, The British Battalion in the International Brigades, 1936–1939*. Pontypool: Warren & Pell.

—. 2012. *Unlikely Warriors: The Extraordinary Story Of The Britons Who Fought In The Spanish Civil War*. London: Aurum Press.

Beckett, Samuel. 2009. *Murphy*. London: Faber.

Beevor, Antony. 2006. *The Battle for Spain*. London: Weidenfeld & Nicolson.

Borgonovo, John. 2007. *Spies, Informers and the 'Anti-Sinn Fein Society': The Intelligence War in Cork City 1920–1921*. Dublin: Irish Academic Press.

—. 2013. *The Dynamics of War and Revolution: Cork City, 1916–1918*. Cork: Cork University Press.

Select bibliography

Borkenau, Franz. 2000. *The Spanish Cockpit: An Eyewitness Account of the Spanish Civil War.* London: Phoenix Press.

Branson, Noreen. 1975. *Lansbury and the Councillors' Revolt: Poplarism 1919–1925.* London: Lawrence & Wishart.

Breen, Dan. 1964. *My Fight for Irish Freedom.* Dublin: Anvil Books.

Buckley, Henry. 2014. *The Life and Death of the Spanish Republic, A Witness to the Spanish Civil War.* London and New York: I B Tauris.

Bunyan, John. c1873. *The Pilgrim's Progress.* Newcastle-Upon-Tyne: Adam & Co.

Calwell, Major-General Sir Charles E, and Marshall Foch. 2010 (1927). *Field-Marshall Sir Henry Wilson Bart., G.C.B., D.S.O. – His Life and Diaries.* Vol. 2. Whitefish, Montana: Kessinger Publishing LLC.

Carr, E.H. 1984. *The Comintern and the Spanish Civil War.* London: Macmillan.

—. 1982. *The Twilight of the Comintern 1930–1935.* New York: Pantheon Books.

Carroll, Denis. 1998. *Unusual Suspects: Twelve Radical Clergymen.* Dublin: Columba Books, pp247–68.

Chalmers, Trench. 1996. *Nearly Ninety.* Dublin: The Hannon Press.

Connolly, James. 1983 (1910). *Labour, Nationality and Religion.* Dublin: New Books.

Coogan, Tim Pat. 1991. *Michael Collins.* London: Arrow Books.

Copeman, Fred. 1948. *Reason in Revolt.* London: Blandford Press.

Craig, George, Martha Dow Fehsenfeld, Dan Gunn, Lois More Overbeck (eds.). 2016. *The Letters of Samuel Beckett, Vol I.* Cambridge: Cambridge University Press.

Crowley, John, Donal Ó Drisceoil, Mike Murphy, and John Borgonovo (eds.). 2018. *Atlas of the Irish Revolution.* Cork: Cork University Press.

Davies, Graham. 2018. *You Are Legend, The Welsh Volunteers of the Spanish Civil War*. Cardiff: Welsh Academic Press.

Dimitrov, Georgi. 1972. *Selected Works*. Sofia: Sofia Press. Online at Marxists Internet Archive.

Doyle, Tom. 2008. *The Civil War in Kerry*. Cork: Mercier Press.

Durgan, Andy. 2007. *The Spanish Civil War*. Basingstoke: Palgrave Macmillan.

Dwyer, T Ryle. 2001. *Tans, Terror and Troubles: Kerry's Real Fighting Story*. Dublin: Mercier Press.

Ellis, Peter Berresford. 1985. *A History of the Irish Working Class*. London: Pluto Press.

Euripides. 1906. *The Bacchae*. Translated by Gilbert Murray. London: George Allen.

Evans, Richard J. 2004. *The Coming of the Third Reich*. London: Penguin Publishing Group.

Ferriter, Diarmaid. 2015. *A Nation and not a Rabble*. London: Profile Books Ltd.

Fleming, Lionel. 1965. *Head or Harp*. London: Barrie & Rockcliff.

Foster, R.F. 1988. *Modern Ireland 1600–1972*. London: Allen Lane.

Fox, R.M. 1946. *James Connolly: The Forerunner*. Tralee: The Kerryman Limited.

Fraser, Ronald. 1981. *Blood of Spain, The Experience of Civil War, 1936–1939*. Harmondsworth: Penguin.

Graham, Helen. 2005. *The Spanish Civil War, A Very Short Introduction*. Oxford: Oxford University Press.

Greene, Graham. 1972. *A Sort of Life*. London: Book Club Associates with Bodley Head.

Gurney, Jason. 1976. *Crusade in Spain*. London: Faber and Faber.

Select bibliography

Hilliard, Richard Marmaduke. 1946. *Killarney: A Hundred Years with Hilliards*. Dublin: Rainbow Press.

Hopkins, James K. 1998. *Into the Heart of the Fire, The British in the Spanish Civil War*. Stanford: Stanford University Press.

Hughes, Ben. 2011. *They Shall Not Pass! The British Battalion at Jarama – The Spanish Civil War*. Botley, Oxford: Osprey Publishing.

Irish, Tomás. 2015. *Trinity in War and Revolution, 1912–1923*. Dublin: Royal Irish Academy.

Jacobs, Joe. 1978. *Out of the Ghetto*. London: Phoenix Press.

Joy, Breda. 2014. *Hidden Kerry, the Keys to the Kingdom*. Cork: Mercier Press.

Joyce, James. 1969. *A Portrait of the Artist as a Young Man*. Harmondsworth: Penguin.

Jump, Jim, (ed.) 2010. *Looking Back at the Spanish Civil War: The International Brigade Memorial Trust's Len Chrome Memorial Lectures, 2002–2010*. London: Lawrence & Wishart.

Keane, Fergal. 2017. *Wounds*. London: William Collins.

Kearns, Kevin C. 1994. *Dublin Tenement Life: An Oral History of the Dublin Slums*. Dublin: Gill & Macmillan.

Khayyam, Omar. 1900. *Les Rubaiyat*. Translated by F Roger-Cornaz. Paris: Payot & Co.

Kostick, Conor. 2009. *Revolution in Ireland: Popular Militancy 1917–1923*. Cork: Cork University Press.

Kushner, Tony, and Nadia Valman (eds.). 2000. *Remembering Cable Street: Fascism and Anti-Fascism in British Society*. London: Vallentine Mitchell, pp109–71.

Le Carré, John. 2017. *The Pigeon Tunnel*. London: Penguin Random House.

Select bibliography

Lean, Garth. 1988. *Frank Buchman – A Life*. London: Fount Paperbacks.

Ledbetter, Gordon T. 2010. *Privilege and Poverty: The Life and Times of Irish Painter and Naturalist Alexander Williams 1846–1930*. Cork: Collins.

Lester, Muriel. 1937. *It Occurred To Me*. New York and London: Harper & Brothers.

Lucey, Donnacha Sean. 2011. *Land, Popular Politics and Agrarian Violence in Ireland*. Dublin: University College Dublin Press.

Mahon, John. 1976. *Harry Pollitt: A Biography*. London: Lawrence & Wishart.

Manning, Maurice. 2006. *The Blueshirts*. Dublin: Gill & Macmillan.

McCracken, John. 2012. *A History of Malawi 1859–1966*. Woodbridge: James Currey.

MacDougall, Ian (ed.). 1995. *Voices from War: Personal recollections of war in our century by Scottish men and women*. Edinburgh: Mercat Press, pp111–34.

McGarry, Feargal. 1999. *Irish Politics and the Spanish Civil War*. Cork: Cork University Press.

McLoughlin, Barry, and Emmet O'Connor. 2020. *In Spanish Trenches*. Dublin: University College Dublin Press.

Meenan, James. 1972. *The Irish Economy Since 1922*. Liverpool: The Liverpool University Press.

Mitchell, Seán. 2017. *Struggle or Starve: Working Class Unity in Belfast's 1932 Outdoor Relief Riots*. Chicago: Haymarket Books.

Moore, H. Kingsmill. 1938. *The Work of the Incorporated Society for Promoting Protestant Schools in Ireland*. Dundalk: Tempest.

Morrow, Felix. 1974. *Revolution and Counter-Revolution in Spain*. New York: Pathfinder Press.

Munck, Ronnie, and Bill Rolston. 1987. *Belfast in the Thirties: An Oral History*. New York: St Martin's Press Inc.

Select bibliography

Nussbaum, Martha. 1990. 'Introduction.' *The Bacchae of Euripides, a New Version*, by C K Williams, vii-xliv. New York: Farrar, Straus and Giroux.

O'Conchubhair, Brian (ed.). 2009. *Rebel Cork's Fighting Story 1916–1921*. Cork: Mercier Press.

O'Conchubair, Brian (ed.). 2009. *Kerry's Fighting Story 1916–21: Told by the Men Who Made it*. Cork: Mercier Press.

O'Connor, Emmet. 1988. *Syndicalism in Ireland 1917–1923*. Cork: Cork University Press.

O'Donoghue, Florence. 1971. *Tomás MacCurtain: Soldier and Patriot*. Tralee: Anvil Books.

O'Riordan, Michael. 1979. *Connolly Column, The story of the Irishmen who fought for the Spanish Republic 1936–1939*. Dublin: New Books Publications.

Orwell, George. 2010. *Animal Farm, A Fairy Story*. London: Penguin.

—. 2000. *Homage to Catalonia*. London: Penguin.

Preston, Paul. 2006. *The Spanish Civil War: Reaction, Revolution and Revenge*. London: Harper Perennial.

Riddell, John. 2012 (ed.). *Towards the United Front: Proceedings of the Fourth Congress of the Communist International 1922*. Chicago: Haymarket Press. Online at Marxists Internet Archive.

Rust, William. 1939. *Britons in Spain*. London: Lawrence & Wishart.

Ryan, Frank (ed.). 2003 (1938). *The Book of the XV Brigade*. Pontypool: Warren & Pell Publishing.

Sheehy-Skeffington, Andrée. 1991. *Skeff: A Life of Owen Sheehy-Skeffington 1909–1970*. Dublin: The Lilliput Press.

St Leger, Alicia. 2016. *A History of Ashton School: Rochelle School, Cork High School, Cork Grammar School*. Cork: Ashton School.

Thomas, Fred. 1996. *To Tilt at Windmills*. East Lansing: Michigan State University Press.

Select bibliography

Thomas, Hugh. 1977. *The Spanish Civil War.* Harmondsworth : Penguin.

Toynbee, Philip (ed.). 1976. *The Distant Drum.* London: Sidgwick & Jackson, pp121–130.

Wade, Francesca. 2020. *Square Haunting: Five Women, Freedom and London Between the Wars.* London: Faber, pp153–206.

West, Trevor. 1996. *Midleton College 1696–1996, A Tercentenary History.* Cork: Midleton College.

Wintringham, Tom. 1941. *English Captain.* Harmondsworth: Penguin.

NOTES

PROLOGUE

1   Little or no Irish history was taught in English schools, which perhaps helps to explain the insensitivity of my question.

2   Extracts from the lyric of Christy Moore's song *Viva la Quinta Brigada* are reproduced with the kind permission of Christy Moore. 'Viva La Quinta Brigada!' means 'Long live the Fifth Brigade!' (the Brigade referred to was in fact the Fifteenth). '*No pasaran!*' means 'They shall not pass'. '*Adelante!*' means 'Forward!'. The 'brave young Christian Brother' in Christy Moore's song was Eamon McGrotty, born in 1911, who had entered the Christian Brothers in 1927 and was expelled in 1932. Like a number of other Irish Brigadistas (but not Robert Hilliard), he left the British Battalion while they were training at Madrigueras and instead joined the American Lincoln Battalion. He was killed at Jarama on 23 February 1937, nine days after Hilliard received his fatal wound.

3   Stephen Hilliard also died tragically young, fatally stabbed by a burglar at his home in 1990, at the age of forty-two. His life is commemorated (among other places) in Chapter 10 of *Unusual Suspects* by Dennis Carroll, Columba Press, Dublin, 1998.

4   *Resource*, Spring 1988: *Subversive Memories* by Reverend Stephen Hilliard, reprinted here: *irelandscw.com*: Hilliard, the boxing Parson – Ireland and the Spanish Civil War

5   Jason Gurney, *Crusade in Spain*, Faber and Faber Ltd, London, 1976, p69.

6   Stephen Hilliard wrote his article, as he did everything, in good faith, relying on accounts which he had no reason to doubt. Fresh scrutiny has since been made possible by the advent of the internet. He had no easy access, for example, to the online *Bureau of Military History Witness Statements* or the online National Archives *Census of Ireland*. Some commonly told stories about Robert Hilliard related in Stephen's article have been thrown into doubt or superseded by the later availability of more information.

Notes

CHAPTER 1

1   It's often stated that Hilliard was 'born in Moyeightragh'. This is impossible. The record of his father's purchase of the Moyeightragh house in the Register of Deeds in Dublin shows it did not take place until 1914. Until then the property was an educational establishment owned by a religious order. The 1901 and 1911 censuses show that at the time of Robert's birth the family home was in New Street, Killarney. The 1901 census shows their address as 62 New Street (Lower); the 1911 census shows 14 New Street (Lower).

2   Margaret Martin, aged fifty-one, is shown in the 1901 census as living in their New Street house as housekeeper, but her name does not reappear in 1911. One maidservant lived there in 1901 and two in 1911.

3   This comment comes from a private memoir of her own life by Deirdre Davey, née Hilliard, Robert Hilliard's elder daughter, a source henceforth referred to as DHM.

4   Both Robert Hilliard senior's wives were members of the Martin family, as was his mother. Alice is shown on the 1901 census (compiled before the marriage) as her eventual husband's 'niece-in-law'.

5   This legal prohibition was repealed soon afterwards by the Deceased Wife's Sister's Marriage Act of 1907.

6   The record in the Jersey Archive shows they were married on 21 November 1901 at St Helier town church, by special license.

7   Ellen had married Richard Hillliard, a skilled leather worker employed in his brother-in-law's Tralee 'grindery' (a shop selling shoemaking tools and materials). Richard's father William had once owned a small farm. According to the family story, told to me by Ellen's great-grandson Billy Hilliard, William heard his dog barking one night and suspected a thief in one of his apple trees. He ran outside, firing his gun blindly into the branches, and a dying man fell to the ground; some say it was his ex-steward, others the steward's son. William gave up his farm in reparation to the man's family and moved to Tralee. His four children, including Richard, were obliged to strike out their own path in life without inheriting any land.

8   Ellen would set out on a Monday and walk to Macroom, where she stayed overnight, completing the walk to Cork the next day. On Wednesday she would order her haberdashery stock and on Thursday and Friday she would walk back again. The stock would later be delivered by wagon. She must often have been pregnant when she undertook this walk, as during these years she bore Richard three children. A fourth was on its way in 1853 when the railway line opened and her walks ended. This piece of family history was passed on to me by both Billy and Richard Hilliard, two of Ellen's great-grandchildren.

9   English competition had almost routed the Irish tanning and leather industry and threatened to do the same to the footwear industry: see A Bielenberg Industrial Growth in Ireland; c. 1790–1910. – LSE Theses Online 1994, pp203–05. *etheses.lse. ac.uk/1326/1/U062811.pdf.*

233

Notes

10 In addition to their boot and shoe manufacturing, R Hilliard and Sons of High Street Killarney were still running a haberdashery and hosiery business in 1893, according to *Guy's Directory of Munster 1893*. William's 1870 sale of his leather trade in Tralee is referred to in Richard Marmaduke Hilliard, *Killarney – A Hundred Years with Hilliards*, Rainbow Press, Dublin, 1946, p3. Unless otherwise attributed, all details and quotations in this chapter and its notes about the factory's working methods and the installation of machinery come from this booklet.

11 'The men worked or talked round the clock. Very few came in before 12 o'clock mid-day and at 10 o'clock at night the gas was extinguished, when the men worked by candle light. The door of the workshop was always open and employees could come and go as they chose.'

12 Among other machines, in 1872 the factory installed treadle presses for cutting soles and insoles. Richard Hilliard told me they later installed a Petter oil engine to power the whole factory.

13 Until late in the century Hilliard workers had the alternative of earning a living hand-making shoes as journeymen. Irish shoemakers also often travelled to England.

14 The Fenians aimed to dispossess the propertied class, oust British rule and establish a people's republic. Their supporters were mostly low-paid clerical and skilled manual workers or artisans. Their movement gained the support of the International Working Men's Association in London, in which Karl Marx was prominently active. Their newspaper, *The Irish People*, demanded 'An entire revolution which will restore the country to its rightful owners. And who are these? The people ...' – Peter Berresford Ellis, *A History of the Irish Working Class*, Pluto Press, 1985, p133.

15 The Fenian forces were dispersed into the McGillicuddy's Reeks mountains. The IRB also mounted attacks on Dublin, Cork, Limerick and Chester Castle in England, all of which were defeated.

16 Some of the earliest and most provocative land sales in Kerry were of Kenmare estate land in Killarney – see Donnacha Seán Lucey, *Land, Popular Politics and Agrarian Violence in Ireland – The Case of County Kerry 1872–86*, University College Dublin Press, Dublin, 2011, pp86–8.

17 Formed by Michael Davitt, an IRB member, socialist and ex-Fenian, under the elected leadership of Charles Stewart Parnell MP.

18 As evictions of small landholders rose with the slump, the Land League attempted to enforce the 'three Fs': fair rents, fixity of tenure – the right not to be evicted if rent had been paid, and free sale – the right to sell tenancies without landlord interference.

19 Named after Captain Boycott, a land agent in Co. Mayo. When Boycott tried to evict tenants, the entire community refused to work for him or sell him their goods and services. He was only able to bring in his crops with the help of Orange volunteers, at immense cost and guarded by troops. Boycott left for England (he later returned), leaving behind a new word for a highly effective tactic.

Notes

20 This phrase had been made famous by Wolfe Tone: 'If the men of property will not help us, they must fall; we will free ourselves by the aid of that large and respectable class of the community – the men of no property.'

21 According to Donnacha Seán Lucey, shopkeepers and businessmen in rural Ireland often took the place of banks by making loans at interest to local people. According to Richard Hilliard, a grandson of John Hilliard, old Robert Hilliard (my grandfather's father) made small loans at interest to less well-off families until the turn of the century.

22 I have relied for the whole of William's and Frances's story on Billy Hilliard, one of John Hilliard's grandsons. *Killarney, a Hundred Years with Hilliards* states that Robert and John took control of the factory in 'about 1880'. It was they who instituted the benchwork made necessary by the threat from G.B. Britton in 1882.

23 According to Billy Hilliard, William gave this account of events to family members when he visited Ireland.

24 There's no reference to William, Frances or their children in the New Zealand national archives. According to the archivist there whom I consulted by telephone and email while writing this book, this does not mean the family account is wrong. As she put it, 'the archival record for the late 19th century is very patchy' and 'much hasn't survived'.

25 Again, this phrase comes from Billy Hilliard, in the written records of family information that he has researched and collated over many years.

26 Richard often camped out with a group of other fishermen at the Upper Killarney Lake when the salmon fishing season opened in January. They used a line holding a hundred hooks, stretched between two boats (nowadays illegal). A daily cart came each day from Killarney to bring food and drink and left heaped with fish, to be divided among the men's families and salted down. This account comes from Billy Hilliard.

27 According to family tradition as passed on to me by Moll's son Ken Shellard, Robert senior later told his daughter Moll that this was what his mother had said.

28 Within a few years nearly half the workforce were 'benchmen' and the rest were under pressure to join them.

29 In 1886 the brothers installed power to drive the machines (this could have been when the Petter oil machine was brought into service), with new finishing machines and cutting presses.

30 This pencil portrait appears in Hilliard, p2.

31 The Register of Deeds shows three transactions in which John and Richard purchased dwelling houses and property in Hogan's Lane in 1886 and 1889.

32 Donnacha Seán Lucey, p177.

33 'Hocking' means cutting the ligaments on an animal's back legs so that it can't walk.

34 One murder, in Firies, ten miles from Killarney, in 1885, became a national cause célèbre. Catholic farmer and League member John Curtin paid his rent in defiance of a rent strike. When raided by Moonlighters he refused to part with money or arms – see Donnacha Seán Lucey, p179. Shots were exchanged, fatally wounding one

Notes

of the raiders and Curtin himself. When his daughters gave evidence leading to the conviction of some of the raiders, the entire family was boycotted until they sold their farm at a fraction of its value and moved away – see Fergal Keane, *Wounds*, William Collins, London 2017, pp73–4.

35 After the Land Wars, the Hilliards' behaviour changed. John acquired farmland, on which he bred prize cattle. He purchased the Lake Hotel, in which Robert initially had a financial stake, and the brothers embarked on a series of Petty Sessions Court hearings to evict tenants from Hilliard-owned dwellings in the town.

36 Gladstone had already introduced a Land Act in 1870, widely regarded as too limited in its effects.

37 The 'men of no property' gained nothing. Irish MPs – led by Charles Parnell until 1890 – were in many cases landlords themselves. This conflict of class interests in the leadership of the Land League undermined its initial radicalism.

38 This provoked widespread Protestant anger: 'English intervention on the nationalist side in the shape of Gladstone's disestablishment of the Church of Ireland in 1869, followed by the Land Acts gradually transferring ownership from landlord to tenant, was the last straw. Many of the better off Irish Protestants began to consider moving to the neighbouring island [i.e. the British mainland].' Trevor West, *Midleton College 1696–1996, A Tercentenary History*, published in Cork by Midleton College, 1996.

39 Connolly identified the foundation-stone of British rule as class exploitation. He agitated for revolutionary self-activity by Irish workers to both overturn class society and gain independence, and saw anything less as a pyrrhic victory.

40 Arthur Griffith was a printer who in 1899 co-founded the journal *The United Irishman*, eventually *Sinn Féin*, and set up Cumann na nGaedheal, meaning 'The Society of Gaels', a nationalist group that later merged with his new party, also called Sinn Féin (meaning 'We ourselves'). An anti-Semite, Griffith would go on in 1904 to back a pogrom against Limerick's small Jewish population. He was hostile to socialist ideas, believing state power should transfer from British to Irish hands without disturbing existing class relations. Griffith wanted a dual monarchy, advocating a withdrawal from the Westminster Parliament after setting up a parallel Irish ruling structure, and set out this template in 1904, in his work *The Resurrection of Hungary*. Griffith's template continues to exert an influence, for example in the refusal of Northern Irish Sinn Féin MPs to take their Westminster seats.

41 *Petty Sessions Order Books*, National Archives of Ireland, series reference code CS/PS/1, 30 May 1890.

42 See *Petty Sessions Order Books*, 16 December 1890, 1 and 6 January 1891, 2 July 1895, 25 June 1897, 7 September 1897, 18 and 25 January 1898, 21 June 1898, 16 March 1900, 1 September 1903, 5 April 1904, 16 April 1905, 2 July 1907, 11 May 1909, 6 September 1910 and 14 February 1911. The properties from which tenants were evicted were in Hogan's Lane, Ball Alley Lane, Duckett's Lane and Well Lane. On 16 March 1900 the Hilliards went to court to evict tenants from a property in Killorglin, co-owned with the Huggard family.

43 Hilliard, p18.

Notes

44 They bought four more dwelling houses in Hogan's Lane as well as more land. All information in this chapter or the next about land and properties purchased by Robert or John Hilliard, apart from additional details of the hotel purchase supplied by Richard Hilliard, comes from the Register of Deeds in Dublin.

45 _Petty Sessions Order Books_, National Archives of Ireland, series reference code CS/PS/1, 14 November 1903.

46 The displaced brother, also called Richard, opened a hardware shop. See Hilliard, p3.

47 He took on four female servants at the hotel, including his step-sister's daughter, Helen Amy McCarthy, who was known as Cousin Nellie and worked for the family as a housemaid.

48 Richard Hilliard, one of John's grandsons, told me that some of John's children later expressed hurt and anger at having been farmed out from their home to make way for paying customers.

49 Gordon T Ledbetter, _Privilege and Poverty, The Life and Times of Irish Painter and Naturalist Alexander Williams 1846–1930_, Collins, Cork, 2010, p55 and p194. The paintings and stuffed trout were still there when I paid a visit in 2014.

50 This information comes from Richard Hilliard.

51 _Kerry Evening Post_, 27 November 1907.

52 Letter written to his son Geoffrey William in 1931, shown to me by Geoff's son Martin Hilliard.

CHAPTER 2

1 _TCD_ (the college magazine of Trinity College Dublin), 9 March 1922.

2 _Kerry Evening Post_, Saturday 1 October 1910, p2.

3 This information comes from Alison Dunlop, Moll's eldest daughter.

4 Letter written to his son Geoffrey William in 1931, shown to me by Geoff's son Martin Hilliard.

5 DHM.

6 Moll's son Ken Shellard told me this story.

7 These two anecdotes come from Moll's daughter, Alison Dunlop.

8 This comes from Moll's son Ken Shellard. Moll was determined not to feed the myths she feared were forming around her brother Robert and in general would only repeat a few well-worn tales. Both she and their cousin Robin died in 2004, the last of Robert's generation who were close to him in his childhood.

9 Childhood memories, dating back to this period, of the circus, film shows, dances and boxing events in this chapter feature in the online source _Notes of Joe Wilkie – Killarney memories_.

10 James Connolly, _Labour, Nationality and Religion_, First published 1910, Dublin and Belfast New Books, Dublin, 1983, p62.

11 At this time Connolly was the ITGWU's Belfast organizer.

12 There had been previous attempts to introduce Home Rule, defeated by Unionists in the North.

Notes

13 For example it could not take decisions about defence, or the relationship with Britain.

14 A former barrister who had presented the successful prosecution case against Oscar Wilde.

15 Carson was the instigator and first signatory of the Ulster Covenant, a public document containing this pledge.

16 T Ryle Dwyer, *Tans, Terror and Troubles, Kerry's Real Fighting Story 1913–23*, Mercier Press, Dublin, 2001, p33.

17 Tens of thousands of union members had held out for many months of desperate hardship for themselves and their families as they struck for the right to a trade union.

18 The strike was betrayed by full-time officials of the English TUC who engineered a vote against the blacking of Irish imports into the UK ('blacking' is a refusal to handle goods or deal with a particular individual or firm). Without this blacking, the strike was doomed. Larkin and Connolly had no strategy for appealing to British workers over the heads of the TUC leaders or regrouping their own supporters, and no political party strong enough to unite militants round an understanding of what had gone wrong. The Irish Socialist Republican Party founded by Connolly had folded in 1904 after he left for the US and the party he founded on his return was little more than a shell that could not play this role.

19 Field Marshall Sir John French's promise was arguably a mutinous act and he was made to resign.

20 Óglaigh na hÉireann, Bureau of Military History (1913–21), Witness Statement (WS) 132, p4.

21 Witness Statement (WS) 132, p4.

22 The explanation that the guns displayed on this march-past came from the Kalem film company is given in T. Ryle Dwyer, *Tans, Terror and Troubles*, Mercier Press, 2001, p39. An alternative explanation comes from WS132 p4, which tells of the purchase of arms for the Killarney Volunteers in Dublin at this time. These explanations are not mutually exclusive as guns probably reached them from more than one source.

23 The last army recruitment meeting in the Killarney area took place in 1915. Volunteers disrupted it so completely that no further such meetings ever took place – WS132, p5.

24 The Representation of the People Act of 1884 and the Redistribution Act of 1885 had extended the franchise to the majority of males.

25 *Killarney Echo and South Kerry Chronicle*, 14 February 1914.

26 Registry of Deeds, Henrietta St, Dublin.

27 Robin Hilliard, his cousin, now deceased, told me in 2004 that this was what they used to say when Robert arrived.

28 This detail comes from Billy Hilliard, Robin's son.

29 Notably in a letter to his wife, written shortly after their marriage, referred to in Chapter 11.

30 Phil Hilliard's reminiscences are preserved in a recording held at the Irish National Archives in Dublin.

Notes

CHAPTER 3

1   The house was probably a private home when built in the 1870s. Cork Grammar School was founded there in 1882 by the Cork Grammar School Company Ltd under a Board of Management headed by the Bishop of Cork, Cloyne and Ross. Alicia St Leger: *A History of Ashton School – Rochelle School, Cork High School, Cork Grammar School* published by Ashton School, Cork, 2016, p88.

2   St Leger, p94

3   This dream story features in a piece called *A Glimpse of Future Grammar*, published in the Midsummer 1919 issue of the school magazine.

4   The school had close ties to the Church of Ireland and most of the boys followed that denomination, though the school had also catered for Methodist, Presbyterian and Jewish pupils since its founding in 1882.

5   1891: (Guy's) City & County Almanac and Directory, p79.

6   John Borgonovo, *The Dynamics of War and Revolution: Cork City, 1916–1918*, Cork University Press, 2013, p15. Borgonovo bases this summary on entries in *Guys Directory* for 1915. All references to Borgonovo's work in this chapter and the next are to this book, unless otherwise stated.

7   'This [soldiers' home] was originally opened as a place of leisure,' according to Sean Healy in his Witness Statement (Bureau of Military History *Witness Statements*, WS1643). He goes on to say that it later became a 'rendezvous for all Crown agents' and that 'spies and informers frequented the place at all hours of the day and night'. It was located in Glanmire Road.

8   Cork had more than thirteen times the population of Killarney, according to the 1911 census figures, which give Killarney's population as 5796 and Cork's as 76,673.

9   The field was in Sunday's Well, to the west of the city centre.

10 St Leger, p120.

11 St Leger, p113.

12 This can be viewed in the online records of the Imperial War Museum at New Scale of Separation Allowances (Art.IWM PST 5116), 841

13 Infant mortality was 132 per 1000 live births, nearly one in eight. J. C. Saunders, *Annual Report of the Medical Officer of Health, 1935*, Cork: Guy and Co Ltd, 1936, quoted in John Borgonovo, p7.

14 This was when Germany declared British waters, which still included Irish waters, to be a warzone.

15 Armstrong, *Cork Grammar School*, The *Grammarian* (School Magazine), 1965, p13, quoted in Alicia St Leger, p111.

16 RIC County Inspector's Monthly Report for Cork City and East Riding (from now on referred to in these notes as CI Report) for March 1916, Public Record Office, The National Archive, Kew, London, 904/100, quoted in John Borgonovo, p39.

17 James Connolly had visited Tralee the previous October and addressed a rally of about 3,000 people organized by the local Trades Council in Tralee's Town Square. This was the official launch of the ITGWU in Kerry. Over 160 joined, though several trade

Notes

unionists, including Michael J O'Connor, secretary of Tralee Trades Council, lost their jobs because of their involvement (See Kieran McNulty, letter, *The Kerryman*, 7 October 2015). One of Connolly's organizers, William Partridge, founded the ITGWU's first Killarney branch by standing on a box outside the Town Hall on Christmas Eve and making a speech about 'a free nation and a free people'. Francis Devine describes these events in *The Irish Transport & General Workers' Union in Kerry 1909–1930*, Kerry Archaeological and Historical Society, Webinar series, No.2.

18 There were trade union defeats in Kerry as well as victories, for example a three-year-long strike in Tralee by members of the Irish Drapers' Assistants Association was unsuccessful. Borgonovo, pp161–62 discusses the reasons why the war had nevertheless created favourable conditions for the ITGWU to make gains.

19 Adrian Hilliard and his father Richard Hilliard confirmed to me that the Hilliard factory was unionized by the ITGWU in 1916 and shared the family's opinion of trade unions.

20 An account of the discovery of the attempted arms landing and the arrest of Casement is given in *Kerry's Fighting Story*, edited Brian O'Conchubhair, Mercier Press, Cork, 2009 (originally published by *The Kerryman* in 1947), pp111–13.

21 *Kerry's Fighting Story*, pp90–1.

22 Among them was James Connolly's Irish Citizen Army, a paramilitary group of volunteer ITGWU members formed during the Dublin Lockout to protect workers from police attacks, and a contingent from Cumann na mBan, the women's Volunteer organization. The rebels' leaders came mainly from the IRB and the Volunteer movement but included James Connolly.

23 Conor Kostick, *Revolution in Ireland: Popular Militancy 1917–1923*, Cork University Press 2009, p26.

24 See account by 'Old Soldier', *Kerry in Holy Week 1916 and After*, from *Kerry's Fighting Story*, p128.

25 Cork in early 1916 had been 'one of the strongest centres of Volunteer activity in the country'. John Borgonovo, *Spies, Informers and the 'Anti-Sinn Féin Society'*, *The Intelligence War in Cork City 1920–1921*, Irish Academic Press, Dublin, 2007, p3.

26 Borgonovo, pp42–3 gives a more detailed narrative of these events.

27 Despite Carson's threat to lead an armed revolt, he was treated as a mainstream politician. By this time he was a respected member of the Coalition government.

28 Borgonovo, p47.

29 On 2 May the RIC tried to arrest brothers Thomas, David, Richard and William Kent, apparently because they were republican sympathizers. The brothers, who had stayed at home during the Rising, resisted arrest. There was a gun battle in which an RIC officer and one Kent brother were killed and another brother was seriously wounded. The three surviving brothers were court-martialled; one was acquitted and another condemned to death (his sentence was commuted). Accounts vary; I have relied on this one: Thomas Kent & Cork's Rising Experience | Century Ireland - RTÉ *www.rte.ie/centuryireland/index.php/articles/the-kent-family-corks-rising-*

Notes

experience. Glanmire Road railway station was later renamed after Thomas Kent and a bust of him stands outside.

30 Empire Day was supposed to be an occasion for saluting the union flag and singing 'Jerusalem' and 'God Save the King'. Those things probably happened as usual inside Cork Grammar School, but for the first time there were no celebrations in the city or Union Jacks in St Patrick Street – Borgonovo, p47.

31 Borgonovo, pp47–8.

32 The demonstration followed a meeting at City Hall called by two Irish Party MPs. Their audience shouted them down and broke up the meeting – Borgonovo, pp50–51.

33 Lloyd George had proposed immediate Home Rule for the south, with six counties in the north partitioned off and separately governed. Since 1914 Irish MPs in the House of Commons had promised Home Rule for the whole of Ireland after the war, which now looked like a confidence trick. The proposal pleased few and went nowhere, though some have suggested it was not so very different from the eventual Treaty.

34 These, with examples of other relatively minor breaches of the DORA, are detailed in Borgonovo, pp52–6.

35 George Monbiot, *Boarding schools warp our political class – I know because I went to one,* *The Guardian,* 7 November 2019.

36 Robert recorded how tired this early study period made him feel in some verses he published in the Michaelmas Term 1919 edition of the school magazine: 'In Grammar, when the darkness dies/The boarders rub their sleepy eyes/And wish it were not time to rise/And go to morning study.'

37 St Leger, p112.

38 His future wife, Rosemary Robins, often told my mother (her eldest daughter, Deirdre) about this, when reminiscing about their courtship.

39 Robert later discussed this schoolboy sense of conflict in an examination paper written during his Divinity studies at Trinity College Dublin in 1931. At that time, under the influence of Frank Buchman, he had swung heavily against reason in favour of divine revelation.

40 Subjects taught at the school are listed in 1916: (Guy's) City & County Almanac and Directory, p85.

41 St Leger, p88.

42 Alicia St Leger, the school's historian, told me she could find no record of boxing being taught at all.

43 St Leger, p103.

44 There was a high correlation between the social class of a school's pupil intake, the sports it played and its political culture. Catholic schools with an intake from lower middle class and 'respectable' working class families generally played traditional Irish sports; their teachers were more likely to speak and read Irish and hold republican views and their ex-students were more likely to become active republicans. The more prestigious Catholic schools played rugby as well as Gaelic sports and were less nationalist. The elite Christian Brothers College took pride in their rugby prowess

Notes

and sent almost as many young men to the Western Front as Cork Grammar. See John Borgonovo, p87.

45   According to Deirdre, Robert's daughter and my mother. She says he loved playing rugby all his life and that his preferred position was fly-half.

46   St Leger, p101.

47   Drill instruction was a well-established tradition at the school. Until 1913 it had been taught by an ex-British Army sergeant – see Guys *Cork Almanac 1913*, p101. St Leger, p96.

48   St Leger, p111

49   St Leger, pp114–15. School song lyrics reproduced with the kind permission of Ashton School.

50   St Leger, p111

51   His Scouts membership is recorded in a handwritten note next to a poem of his in the school's archived copy of its magazine.

52   Military historian Tom Burnell has compiled a list of Irish war dead from a comprehensive range of sources: https://irelandsgreatwardead.ie. Of the 674 Kerry-related war dead on his list, approximately 62 were born, or lived, in Killarney.

53   Kostick, p32, citing R F Foster, *Modern Ireland 1600–1972*, Allen Lane, London, 1988, p471.

54   Sinn Féin MPs did not take their seats in the House of Commons.

55   Kostick, pp28–30.

56   As well as these strikes, the union also won pay rises for its members in the coal trade, grain mills and two shipping lines. Its new sister union for women won pay rises for female paper factory workers and the male colleagues who had picketed with them. Its successes fired other unions. The National Federation of Women Workers won victories at the city's new artillery shell factory and a woollen mill. The ITGWU also established nine agricultural branches for farm workers on the edges of Cork – see Borgonovo, pp162–63. The beginning was in 1917; this wave of workers' struggles would continue throughout 1918 and beyond, unquelled until the Irish Civil War.

57   CI reports for February, March and April 1917 cited by Borgonovo, pp85, 276.

58   A full account of these disturbances is given by Borgonovo, pp64–8

59   The sight of Irish women walking through Cork with US sailors after the May 1917 arrival of US navy ships in Queenstown prompted moral panic from the city's priests. Some republicans physically assaulted women seen with US servicemen – See Borgonovo pp120–38.

60   St Leger, p108.

61   Bureau of Military History, Witness Statement *WS1656*, pp2–3.

62   Florence O'Donoghue, *Tomas MacCurtain, Soldier and Patriot*, Anvil Books, Tralee, 1971, p132.

63   St Leger, p108.

Notes

64 Borgonovo, p126.

65 St Leger, p112.

66 Cork's Lord Mayor asked Sinn Féin to patrol the streets but they refused – Borgonovo, p72.

67 The prison death of republican hunger striker Thomas Ashe prompted a major disturbance in September. Ashe, a former Kerry school teacher, died from injuries inflicted by forcible feeding during imprisonment for sedition. His funeral procession in Dublin attracted 30,000 people. The hunger strike and funeral are described in Tim Pat Coogan, *Michael Collins*, Arrow Books, London, 1991, pp73–4.

68 These arrests were made after one of a series of formal, orderly events in which Volunteers, accompanied by their pipe band, Cumann na mBan members, and contingents of republican girl and boy scouts, marched from their HQ in Sheares Street into the countryside for drilling. John Borgonovo, p92.

69 Borgonovo p71. The RIC who returned to smash the instruments and attack the language class, which was run by Sinn Féin, were senior officers led by the notorious District Inspector Oswald Swanzy. The Brian Boru band was the first pipers' band to be established in Cork City and had links with its Mayor, Thomas MacCurtain, himself a two-drone warpipes player.

70 These were in North Roscommon, South Longford, East Clare and Kilkenny City. The elected candidates were George Noble Plunkett, Joseph McGuinness, Éamon de Valera and WT Cosgrave.

71 Demonstrations towards the end of 1917 included the annual Manchester Martyrs commemoration parade of 3000 Sinn Féin and 3000 ITGWU members on 23 November (with up to 15,000 in the crowd), and a parade in December for a visit by Éamon de Valera, leader of the Volunteers and Sinn Féin. De Valera was escorted from the station to his hotel by a noisy crowd before addressing a rally of 6000–8000 in the city centre the next day. The RIC left well alone – see Borgonovo, pp94–5.

CHAPTER 4

1 Michael Spillane and Michael J O' Sullivan, Bureau of Military History, *WS862*, p5.

2 Home-grown produce was still being exported to Britain (despite the blockade) because it fetched better prices. Potatoes cost more in Cork than anywhere else in the country. Milk was so dear that Bishop Cohalan set up a Poor Children's Milk Fund – Borgonovo, p176.

3 This followed pressure on the Lord Mayor to form a Cork 'People's Food Committee' which banned meat exports. Borgonovo, p179.

4 Livestock exports were substantially reduced – see Borgonovo, p183, Table 10.6 and p184, Tables 10.8 and 10.9 – and dead meat exports stopped – Borgonovo, p184.

5 Borgonovo, p182. Sinn Féin clamped down on agrarian unrest and direct action by Volunteers to secure food supplies in February 1918. It was a nationalist movement rather than a workers' movement and had no wish to antagonize those of its supporters who were landowners or had wealth. – Borgonovo, p183.

Notes

6　Milk was 3d (three old pence) per pint in both January and November 1918 and bread had remained at 9d per 4lb loaf. Potatoes only went up from 18d to 20d per weight and boiled beef from 14d to 16d per pound but some eggs were dear and became even dearer – 50d per dozen in January rising to 75d in November, by which time butter was up from 26d to 31d per pound and bacon had risen from 24d to 34d per pound of rashers – See Borgonovo, p185.

7　During 1918 food supplies were further eased as German U-boats were beaten back by US and British submarines. Another factor increasing supply was that Britain introduced food price controls, an admission that market forces must be reined in.

8　After the Russian revolution, Russia signed the treaty of Brest-Litovsk with Germany, on 3 March 1918. Germany was then able to move forces to the Western Front and mount a successful spring offensive. The decision to introduce Irish conscription was prompted by the resulting need to bolster Allied forces on the Western Front. One senior military figure put the cause of the Allied quandary as follows: 'The really dominating event ... had been the gradual elimination of Russia as a factor in the struggle following on the revolution of March. This had upset all the calculations of the Allied chiefs ...' – Major-General Sir Charles E. Calwell and Marshall Foch, *Field-Marshal Sir Henry Wilson Bart., G.C.B., D.S.O. – His Life and Diaries, Volume 2*, Kessinger Legacy Reprints, Charles Scribner's Sons, New York, 1927, pp36–7.

9　Borgonovo, pp189–190.

10　Cork Grammar School magazine, quoted in Alicia St Leger, pp108–09.

11　The Military Service Act 1918 can be found on the Legislation.gov.uk website.

12　The Corporation, the Poor Law Guardians, the Cork Harbour Commission, the Cork District Trades Council, the city High Sheriff, trading groups, a university student group, trades unions – all denounced the measure. On the day the Bill was passed a demonstration drew several thousand behind a banner reading 'Cork's Resolve – Death before Conscription'. The following Sunday Cork's Catholic churches prayed for the end of conscription at special masses. Congregations were huge. John Borgonovo, pp192–194.

13　T Johnson and C O'Shannon, *Irish Labour and Its International Relations*, Cork Workers' Club reprint, no date, pp13–14, quoted in Conor Kostick, *Revolution in Ireland – Popular Militancy 1917–1923*, Cork University Press 2009, p39.

14　*The Irish Times*, 24 April 1918, cited Kostick, p40.

15　Callwell, p94.

16　Borgonovo, p199.

17　Seventy-three republicans were arrested across Ireland in one night on 17 May and deported to England without charge or trial – see Kostick, p42. Little or no evidence was ever set out that any such plot existed.

18　*Cork Examiner* 24 May 1918, cited Borgonovo, p200.

19　Sinn Féin's women's organization

20　Kostick, pp42–3.

Notes

21 Sinn Féin repeatedly defied the ban by giving out false locations to decoy the RIC – Borgonovo, p208.

22 Borgonovo, pp205–6.

23 This act of mass sporting defiance, known as Gaelic Sunday, further eroded the political authority of the British state. My thanks to Eimhin Murgan-Fennessy, tour guide at the GAA Museum in Croke Park when I visited in October 2023, for his lively account of this event, which is also recorded by Borgonovo p208.

24 *Cork Constitution*, 10–11, 15, 21 October 1918; *Cork Examiner*, 13–14 September, 3, 11, 21–22 October 1918, all cited in Borgonovo, pp209–10.

25 French's national target of 50,000 recruits was reduced to 10,000 but still missed – Borgonovo, p210.

26 The speakers had to be rescued by a police baton charge – Borgonovo, p211.

27 St Leger, p112. 2,000 caught the infection in the city and forty-nine would die – Borgonovo, p211.

28 Sinn Féin stood unopposed in many constituencies, including South Kerry (the Hilliards' constituency) and mid-Cork (where the school was). They now had seventy-three elected MPs out of 105 Irish constituencies, helped by the Irish TUC and Irish Labour Party's decision not to stand against them.

29 St Leger, p112.

30 My thanks to Alicia St Leger, who shared with me the details of when Hilliard earned this medal.

31 St Leger, p116.

32 The declaration was made by those who were not in prison. Forty-seven Sinn Féin MPs were still in jail for the so-called 'German Plot'. They also passed a radical-sounding Democratic Programme, some of its promises apparently designed to keep the labour movement onside. Dáil Éireann - 21/Jan/1919 DEMOCRATIC PROGRAMME. *oireachtasdebates.oireachtas.ie › ... › Dáil Debates › 191*, p16.

33 The shots killing these policemen are usually seen as the first shots in the Irish War of Independence. Dan Breen and Sean Treacy, who mounted the ambush, wanted to ensure the Volunteers' independence from Sinn Féin: 'The Volunteers were in great danger of becoming merely an adjunct to the Sinn Féin organisation ... We had thoroughly discussed the pros and cons and arrived at the conclusion that it was our duty to fight for the Irish Republic that had been established on Easter Monday 1916.' Dan Breen, *My Fight for Irish Freedom*, Anvil Books, Dublin 1964, p31.

34 Kostick, pp53–4.

35 Preparations for a guerrilla war had been gaining pace during 1918, accompanied by confrontations and reprisals which could in turn prompt mass resistance. For example, two weeks after Easter, on 13 April 1918 in Gortatlea, between Killarney and Tralee, a group of Volunteers tried to capture weapons by holding up an RIC station at gunpoint. They fired no shots, but police shot two of them dead. About 6,000 people attended their funeral. Boycotts of the RIC began in Kerry following these shootings and there were similar boycotts elsewhere. *Kerry's Fighting Story 1916–1921*, pp201–3.

Notes

36 Engineering, shipyard, gas and power station workers walked out in a dispute about over-long working hours. By the evening Belfast was in darkness. By 27 January the strike committee was in charge of the city. Other workers joined in: railway engineering shops, graveyard workers (they later went back to work), women rope workers, crane men, carpenters, joiners, women workers from spinning mills; a rent strike also began. See Kostick, pp57–60.

37 Emmet O'Connor, *Syndicalism in Ireland 1917–1923*, Cork University Press 1988, p71.

38 The strikes were undermined, partly by the ending of the parallel strike in Glasgow (Kostick pp59–60) but even more importantly by the conservatism of the strike committee and its reluctance to expand the strikes, causing a loss of momentum. Many of those on the strike committee were union leaders, afraid of losing control of their members (Kostick pp60–2). The strike did, however, prompt Lord French to advocate releasing the 'German Plot' prisoners, with the long-term aim of reaching a deal with 'moderate elements in Sinn Féin'. The British government was anxious to avoid a revolutionary, cross-sectarian revolt by Irish workers. Kostick, pp62–3.

39 *The Manchester Guardian* described it as a 'Soviet' - see Kostick, p58.

40 Kostick, p59, citing C Rosenberg, *Britain on the Brink of Revolution 1919*, Bookmarks, 1987, p42.

41 Kostick, pp74–93, gives a full and fascinating account of the Limerick Soviet.

42 Kostick, p91.

43 Kostick, p92.

44 Kostick, p72.

45 Raids were commonplace even before the autumn of 1919. Kostick, p94, states that between January and September 1919, 5588 raids on individual homes were reported in the Irish press. This repression would however worsen from then on, in particular after the arrival in 1920 of the Black and Tans and Auxiliaries.

46 It continued to meet in secret.

47 *The Westminster Gazette*, a Liberal London paper, described Lord French's programme as 'a system of coercion such as there has not been seen in living memory' – Kostick, p94.

48 The change of name followed the taking of an Oath of Loyalty to the leadership of Sinn Féin, at which point the Volunteers became Ireland's new army in the eyes of nationalists.

49 Across Ireland 400 RIC officers and 160 soldiers were killed by the IRA before the Truce of 1921, according to Foster, p497.

50 This was one way the Dáil set out in 1919 to present itself as an alternative government. It also set up an alternative court system, called a nationwide boycott of the RIC, instigated a compulsory Oath of Allegiance for Volunteers (Dáil Éireann - 20/Aug/1919 OATH OF ALLEGIANCE.*oireachtasdebates.oireachtas.ie › Current Debates › Dáil Debates › 1919*) and sought recognition and funding abroad.

51 The plaque holds forty-six names and is pictured in Alicia St Leger, p115. It is still on display at Ashton School.

Notes

52 These plans for expanding the school became 'impossible in the disturbed conditions of Ireland in the years after 1919' – St Leger, p116.

53 St Leger, p113.

54 Kostick, p96.

55 DI Swanzy, the officer who had smashed up the instruments of the Brian Boru band and attacked a nearby Irish language class in 1917 (see Chapter 4), was District Inspector for the North District of Cork at the time of MacCurtain's murder. The coroner held him responsible for ordering the killing. He was tracked down and shot in Lisburn in August, sparking a pogrom by Protestant civilians against Catholics in that town.

56 See British Pathé News footage https://www.youtube.com/watch?v=G2kOqqnkS84

57 St Leger, p113.

58 Report in the school magazine, quoted by Alicia St Leger, p117.

59 Recruitment to the 'Tans' relied heavily on veterans from the trenches, brutalized by their wartime experiences.

60 See, for example, Bureau of Military History, *WS Ref #: 1737,* Witness: Seamus Fitzgerald, Officer IRA, Cobh, County Cork, p30.

61 Tim Pat Coogan, *Michael Collins,* Arrow Books, London, 1991, pp126–27, pp144–45.

62 This family story about Moll comes from her son Ken Shellard.

63 My grandmother, Rosemary, used to relate to my mother the stories of the Black and Tans which Robert told her when they first met. She also talked about the traumatic effects of some of what he had seen and heard.

64 St Leger, p116.

65 *Cork Examiner:* '... not a shop is open. The trams are off the streets – in fact there is not the slightest indication of business being applied, even the hackney cabs are off the stands.' Quoted by Kostick, p132.

66 More than a hundred prisoners were in the same situation at the prison. The number who started the hunger strike was sixty-six. Later others joined it.

67 Many were labour activists and socialists. *The Manchester Guardian* interviewed one, and reported that 'he is as keen that the Irish nation should become a workers' republic as that it should become a republic at all' – *The Manchester Guardian,* 28 April 1920, quoted by Kostick, p130.

68 *The Manchester Guardian* described how: *'The direction of affairs passed during the strike to these councils, which were formed not on a local but a class basis. In most places the police abdicated and the maintenance of order was taken over by the Workers' Councils.'* Quoted by Kostick, pp134–5.

69 *Cork Examiner,* 14 April 1920, cited in Kostick, p132.

70 The release of untried prisoners (the vast majority) was announced on condition they signed a promise to come back. The prisoners refused to sign and were simply set free. Kostick, pp136–7.

71 'It was common practice for the military authorities to get up on the footplate of an engine and say to the driver "you have got to drive this train". Put a revolver to his

Notes

head and say "you will get this if you don't drive". And to the everlasting credit of the railwaymen they said "no".' Tom Farren in ILPTUC reports 1921 pp88–9, quoted in Kostick, p143.

72 Kostick, p146.

73 Colonel Gerald Bryce Ferguson Smyth had been appointed Divisional Police Commissioner for Munster on June 3.

74 There are slightly divergent versions of Smyth's speech. This extract is from Tim Pat Coogan, *Michael Collins*, Arrow Books, London, 1991, p150.

75 One Listowel policeman immediately handed in his police insignia. His colleagues backed him, and it became a case of arresting all or none, so none was arrested. In Killarney Smyth was greeted by rebellious RIC members with shouts of 'Up Listowel!' See Kostick, p108.

76 Garda Síochána Historical Society www.policehistory.com/listowel.html, *Listowel Police Mutiny*. See also Bureau of Military History 1913–1921, *Witness Statement 832*, page 17, for a list of names of RIC members who resigned in Killarney and nearby towns.

77 Bureau of Military History, *WS Ref #: 1643*, Third Witness Statement by Sean Healy, p3.

78 The burned RIC stations were St Luke's, the already wrecked King Street and Lower Glanmire Road.

79 The IRA men who shot him included Daniel Healy, who had stood as lookout for the 1917 raid on Cork Grammar School. Bureau of Military History, *WS Ref #1656*,. pp9–11.

80 *Rebel Cork's Fighting Story* 1916–1921, ed. Brian O'Conchubhair, Mercier Press, Cork 2009, p133.

81 Emmet O'Connor, pp45–6.

82 He would not personally witness workers winning a victory again until the Outdoor Relief struggles in Belfast twelve years later.

83 Robert's wife, my grandmother Rosemary, told my mother this.

CHAPTER 5

1 Dublin had once been an elegant European capital, but had visibly decayed since the Act of Union of 1800.

2 For example, the new La Scala Theatre – a cinema – had just been built in Prince's Street, off Sackville Street (now O' Connell Street) on the site of the *Freeman's Journal* office, which was destroyed during the Rising.

3 Breen, p130.

4 The contemporaneity of this name is disputed; for example one internet account – www.cairogang.com – (which questions the most commonly reprinted photo of the gang) states: 'There is no findable mention of "Cairo Gang" in books or documents of the 1919–1922 period. The earliest reference found so far is 1958.'

Notes

5 Some claim their nickname came from the Café Cairo, others from their experience of operating as enforcers of the British occupation of Egypt. It's also claimed that this nickname is of more modern origin.

6 Delia Larkin, socialist activist and actor, founded the Irish Women Workers' Union and the Irish Workers' Dramatic Club.

7 C Desmond Greaves, *The Political Evolution of Sean O'Casey*, Desmond Greaves Archive.com, Section III. The raid took place on Good Friday, so Robert would not have witnessed it.

8 The Dáil had met at number 3 Mountjoy Square North in 1919.

9 This pub's importance as an IRA meeting place is well documented, see for example Patrick Colgan, *Witness Statement 850*, Bureau of Military History, p65.

10 Breen, p153.

11 Coogan, *Michael Collins*, p134.

12 Breen, p146.

13 The source of all these figures is the school attendance registers and payment records of Mountjoy School, now held by Mount Pleasant School (Mountjoy's successor school).

14 Liam Wegimont, the Head of Mountjoy School, told me that after Irish independence the school was one of the first Protestant schools to admit Catholics, Jews, Muslims and atheists. In 1920 sectarian attitudes prevailed, at least as regards the administration of land held by the school. Minutes of dealings concerning the school's endowment properties show that in at least one case the school's solicitor was asked to prevent the sale of an endowment property lease to a Catholic: 'We understand that Flannery [and] Carter ... have forwarded proposals ... he [Carter] is a decent member of the Church of Ireland, and his farm adjoins the place. Flannery as no doubt you are aware is an RC [Roman Catholic] and would not be a desirable tenant.' (Letter, 2 December 1919, in papers of Mount Temple School). Later correspondence, also held by the school, ensured Carter got the lease.

15 The school was run by the Incorporated Society for Promoting Protestant Schools in Ireland. As well as fees, it was funded by income from endowments of land and property, managed by a board of Governors and a standing Committee – see H Kingsmill Moore, *The Work of the Incorporated Society for Promoting Protestant Schools in Ireland*, Tempest, Dundalk, 1938, p43.

16 Tom Barry, *Guerrilla Days in Ireland*, Anvil Books, Dublin, 1962, p37.

17 Coogan, pp159–60.

18 Bloody Sunday was to become still bloodier. That night two IRA men and an unconnected member of the Gaelic League were tortured, beaten and killed by British forces at Dublin Castle. See Coogan, p161.

19 Identities of service personnel were not given at this enquiry. Though their witness statements were frequently contradicted by those of spectators, they were given without cross-examination. The RIC's firing was described as 'indiscriminate and unjustified' but the army and Auxiliaries suffered no consequences. See Tim Carey in

Notes

History Ireland: Bloody Sunday: new evidence, Issue 2 (Summer 2003), Revolutionary Period 1912–23, Volume II.

20 Under martial law civil courts were replaced by courts martial and coroners' courts by courts of military enquiry. Civilian life was harshly affected. Curfew restrictions were introduced, travel by car or bicycle was limited by a special permits system, fairs and markets in some areas were banned and internment without trial was drastically stepped up.

21 The letter was from K Company Auxiliary Charles Schulze, a former British Army Captain who was later 'conjectured to be one of the main organisers of the burning'. It was unearthed in research by historian and genealogist Jim Herlihy and quoted in The Auxiliaries Website, The Burning of Cork.

22 The alternative was to escalate it, seeking support from other unions in Ireland or Britain. Train drivers had held out under great pressure but were being relentlessly sacked. Union leaders had either to escalate the sanction to other workers or call it off. They called it off, from 11 December 1920 – see Kostick, pp140–46.

23 *Witness Statement (hereafter WS) 862*, p18.

24 *WS 862*, p20.

25 Richard Hilliard told me in 2014 that during this period Auxiliaries stormed into the Hilliards' shop and looted blankets. He gave no date but going by the account in WS862 it's likely that this was the same occasion. He added that the family made a claim and were awarded compensation for the value of the blankets. I do not know whether similar compensation was successfully claimed by shopkeepers who did not share the Hilliards' history of loyalism to the Crown.

26 *WS 862*, p20.

27 Mountjoy School register 1920–21, held at Mount Pleasant School.

28 Three locations, Cork County, Dublin city and Belfast, saw over 50 per cent of the fatalities in the Irish revolution.

29 Mount Temple School records.

30 Robert may have been helped by the school Matron, who was supposed to provide pastoral care and a sympathetic ear. The school's papers show Mountjoy School's Matron left midway through the year, and her departure may have been a blow to Robert if he had confided in her. It's startling to read some of the attributes and experience claimed by candidates to replace her. One applicant, for example, claimed to have involved herself in the street battle to suppress the Easter Rising (she was not appointed).

31 The popularity of new dances was boosted by their appearance in films. Robert would enthusiastically defend popular cinema in a debate during his first term at Trinity.

32 See *TCD*, the college magazine, 23 February 1922.

33 The Monto was bounded by Gardiner Street, Amiens Street, Talbot Street and Gloucester Street.

34 James Joyce, *A Portrait of the Artist as a Young Man*, Penguin, Middlesex, 1969, p100 & p102.

Notes

35 Kevin C. Kearns *Dublin Tenement Life: An Oral History of the Dublin Slums,* Gill & Macmillan Ltd, 1994.

36 Misbehaviour outside school hours would have been made even more difficult than it already was for a school boarder like Robert by a change in the curfew from 10.00 p.m. to 8.00 p.m. in February 1921.

37 No secret was made of this policy, which was shown in at least one newsreel – see British Pathé, *British Troops in Ireland 1916–1922, All's Fair In ... (1921).*

38 Tom Barry, an IRA commander from Co. Cork, described the psychological damage done to those using some of the methods adopted by the IRA at this time.'The British ... had gone down in the mire to destroy us and our nation, and down after them we had to go to stop them. The step was not an easy one, for one's mind was darkened and one's outlook made bleak by the decisions which had to be taken.' Tom Barry, *Guerilla Days in Ireland,* The Irish Press, 1949, p112.

39 On 5 March, for instance, one civilian was killed and four wounded in two IRA ambushes of troops in Dublin, one near Parnell Square and another in Clontarf. On 11 March 1921 the Dáil empowered Éamon de Valera to make a formal declaration of war, though he never did so. On 14 March, following news that six IRA prisoners had been hanged in Mountjoy Prison, two civilians, two policemen, and three IRA men were killed in a long gun battle on Brunswick Street (now Pearse Street).

40 He used this phrase in the letter to his son Geoff quoted in Chapter 2.

41 Bureau of Military History, *WS862,* p15.

42 Barry, p80.

43 The Killarney IRA had formed a new unit in March 1921. While they trained, another company was sent to find rations for them as well as for two other units. It's therefore likely that this visiting company took food away from Moyeightragh as well as having a meal themselves. See Bureau of Military History, *WS 862,* p22.

44 Stephen Hilliard's account implies Robert was an undergraduate ('at college'), but the vagueness of his phrase 'On at least one occasion' raises questions about timing. Robert didn't start university until after the Truce began in June 1921. During the Truce IRA members would not have been looking for food and shelter. This therefore must have happened while he was at school, probably at Mountjoy School. Clandestine IRA operations resumed with the Civil War, but Robert could not reach Killarney at that time and newspaper reports show him in Dublin throughout the Civil War (see Chapters 6 and 8).

45 Stephen Hilliard, *The Boxing Parson, Resource Magazine* 1988, *irelandscw.com/ibvol-Hilliard.htm*

46 Mount Temple School papers.

47 Her letter is in the Mount Temple School papers. 'Such a thing is not to be tolerated in the twentieth century,' she wrote, '... we thought [our boy] would be treated as a schoolboy, not as a convict.' The school's ultimate managing body (The Incorporated Society for Promoting Protestant Schools in Ireland, to whom the boy's mother complained) replied: "... we can find no evidence of any undue severity".

Notes

48 Emmet O'Connor, p25.

49 The slump took effect from May 1920 onwards. Unemployment rose fast, reducing the numbers of union members, especially in the ITGWU. Emmet O'Connor, p90.

50 Emmet O'Connor, p88: 'Despite the proven value of the strike as an instrument with which to embarrass the government or hamper the military, Dáil Éireann never sought to invoke it, or attempted to manipulate political strikes once they had begun. Employing a weapon of social conflict would have run counter to Sinn Féin's integrationist strategy'.

51 None took their Westminster seats.

52 Diarmaid Ferriter, in *A Nation and not a Rabble*, Profile Books Ltd, 2015, p242, quotes 100 captured. Coogan p207 states seventy.

53 After his return from the US at the end of 1920, Éamon de Valera began pushing for the abandonment of guerrilla tactics in favour of formal pitched battles. One such was the burning of the Custom House on 25 May 1921. Instead of a few men making a quick attack and disappearing, a large contingent was ordered into the building to set fire to it, leaving a covering party outside. The attack disabled local administration, but six Volunteers were killed, twelve wounded and between seventy and one hundred captured (see note 52): a military disaster for the IRA. Two civilians were also killed.

54 Tim Pat Coogan, *Collins's place in history*, article in the *Irish Independent*, 22 August 2002.

55 The new armed police force in the North, set up in October 1920 and divided into the A, B and C Specials, was recruited from the explicitly anti-Catholic UVF and Orange Lodges.

56 Kostick, p171.

57 'The poverty of the Candidates is one of the qualifications to be inquired into before they are admitted as Sizars.' See *General Information on Sizarships* in Calendar 1922–23, Trinity College Dublin.

CHAPTER 6

1 Kieran Allen, *1916 – Ireland's Revolutionary Tradition*, Pluto Press, London, 2016, p101.

2 Letter to his wife Rosemary's Uncle Louis dated 18 October 1930.

3 Lionel Fleming, *Head or Harp*, Barrie & Rockliff, London 1965, p98.

4 *Dictionary of Irish Biography Online* © 2016 Cambridge University Press and Royal Irish Academy. My thanks to Cyril Smith for establishing that Thrift was Robert's tutor and pointing out this information about him.

5 Fleming, p99.

6 Fleming, p99.

7 Fleming, p97.

8 Richard Hilliard told me this anecdote in 2014.

9 Mahaffy famously dismissed the Irish language as 'sometimes useful to a man fishing for salmon or shooting grouse in the West', but later changed his view – See Tomás Irish, *Trinity in War and Revolution, 1912–1923*, Royal Irish Academy, 2015 pp22–5.

Notes

10 Irish, p169. The oft-told story that Robert Hilliard founded or co-founded the Thomas Davis Society cannot be true, as this society began meeting before Robert had even left school.

11 Fleming, p101.

12 Robert was reported to have made 'bi-weekly' contributions to the Historical Society (*TCD*, 18 May 1922), for example, but what he said was not always reported.

13 Denis Carroll: *Unusual Suspects*, The Columba Press, 1998, p249.

14 The motion was 'A Plebiscite is useless in discovering national opinion in times of stress' and the debate was reported in *TCD*, 17 November 1921. Other debates that he attended, for instance one about Queen Victoria (*TCD*, 8 December 1921) reports that ('Mr RM Hilliard was admirably brief') and another about the Irish language, (reported in *TCD* 8 December 1921), also offered opportunities to air the nationalist cause, though there is no report of what he said.

15 *TCD*, 8 December 1921.

16 *The Kid* dealt with lives of extreme poverty and was implicitly subversive, *The Four Horsemen* had an anti-war message and *The Sheik* dwelt on the white-skinned heroine's forbidden erotic attraction to an apparently dark-skinned man. Rudolph Valentino, the star of two of these films, was disapproved of by many for having done time in prison as well as his reputation as a sex symbol.

17 Neophyte Debating Society, reported *TCD*, 24 November 1921.

18 The description of Robert as a Marxist and atheist during his time at Trinity from 1921 to 1926 has been copied from one account to another without any direct, non-hearsay evidence of either belief. That he was not a Marxist at this time is proved by some of his debating contributions, which show little inclination to take class politics seriously. Nor, among all the *TCD* reports and Society minutes, is there any record of his expressing atheistic opinions.

19 Minutes of Neophyte Debating Society 1921.

20 In November Robert made a speech supporting Horace 'for making literature out of women' (*TCD*, 1 December 1921). Since several Horace odes about women were regarded as obscene, in particular Odes 1.25, 3.15, and 4.13, and since Horace is often seen as the least sympathetic to women of the best-known classical Roman poets, it's fair to guess Robert was looking for sexist laughs with this speech. He did so again, days later, comparing the decline of social etiquette 'to a female removing her clothes' (*TCD*, 8 December 1921).

21 Irish, p14. It would be longer still before women were first awarded degrees by Oxford (1920) or Cambridge (1948).

22 Trinity College Dublin website, Equality Home Page.

23 *TCD*, 15 December 1921.

24 *TCD*, 15 December 1921.

25 He would later speak at least twice about women's equality, on both occasions ironically. In March 1922, referring to his National schooldays (before he went to Cork Grammar), he 'objected to seeing "the inferior female" at the head of the class while he

Notes

was at the bottom' – *TCD*, 9 March 1922. A week earlier he had carried advocacy of women's rights to a deliberately absurd pitch: 'Mr R M Hilliard proved ... that women alone were fit to govern the state' – *TCD* 2 March 1922.

26 Ireland also had to take on some of the UK's debt.

27 Kerry County Council had cut its road maintenance workforce from 480 to fifty – See Tom Doyle, *The Civil War in Kerry*, Mercier Press, Cork, 2008, pp74–5.

28 These fears later worsened – see Doyle, pp86–7. However, many business people like the Hilliards also hoped the Treaty would revive normal commercial activity.

29 Doyle, p72.

30 Kostick, pp185–7.

31 The RIC were due to leave their barracks in February. Doyle, p68.

32 Volunteers at this camp carried out 'Field training ... field engineering, signaling, tactics, physical training ... [and] night operations'. *Witness Statement 862*, p32.

33 Doyle, p73.

34 Doyle, p78.

35 Robert's parents could not afford his university fees without a Sizarship and would find it difficult to support him in Dublin during the holidays. I have therefore assumed he returned home if he could. Later on in the Civil War this became impossible to do safely. My thanks to Cyril Smyth for term dates listed in College records.

36 Ireland's revolution was fast becoming a beacon for independence movements in other nations struggling to extricate themselves from the British Empire, including Egypt.

37 *TCD*, 9 February 1922.

38 *TCD* noted that the other anti-Treaty speaker in the room was a Unionist and that the two of them 'made strange bedfellows' – *TCD*, 16 February 1922.

39 Robert took an active part in the discussions of the Classical Society. On 10 February 1922, in a discussion of a paper on 'Greek Federalism' in the 3rd and 2nd centuries BC, he is reported as commenting that 'The geographical conditions of Greece were responsible for the various attempts at federal government but such attempts were ruined by the selfishness of the Greek character' – *TCD*, 16 February 1922. Stereotypical remarks about character and race or national origin strike a dissonant note today but were common at the time. On 24 February 1922 he supposedly 'commended Sulla's cruelty' – *TCD*, 2 March 1922.

40 By applying empirical archaeological study to classical texts, Jane Harrison, a pioneering research fellow at Newnham College, Cambridge, had concluded that the pantheon of deities headed by Zeus had little to do with the mystical and ritual qualities of ancient Greek popular religion, and were instead sanitized figures created by later interpretations, shorn of their power to express the unconscious mind – see among others Francesca Wade, *Square Haunting*, Faber, London 2020, pp167–68.

41 My mother still has these translations.

42 For example, he debunked one motion supporting 'Psychical Research' by pretending to classify species of ghosts scientifically and 'expressing strong disapproval of those which absconded with his bedclothes' – *TCD*, 23 February 1922. He mocked another

Notes

that 'the interest taken in athletics is excessive' with a jokey rhetorical question: 'Con of the Hundred Battles was a remarkable athlete and who didn't take an interest in him?'- *TCD*, 9 March 1922.

43 *TCD*, 23 February 1922.

44 Gilbert Murray's translation of *The Bacchae*, George Allen, London, 1906, p54.

45 The chorus goes on to speak of escaping from fear to the safety of wild places:

   'Leap of the hunted, no more in dread,

   Beyond the snares and the deadly press :

   ... Is it joy or terror, ye storm-swift feet? ...

   To the clear lone lands untroubled of men ...'

Euripides ends the lyric by bringing together the wild joy of the dance, the escape from fear and hatred, and the attainment of wisdom:

   'What else is Wisdom ? What of man's endeavour

   Or God's high grace, so lovely and so great?

   To stand from fear set free, to breathe and wait

   To hold a hand uplifted over Hate

   And shall not Loveliness be loved for ever?'

The last line is Murray's attempt to render an ambiguity in the original Greek, well explained by Martha Nussbaum: 'Literally the Greek says "Whatever is kalon is also philon". Kalon is a word that signifies at once beauty and nobility [which is] either aesthetic or ethical, and is usually both at once, showing how hard it is to distinguish these spheres in Greek thought ... Philon means "beloved", "precious", "a friend to", "dear", "welcome". This ambiguous line, then, is the ancestor of "A thing of beauty is a joy forever". It expresses love for what is truly noble, truly fine.' (Martha Nussbaum, *Introduction* to C K Williams, *The Bacchae of Euripides, a New Version*, US Macmillan, 1990). For Robert these lines would have evoked his childhood wanderings in the wild places by the Killarney lakes, and his later longing, while at school, to 'stand from fear set free, to breathe and wait/to hold a hand uplifted over Hate'.

46 This was preceded by a split in the Sinn Féin women's organization, Cumann na mBan, in February 1922, when a large majority voted against the Treaty.

47 Kostick, pp202–4.

48 *Irish Worker*, 14 March 1914.

49 *Kerry People*, 8 April 1922.

50 *Irish Independent*, 20 March 1922, quoted in Coogan, p320.

51 Doyle, p89.

52 *TCD*, 1 June 1922.

53 The motion referred to France's division of Syria into separate areas in 1922.

54 As armed clashes increased, Collins and de Valera made a pre-election pact that both Sinn Féin factions would stand as a unified party and form a coalition after the results were announced. The British cabinet wanted no such compromise and threatened Collins that without an unequivocal electoral endorsement of the Treaty they would mount a full military invasion.

Notes

55 Smyllie later edited *The Irish Times*, and wrote for it under the pseudonym 'Nichevo'.

56 *The Irish Times*, 13 May 1944.

57 Pro-Treaty Sinn Féin candidates won fifty-eight seats and anti-Treaty Sinn Féin thirty-six. In the January 1922 election they had won sixty-four and fifty-seven seats respectively, so electoral support had dropped away from both factions.

58 The Labour party won more than 21 per cent of first preference votes. The intentions of its leadership were far less radical than their electoral rhetoric, as their subsequent behaviour shows.

59 In January 1922 Cork railworkers mounted a successful strike to defend their hours. In February two Cork flour mills were seized and run under workers' control. In March, Tipperary gasworkers occupied and ran their workplace as a soviet. Farmworkers in counties Dublin and Meath successfully struck against a wage reduction, forming an alliance with local unemployed groups and demanding more jobs. Kildare council chambers were occupied by workers carrying red flags in a successful protest against pay cuts. In May roadworkers occupied Tipperary council and in the name of the workers' republic awarded themselves a pay rise. In the same month 300 people seized a shut-down sawmill in Ballinacourty and reopened it. On 12 May a Clonmel creamery was taken over and the red flag raised to protest against an attempted 33 per cent pay cut. This was followed by a coordinated campaign to take over another hundred creameries, which were successfully run under workers' control for weeks. For these and other examples of workers' direct action in 1922 see Kostick, pp202–4.

60 Wilson was an Ulster Unionist who had encouraged the 1913 Curragh mutiny. He took a leading role in advising the wartime British government, including advice on military policy in Ireland and the use of troops to break strikes in mainland Britain. Since the war he had become the hawkish MP for North Down.

61 Hansard, 26 June 1922.

62 On 8 August the attack began which ultimately drove the anti-Treatyites out of Cork city. They were also forced out of Tipperary, Clonmel, and most of the Midlands.

63 Lionel Fleming, whose time at TCD overlapped with Robert's and whose family lived near Cork city, reports that 'At the end of my first term at Trinity I had to travel all the way round to Cork by sea; it took twenty hours and I was horribly sick'– Fleming, p85. Kerry ports were held by anti-Treaty forces and about to be attacked by the Free State, so – unlike his friend – Robert was unlikely to travel home by sea.

64 *Cork Examiner*, 21 October 1922.

65 Newspaper reports however indicate that throughout this period of acute food shortages, John Hilliard was still able to feed his herd of prize cattle and win prizes at shows.

66 Fleming, p83.

67 Chalmers (Terry) Trench, *Nearly Ninety*, The Hannon Press, Dublin, 1996, p24.

68 Trench, p24.

69 Some accounts say Robert fought as a combatant on the Anti-Treatyite side in the closing months of the civil war. No primary evidence supports this idea and

Notes

circumstantial evidence is against it. Although the opportunist filching of guns from a college OTC store shows where his loyalties lay (see next note), none of the witnesses giving statements to the Irish History Bureau mentions Robert Hilliard as a combatant. Specifically, the assertion sometimes made that he joined an active service unit in Kerry during the later stages of the civil war cannot be correct because a) he could not travel there and b) in spring 1923 he was training intensively in Dublin and fighting his way through the qualifying stages for the All-Ireland boxing championships in May 1923. Newspaper and TCD reports show him taking part in cross-country runs through Dublin as part of this training, still speaking in occasional debates at Trinity in February and March and therefore frequently in the public gaze in that city. There are too many of these reports and they are too close together for him to have been able to participate in an active service unit in Kerry at the same time. But the most decisive evidence is what Robert himself said. His comments about both sides in the November 1922 debate (*TCD*, 23 November 1922) point decisively away from his becoming an active combatant in the ensuing weeks.

70 Records of Johana Mary Cogley's pension are here: http://mspcsearch.militaryarchives. ie/docs/files//PDF_Pensions/R5/MSP34REF60812%20%20Johanna%20Mary%20 Cogley/MSP34REF60812%20%20Johanna%20Mary%20Cogley.pdf Better known as Daisy Bannard Cogley, this multi-talented woman was well-known for her acting as well as her republican activities - see Elaine Sisson and Brian Trench, *The Many Parts of Daisy Bannard Cogley*, History Ireland, Issue 5 (September/October 2022), Volume 30.

71 *TCD*, 23 November 1922.

72 His contributions to discussions of class politics were invariably flippant. For example, when speaking to a motion in February 1922 'That the present industrial situation calls for radical reform', he declared that he found his 'ideal in a "pub", drink in one's middle and money at one's back for nothing' (*TCD* 2 March 1922). In November 1922 a strike affected student life and a Neophyte Society motion deplored 'the action of a trade union in preventing students from making proper ablutions'. Instead of supporting these workers' right to take industrial action, Robert 'illogically proved to his own satisfaction that both sides of the motion were wrong' – *TCD*, 23 November 1922. It's sometimes suggested, again without evidence, that Robert joined the Communist Party of Ireland (CPI) at this time, but this notion is contradicted by views he expressed in debates, which as we have seen do not accord with those of the CPI. Possibly CPI membership has been assumed, despite lack of evidence, merely because he joined the Communist Party of Great Britain thirteen years later.

73 Minutes of Neophyte Debating Society, 6 November 1922.

74 The upper weight limit for a bantamweight was eight stone six pounds. When Robert was heavier than this he had to fight at featherweight only. When he was lighter he sometimes chose to fight at both weights.

75 He played hockey, but not well: 'Hilliard was inclined to be slow on the ball' – *TCD*, 25 February 1922.

76 John Le Carré, *The Pigeon Tunnel*, Penguin Random House UK, 2017, p80.

Notes

CHAPTER 7

1   *The Handbook of Nyasaland, 1910.*

2   The British had consolidated their conquest of the British Central Africa Protectorate, later renamed Nyasaland, in the 1890s, using Sikh troops to suppress both Portuguese claims and local resistance. In 1915 John Chilembwe, a Baptist pastor, would lead an unsuccessful uprising against the British, but during Rose's brief time in the territory there were few challenges to British rule.

3   Tax collection and British rule depended on men like Pemba: 'Over much of the territory … [few] resources were available to collectors and hence greater reliance was placed on African intermediaries … they played a role of considerable significance at the cutting edge of imperial authority, collecting taxes, seizing hostages, forcing labour and even, on occasions, "beating up people and robbing the men who had gathered to pay their tax".' John McCracken, *A History of Malawi 1859–1966*, James Currey, Woodbridge, Suffolk, 2012, p71. The quotation he gives is from Lewis Matak Bandawe, *Memoirs of a Malawian*, Blantyre, Malawi, 1971, p71.

4   One of Pemba's wives was known as 'Ruth' and the other as 'Grace'. According to a letter from Rose, they told her and Stephen that they previously had 'no names' (unlikely) and that these names came 'from a book'.

5   Rose's letters to her mother are peppered with the 'n'-word and show that she and Stephen shared the racist, colonial attitudes of the day. Although the couple regarded Pemba as superior in worth and intelligence to other local people by virtue of his association with the British, Rose would have found it a very novel idea that a sudden rupture of Rosemary's close bond with her African carers would cause emotional damage.

6   Rosemary kept these letters. Much information in this chapter comes from them or Rose's journal.

7   Many of the species routinely shot by British colonists in Africa are now endangered and require protection.

8   This body was called the Corporation of the Sons of the Clergy.

9   This description and much of the other information in this chapter about Rosemary's early life and the household at Kingswood Hanger is from DHM.

10   Rose took Rosemary to a series of these shows and kept all the programmes.

11   Muriel Lester, *It Occurred to Me*, Harper and Brothers, New York and London, 1937, p29.

12   In 1923 the Lesters also founded a 'Children's House' on Bruce Road, formally opened by H.G. Wells, which is still a nursery today.

13   British intelligence officer Basil Home Thomson, quoted in Conor Kostick, p59.

14   Noreen Branson, *George Lansbury and the Councillors' Revolt: Poplarism 1919–1925*, Lawrence and Wishart, London, 1979, pp20–1.

15   The uplifted pay was conditional on the employee joining a union – Branson, p22.

16   Respectively the Metropolitan Police Authority, the Metropolitan Water Board and the Metropolitan Asylum Board, which ran the Poor Law hospitals – see Branson, p27.

258

Notes

17 Branson, pp27–8.

18 Lester, p96.

19 Branson, p30.

20 Lester took up the vacancy left by Minnie Lansbury, George Lansbury's daughter-in-law, one of the imprisoned councillors, who had died after release. Lester, p98.

21 Decades later Warner played George Dixon in *Dixon of Dock Green*, his most famous role.

22 At least two of the Poplar councillors, Julia and John Scurr, were Irish or of Irish descent. Both had long political careers as activists in the Irish and labour movements; both supported women's suffrage and social justice for women; both served as Poplar Guardians. John Scurr was Member of Parliament for Mile End, Stepney 1923-32. Branson, pp236-7.

23 Lester, p82. Lester also describes how Black and Tans burst into the bathroom of Hanna Sheehy-Skeffington's house while she was bathing her children, one pressing his bayonet against the children's bodies. The officer who killed her husband, Captain John C. Bowen-Colthurst, killed others the same night, including Richard O'Carroll, prominent trade unionist, socialist and Irish republican.

24 Their friendship would last for much of Lester's life, as shown by their continuing correspondence. Letters were exchanged for decades after this period, often kept by Rosemary, and Lester would visit Rosemary and her children in Ireland in 1934.

25 Markievicz had taken part in the Easter Rising. She had been Minister of Labour in the Dáil during the Irish revolution and at this time represented Dublin South in the Dáil.

26 Chalmers (Terry) Trench, p121.

CHAPTER 8

1 I am indebted for the descriptions of the old boxing gyms in this chapter to boxer Jimmy Clark, who tells me little had changed between the 1920s and 1930s and his own training days in the early 1950s.

2 Fleming, p85.

3 This story comes from the notes to the family tree provided by Billy Hilliard.

4 *Cork Examiner* 21 October 1922, quoted in Tom Doyle, p202.

5 The blitz of destruction carried out against key parts of the Kerry rail network during the first three weeks of January 1923, and the subsequent operations to hunt down and in many cases summarily execute those held responsible, is detailed in Tom Doyle, *The Civil War in Kerry*, pp241–54.

6 Doyle, p248.

7 Doyle, p253.

8 Doyle, p249.

9 Neophyte Debating Society Minutes, 5 February 1923.

10 Neophyte Debating Society Minutes, 12 February 1923

11 Neophyte Debating Society Minutes, 19 February 1923.

12 *TCD*, 1 March 1923.

Notes

13 Neophyte Debating Society Minutes, 5 March 1923.
14 *The Irish Times*, 10 November 1922.
15 *TCD* 8 March 1923.
16 His legs were so badly injured that they had to be amputated – Doyle, p271.
17 Doyle, p272–74.
18 Doyle, p279.
19 *TCD*, 24 February 1924.
20 *Freeman's Journal*, 28 April 1923.
21 *Freeman's Journal*, 25 April 1923.
22 *TCD*, 10 May 1923.
23 His habit of smiling even when things went against him would be noted in a report of his Olympic fight in Paris.
24 As only three semi-finalists were able to take part, lots were drawn to determine which one need not fight.
25 *The Irish Times*, 21 May 1923.
26 *The Irish Times*, 15 June, 1923.
27 *Dublin University Calendar 1922–23*, pp44–5.
28 The cities were Oxford, Cambridge, London, Dublin, Liverpool, Birmingham and Bristol. On 6 November 1923 the Dublin University Boxing Club records show a grant of £22.10s.0d for event expenses.
29 The featherweight limit was 9 stone.
30 *The Irish Times*, 7 December 1923.
31 *Irish Independent*, 17 December 1923
32 Founded in April 1923.
33 Lee was in fact Scottish, the first Scot to win a Lonsdale belt.
34 This exclusive focus on boxing kept him out of debates. His last recorded debate before leaving Trinity in 1925 was in February 1924.
35 Paddy Trench's sister Shamrock went to St George's, Harpenden (see Chalmers (Terry) Trench, pp119–20), the same school as Rosemary, and they may have known each other there.
36 This comment by Rosemary is recorded in DHM.

CHAPTER 9

1 Dublin University Central Athletic Club minutes, 28 April 1924.
2 The term is the Irish equivalent of 'Private' – Flaherty was a soldier.
3 *The Irish Times*, 8 May 1924.
4 Robert had lost to H Rubinstein at the Civic Guards' Tournament in McKie Barracks, a five-round fight reported in *The Irish Times* on 29 May 1924.
5 *Irish Independent*, 3 June 1924.
6 *Irish Independent*, 5 June 1924.
7 *The Irish Times*, 6 June 1924.

Notes

8   *The Irish Times,* 7 June 1924.

9   *The Irish Times,* 9 June 1924.

10   Won by Constable John O'Driscoll.

11   '*An tÓglách*' means 'The Volunteer'.

12   *An tÓglách,* 21 June 1924. A week later the paper again said Flaherty was 'unlucky' to lose to Hilliard.

13   *An tÓglách,* 5 July 1924.

14   *Freeman's Journal,* 7 July 1924. The paper writes of a swimming team; in fact they were water polo players.

15   The Games had started in May but this ceremony was a lot later.

16   All information in this chapter about the Irish Olympic boxing team's stay in Paris, and the matches they fought there, is from *An t-Óglách* (the Irish Army newspaper) 19 July, unless otherwise referenced.

17   *Irish Independent,* 17 July 1926.

18   This is according to Rosemary's recollection and is something she spoke of to both her daughter Deirdre and me.

19   Weather details are from the Netweather website.

CHAPTER 10

1   Rose's Visitors' Book also gives an address he had rented in Dublin for the summer: 13 Dawson Street. Thanks to Rose's carefully kept notes of all visitors in this book, we have a record of every visit that Robert paid to Kingswood Hanger during his courtship of Rosemary, up until his departure from Ireland. I rely on it for all dates of his visits given in this book.

2   Omar Khayyam: *Les Rubaiyat – Traduction nouvelle par F Roger-Cornaz,* Payot & Co, Paris.

3   Robert Hilliard's letter to Rosemary's Uncle Louis, 1929.

4   *The Irish Times,* 2 September 1924

5   *Freeman's Journal,* 13 November 1924

6   Neophyte Debating Society Minutes, 24 November 1924.

7   R.F. Foster, p520.

8   James Connolly, *Workers' Republic,* 1899, *Let Us Free Ireland,* quoted in R.M. Fox, *James Connolly: The Forerunner,* The Kerryman Ltd, Tralee, 1946, p137.

9   He would be assassinated for this by anti-Treatyite IRA members in 1927.

10 J. Knirck, *Afterimage of the Revolution: Cumann ne nGaedhael and Irish Politics, 1922–1932,* University of Wisconsin Press, Madison, 2014, p43, quoted by Allen, p105.

11 *Courts of Justice Act 1924* – See also Allen, p106.

12 See, for example, Diarmaid Ferriter, *A Nation Not a Rabble,* Profile Books, London 2015, p265: 'What was instructive during this period … was the government's determination to crack down on labour unrest on security grounds.' Ferriter gives a

Notes

number of instances and quotes a government proclamation effectively outlawing any strike action by public servants.

13 *Old Age Pension Act, 1924.*

14 Allen, p106.

15 *Enforcement of Law (Occasional Powers) Act, 1924*

16 R.F. Foster, p519.

17 See Allen, p110.

18 *Censorship of Films Act, 1923* and the *Censorship of Publications Act, 1929.*

19 Robert had spoken in support of press freedom in 1922: see Neophyte Debating Society Minutes 3 February 1922.

20 James Meenan, *The Irish Economy Since 1922*, Liverpool University Press, 1970, p34.

21 This moveable feast, on the first Thursday after Trinity Sunday, is not celebrated by Protestants.

22 DHM.

23 Allen, p114.

24 According to my mother, Robert often spoke to Rosemary of his dismay at the sectarian feelings which were widespread in Ireland after 1922. When he returned after 1930, however, he apparently believed that southern Protestants were able to feel more at ease in the new Irish state than previously, a view he expressed in a debate during his second period at Trinity.

25 Neophyte Debating Society Minutes for 19 February 1923. See Chapter 10.

26 *College Calendar* 1924–25. My thanks again to Cyril Smith for researching all these dates and the titles under which Robert was listed.

27 *Irish Independent*, 19 February 1925

28 *Irish Independent*, 15 June 1925.

29 *The Irish Times*, 17 June 1925.

30 I have been unable to confirm this. For example, Robert is not mentioned in Richard Evans's biography *From the Frontline: The Extraordinary Life of Sir Basil Clarke*, History Press, 1913 (though it would be surprising if any biography were to list Clarke's staff).

31 Merchandise carrying this slogan from the 1920s onwards can be found online.

32 Kit Laidley later acted as godfather to the couple's fourth child, also called Kit.

CHAPTER 11

1 This letter, published by the *Daily Mail* days before the election, was supposedly sent by Grigory Zinoviev, head of the Communist International, or Comintern, to the Communist Party of Great Britain. The Labour government had that year signed a trade agreement with Russia and was likely to make a loan to the Russian government. The letter claimed this would 'make it possible for us to extend and develop the propaganda of ideas of Leninism in England and the Colonies' – in effect suggesting that Labour foreign policy could eventually lead to a Bolshevik Britain.

Notes

Most historians agree the letter was a forgery. The Labour vote was undiminished but Liberal Party voters turned to the Conservatives, who came to power in a landslide. The letter is held by The National Archive, Kew, London.

2   Graham Greene, *A Sort of Life*, Book Club Associates with Bodley Head, London, 1972, p175.

3   Lester, p124.

4   Lester, p127.

5   The article was torn by Rosemary from an Irish newspaper. The name of the paper is torn off, but the date is visible: 14 May 1927.

6   Rosemary relayed the story of this journey to Rose in a letter.

7   Fleming, p109.

8   Family tradition has it he worked for *The Times* during some of this period.

9   Greene, p175.

10 All quotations from Deirdre in this chapter, unless otherwise attributed, are from DHM.

11 UK law did not recognize marital rape as a crime until 1991. As late as 1983 the UK's Criminal Law Revision Committee (which advised the Home Secretary until replaced by the Law Commission) explicitly rejected the idea that forced sex by a husband constituted rape. The first country to criminalize marital rape was Soviet Russia in 1922. The first outside the Eastern bloc was Sweden, in 1965. Ireland did so in 1990.

12 Kingswood Hanger Visitors' Book shows that Robert, the pregnant Rosemary and baby Tim spent Christmas 1927 at Kingswood Hanger. On 9 April 1928 they took Timothy (and Boreas) to join a family party at Kingswood Hanger celebrating Marianne's ninety-sixth birthday.

13 Both Tim and Deirdre would speak as adults of the insecurity caused by the suddenness of these separations and the fact that they never knew how long it would be before they saw their parents again.

14 Paddy Trench had by this time left Francie Baker and moved to London with his second wife Eve Hayden. From this period onwards, Rosemary regarded him as an unscrupulous libertine and would never lose her intense dislike. Links with the Trench family however remained strong. Paddy and Terry's father, Wilbraham, had visited Kingswood Hanger in 1926 (recorded in the Visitors' Book). Paddy Trench was also a friend of Francie's sister Lettice, who had married the distinguished Cambridge mathematician Frank Ramsey. Rosemary, who continued to mix socially with Lettice but distrusted her ethos of open marriage, was convinced that Robert was having an affair with her during this period, an allegation she repeated many times to Deirdre in later years.

15 Chalmers (Terry) Trench, p24.

16 It has not proved possible to confirm from publicly available land records that the house was transferred in payment of a gambling debt. It is however highly plausible, since this was the story told on both sides of the family and Robert and Rosemary received no proceeds for the house they lost.

Notes

17   This and other quotations from Robert in this chapter are from the letter written in October 1930 to Louis Reynolds, Rosemary's uncle, passed to his son Christopher Reynolds, who gave it to my mother in 1972.

18   These words are written in Rose's Visitors' Book.

CHAPTER 12

1   *The Irish Times*, 26 November 1930.

2   *The Irish Times*, 27 January 1931.

3   *The Irish Times*, 11 February 1931.

4   *TCD*, 9 February 1931.

5   *TCD*, 4 December 1930.

6   *The Irish Times*, 24 February 1931.

7   See Chapter 2.

8   *The Irish Times*, 1 December 1930.

9   *The Irish Independent*, 29 May 1931, p31.

10   *The Irish Times*, 29 May 1931. This victory allowed him to represent Trinity at the Intervarsity championships, but his name doesn't appear in the coverage in *The Irish Times* on 5 June. This was probably when he was in Surrey.

11   DHM.

12   *The Irish Times*, 21 September 1931.

13   *TCD*, 29 October 1931. The verse parodies 'Tis the Voice of the Sluggard' by Isaac Watts, already famously parodied by Lewis Carroll.

14   Samuel Beckett's 1980 interview with Maeve Binchy in *The Irish Times*, recalled here: *www.irishtimes.com/culture/stage/when-beckett-met-binchy-1.54140*

15   Smyllie amused his peers by improvising obscene lyrics to well-known tunes – see Fleming, p122.

16   As detailed in a later chapter, in 1935 Beckett would mention Robert in a letter to McGreevy, in terms which make clear that Robert was well-known to both of them.

17   Andrée Sheehy-Skeffington: *Skeff: The Life of Owen Sheehy Skeffington 1909–1970*, The Lilliput Press, Dublin, 1991, p83. Owen Sheehy-Skeffington's mother Hanna had stayed with Rosemary's friend Muriel Lester in London – see Chapter 7.

18   Not the bantamweight title, as mistakenly reported in *TCD* on 5 November 1931.

19   *The Irish Independent*, 31 May 1931.

20   *TCD*, 26 November 1931.

21   Denis Carroll, p252, quoting *TCD*.

CHAPTER 13

1   *The Liberator* (Tralee), 29 December 1931

2   *TCD*, 11 February 1932.

3   Fearghal McGarry, *Irish Politics and the Spanish Civil War*, Cork University Press, 1999, p5.

Notes

4 Kieran Allen, *Fianna Fáil and Irish Labour 1926 to the Present*, Pluto Press, London, 1997, p15.

5 Allen, p120

6 Kieran Allen, *Fianna Fáil and Irish Labour – 1926 to the Present*, p26.

7 Donal McAnallen *Rev R M Hilliard and the Trinity Hurlers* – reprinted on *irelandscw. com/docs-hilliardGAA.htm*. Donal McAnallen has told me he now believes some of the accounts given to him and included in this article cannot be reliably verified; for example, the story that government detectives in trench coats and hats were scrutinising Hilliard's movements from the sidelines of a hurling match. I am most grateful to him for a discussion of this article by phone. The article also quotes from a piece by 'Mutius' in *An Phoblacht*, the Sinn Féin newspaper, denouncing Hilliard as a 'West Briton'. I have not succeeded (despite best efforts) in tracing this article, but it hardly needs saying that 'Mutius' was misinformed, as Hilliard was a republican and anti-imperialist all his adult life.

8 TCD, 11 February 1932.

9 This motion was debated by the Historical Society on 18 May 1932.

10 *TCD*, 12 May 1932

11 Quoted in Denis Carroll: *Unusual Suspects*, p252.

12 Deirdre still holds his ornate certificate of membership.

13 DHM.

14 DHM.

15 These limericks in Robert's handwriting were found among Rosemary's papers after her death.

16 *Cigarettes, cleric, characters and cards*, Lisburn.com (online local history site)

17 Seán Mitchell, *Struggle or Starve – Working class Unity in Belfast's 1932 Outdoor Relief Riots*, Haymarket Books, Chicago, 2017, p60.

18 Mitchell, p62.

19 Mitchell, p71.

20 John Nicholson, eyewitness and participant in the protests, quoted in Munck and Rolston, *Belfast in the Thirties, an Oral History*, St Martin's Press Inc., New York, 1987, p162.

21 'Rarely had Belfast witnessed such a gathering of people … It was impossible to move …' *The Irish News*, 4 October 1932, quoted in Mitchell, p73.

22 Mitchell discusses these plans at pp80, 88, 90 and elsewhere.

23 John Mahon, *Harry Pollitt, A Biography*, Lawrence and Wishart, London, 1976, p183. The term 'deported' seems out of place when Northern Ireland was nominally part of the UK.

24 Seán Mitchell, p113, outlines the terms of the deal and on pp115–116 discusses the pros and cons to be considered before accepting it.

25 I have found no evidence that Robert took any active part in the Outdoor Relief protests.

26 His new appointment was announced in the *Belfast Telegraph* on 3 January 1933.

Notes

27　On 28 February the Hilliard shop in Killarney was burned to the ground. John Hilliard had taken over much of Robert senior's share of the business many years earlier. This fire is not known to have affected Robert's branch of the family financially but may well have made a further call on Alice's energies and attention.

28　*Casti Cunnubii*, Papal Encyclical, 1930.

CHAPTER 14

1　The *News Letter* published notices that Hilliard would preach on – among other dates – 4 March, 10 April and 7 October in 1933 and 10 February and 18 August 1934. Composers of the music sung by the Cathedral choir included Byrd, Tye, Stainer and Tchaikovsky.

2　Carroll, p253.

3　Kingswood Hanger Visitors' Book.

4　According to the Registry of Deeds in Dublin, Alice purchased indentures of a 499–year lease running from 29 September 1905 subject to rent of £6 10s. In August 1935, after Robert had left for England, she assigned her interest to Moll, Phyl, Marjorie and Geoff, that is to say all her children except Robert.

5　All quotations from Deirdre in this chapter are from DHM.

6　Mitchell, p127.

7　Mitchell pp129–31.

8　Cardinal Tomás Ó Fiaich Memorial Library and Archive, Cardinal MacRory papers, Box 2, Folder 2, *Report on the Spread of Communism in Ireland*, 1931, quoted in Barry McLoughlin and Emmet O'Connor, *In Spanish Trenches*, University College Dublin Press, 2020, p9.

9　It would have been extremely difficult for a man in Robert's position to join this party. Even if he wanted to join it, his concern for keeping his job would almost certainly prevent him.

10　John Mahon, *Harry Pollitt, A Biography*, Lawrence and Wishart, London, 1976, pp183–4.

11　Maurice Manning, *The Blueshirts*, Gill and Macmillan, Dublin, pp52–7.

12　Manning, pp82–3.

13　Manning pp121–22.

14　Opposition to fascism was also growing in the Irish labour movement. The Irish TUC described Fine Gael propaganda as '*a facsimile of the ideology of the fascist dictators on the continent*', and on 6 May 1934 an impressive Irish TUC-organized march, 10,000 strong, demonstrated against the Blueshirts in Dublin. See Kieran Allen, *Fianna Fáil and Irish Labour 1926 to the Present*, p53.

15　*Belfast Telegraph*, 13 January 1934.

16　Another family story from this wedding is that Robert reinserted the word 'obey' into Moll's marriage vows, after she had left it out, and that she corrected him mid-ceremony. However the *Belfast Telegraph* report makes clear that the Dean of Ardfert was officiating and he presumably administered the vows. If so this story is unlikely to be accurate.

Notes

17 Seán Murray, the RWG's General Secretary, was reported by British intelligence as suggesting to Moscow in 1932 that Communists in Ireland should weaken their antagonists' arguments by appealing to the Bible – see McLoughlin and O'Connor, p18.

18 Garth Lean, *Frank Buchman – A Life*, Fount Paperbacks, London, 1988, pp207–8. Lean gives a detailed account of Buchman's efforts to make links with Hitler. Lean is here quoting Garrett Stearly, a young Oxford Group member who accompanied Buchman on a visit to Germany in the summer of 1932 and later gave an account of Buchman's comments and reactions. Hitler, of course, had no intention of allowing anyone other than himself to control the German fascist movement and always regarded Buchman with suspicion.

19 Richard J Evans, *The Coming of the Third Reich*, Penguin, 2004, pp380–81.

20 A sign of how far to the right the Oxford Group might in different circumstances have pulled Robert, and of how uncomfortable he felt about it, had come as early as 24 February 1932, when he had opposed a motion 'that Racial Differences should not be a bar to marriage'. TCD reports him as arguing that 'European civilisation would have lacked many of its characteristics had not the Jews been so jealous to preserve their racial purity.' It's hard to discern from this paraphrase exactly what he meant, but such sweeping, stereotypical vocabulary strikes a deeply disturbing note. Buchmanism was happy to accommodate to the antisemitism of the wealthy, powerful figures with whom its founder liked to curry favour (in 1932, for example, Buchman was pursuing an active friendship with car-mogul Henry Ford, whose antisemitic conspiracy theories he never condemned). It seems that Robert sensed his loyalty to his mentor was in danger of leading him to a dark place and the TCD report makes clear his visible discomfort: 'Mr Hilliard's bright, airy playfulness was not so much in evidence as usual, nor his wit, nor the charming qualities which have so endeared him to the Society. Indeed, he spoke haltingly and for a short time.' As far as I can discover, he was never recorded as using this kind of language again. By this time he was expressing support for Fianna Fáil; during 1933 his rejection of Buchmanism and all its insidious trappings became ever more evident and by the end of 1934 he was on the verge of becoming an active communist and anti-fascist.

21 Lean, p178.

22 DHM.

23 The *News Letter* 7 April 1934.

24 Payments didn't always arrive on time and the June payment that year was delayed until August. My thanks to Jean Barber, archivist at St Anne's Cathedral, Belfast, for researching every payment Robert received. Besides his stipend, he was occasionally reimbursed a few shillings and pence for expenses. Fees for weddings and baptisms would be paid to him direct by the relevant parishioners.

25 Very large numbers of working-class people used to queue up to wed on bank holidays because these were the only days they were guaranteed time off work. Statutory holidays on Easter Monday, Whit Monday (the first Monday in August), and Boxing Day had been introduced by the Bank Holidays Act of 1871. The tradition of bank

Notes

holiday weddings did not end until well into the twentieth century, when trade union campaigns at last ensured that more time off became the norm. It is reflected in, for example, Philip Larkin's well-known poem *The Whitsun Weddings*, inspired by seeing crowds of working-class newlyweds on a train platform in 1955.

26 Again my thanks to Jean Barber for tallying these ceremonies.

27 Rosemary told Deirdre many years later that Robert was having an affair during this holiday. There is no way to know whether this was confirmed fact or mere suspicion.

28 Deirdre heard the story of the Dean's refusal many times from Rosemary.

29 Robert is on record as officiating at weddings in January. In February he received reimbursements for kindergarten expenses. He is listed in the Cathedral magazine as one of its clergy until March 1935. In April his name is dropped and a new appointment, Rev G.F. Craig, appears.

CHAPTER 15

1 Samuel Beckett, *Murphy*, Faber and Faber, London, 2009, p12. Reproduced by permission of Faber and Faber, London.

2 See Chapter 6.

3 Trench had married Rosemary's cousin Francie Baker in Dublin in 1926 but soon left her, moving to London with his second wife, Eve Hayden. After a year-long liaison with the artist Barbara Nicholson, with whom he had a child, he settled in 1930 with Eve in Hampshire, where his father bought him a house. The 1935 electoral roll shows him and Eve living at 11b Sinclair Road, Hammersmith.

4 Rosemary disapproved strongly of Trench's morals. My mother believes any mention of Trench in Robert's letters would have contributed to her wish to destroy them.

5 Chalmers (Terry) Trench, p124.

6 Edited by George Craig, Martha Dow Fehsenfeld, Dan Gunn, Lois More Overbeck, *The Letters of Samuel Beckett*, Cambridge University Press, 2016, Letter to Thomas McGreevy of 22 September 1935, Volume I, p279.

7 For example, a physiotherapist, a civil servant, a political organizer and lecturer.

8 Trench is shown as living there in the 1936 Electoral Register.

9 Chalmers (Terry) Trench, p24. Terry Trench's memoir speaks of meeting Robert only once, in 1929, so this 'badly wrong' comment must have come from Paddy.

10 No mention of Robert Hilliard going bankrupt appears in the court records held by the Public Records Office of Northern Ireland (PRONI), or the local press. My thanks to staff at PRONI for checking their records to establish this.

11 His Communist Party membership stamps show he paid the rate for unemployed members for twenty-seven weeks. His severe weight loss, ragged clothing and poor health when Rosemary and the children next saw him (see next chapter) attest to his poverty at this time.

12 See Chapter 11 for an account of Rosemary's destruction of Robert's letters.

13 Breda Joy, *Hidden Kerry, the Keys to the Kingdom*, Mercier Press, Cork, 2014, p225. Joy learned of this encounter from an interview with Moll.

Notes

14 All quotations from Deirdre in this chapter, unless otherwise attributed, are from DHM.
15 Deirdre later transcribed the story and included it in its entirety in DHM.
16 Jason Gurney, *Crusade in Spain*, Faber and Faber, London, 1976, p34.
17 Gurney, p20.
18 Paddy Trench later became a prominent Trotskyist in Ireland – see Chalmers (Terry) Trench, Chapter XII.
19 Gurney, p23.
20 Communist Party of Great Britain pamphlet, *Sixteen Bob a Day for Dockers – Abolish Casual Labour*, People's History Museum, Manchester, CP/LON/CIRC/02/05
21 Letter from Rosemary dated 16 August. This letter was written over a year after Robert had left, and was found in his wallet.
22 Joe Jacobs, *Out of the Ghetto*, Phoenix Press, London, 1978, p148.
23 Fred Copeman, *Reason in Revolt*, Blandford Press, London, 1948, p59.
24 Jacobs, pp165–6.
25 Copeman, p69.
26 Gurney, p61.

CHAPTER 16

1 See Paul Preston, *The Spanish Civil War: Reaction, Revolution and Revenge*, Harper Perennial, London, 2006, p68.
2 Georgi Dimitrov, *The Fascist Offensive and the Tasks of the Communist International in the Struggle of the Working Class against Fascism*, Main Report delivered at the Seventh World Congress of the Communist International, delivered 2 August 1935, Source: *Georgi Dimitrov, Selected Works* Sofia Press, Sofia, Volume 2, 1972, available online at: *www.marxists.org › history › comintern › 7th-congress*
3 The 'united front' had emerged as a key tactic at the Fourth Congress of the Communist International in 1922: 'The united front tactic is an initiative for united struggle of the Communists with all workers who belong to other parties and groups, with all unaligned workers, to defend the most basic vital interests of the working class against the bourgeoisie. Every struggle for the most limited immediate demand is a source of revolutionary education, for it is the experiences of struggle that will convince working people of the inevitability of revolution and the significance of communism.' – extract from *Fourth Congress of the Communist International – Resolutions 1922, On the Tactics of the Comintern,* translated by John Riddell, published in *Toward the United Front: Proceedings of the Fourth Congress of the Communist International, 1922* (https://www. haymarketbooks.org/books/897-to-the-masses), pp. 1149–1163, and reprinted online at *www.marxists.org › history › international › tactics-of-..*
4 E.H. Carr, *The Twilight of the Comintern 1930–1935*, Pantheon Books, New York, 1982, p426. All references hereafter to EH Carr are to this book unless otherwise stated.

269

Notes

5   See Chapter 7 of Joe Jacobs, *Out of the Ghetto*, Phoenix Press, London, 1978 for a thoughtful first-hand account of this change in the line and its effect on party work in London.

6   Stalin's Five-Year Plan could not be achieved without increasing the rate of exploitation of Russian labour. George Orwell would later satirize the extreme work ethic embodied in Stakhanovism by creating Boxer, the loyal horse in *Animal Farm*, whose heart-rending motto is 'I must work harder'. Boxer works himself to the point of collapse. Napoleon the pig, a satirical portrayal of Stalin, then sends him to the knacker's yard without a qualm.

7   Jacobs, p184. This development in CP policy is reflected in, for example, the *Resolution of the LDC Annual Congress of the Communist Party*, in CP/LON/CIRC/02/05, Manchester People's History Museum.

8   Initially the stamps in Robert's party card are marked 'Reduced fee' because he was unemployed, but at the end of October, he began using orange stamps with no 'Reduced fee' marking. Throughout both periods, a brown stamp marked 'International levy' every three months recorded the sub he paid for party work abroad.

9   Literally "Anschluss" means "connection"; in practice it meant German annexation of Austria. Hitler's push to control Eastern Europe, or "Drang nach Osten", had been a goal of German nationalists since the previous century.

10   Labour made a net gain of 100 seats but the National Government, of which National Labour was still part, was returned to power.

11   The National Archives, Kew, '*List of persons who fought in Spain, 1936–1939: H*', Catalogue reference KV 5/112/8. Interestingly, Robert is shown as 'Robert M Hilliard @ H. Roberts'. 'H Roberts' is a reversal of 'Robert H' and may have been a pen name or alias. Some family members have suggested he wrote for the *Daily Worker* at this time but I have not succeeded in finding any articles in that paper under either surname.

12   Excerpt from Samuel Beckett's letter of 9 July 1935 by kind permission of the Estate of Samuel Beckett, c/o Rosica Colin Limited, London. Permission also kindly granted by the Harry Ransom Center, The University of Texas at Austin. My thanks to Lois Overbeck, Director of the *Letters of Samuel Beckett Project* at Emory University, for drawing my attention to the presence of this letter in the Arland Ussher collection, Harry Ransom Research Center, University of Texas.

13   Ed. Craig, Dow Fehsenfeld, Gunn, Overbeck, p279. It was in this letter that Beckett had speculated, incorrectly, that Robert was staying with Paddy Trench.

14   Unless otherwise stated, all quotations from Deirdre and information about Rosemary and the children in this chapter are from DHM.

15   They did not see their father in London and Rosemary may never even have realized that they had formed hopes of doing so. To this day, Deirdre speaks of their disappointment with great sadness.

16   Robert's name disappeared off the electoral register after he moved. Though he kept some of Rosemary's letters, he didn't keep their envelopes, so there's no way of knowing his new address, apart from the postcode SW3 referenced in his secret service file note, which indicates he was still in Chelsea.

Notes

17 The parties forming the Popular Front were the Spanish Socialist Workers' Party (PSOE) and two republican parties, one headed by Manuel Azaña, Spain's new president, as well as the Spanish Communist Party (PCE) and POUM, the Marxist Workers' Unity Party. The Popular Front was supported by the millions-strong anarchist CNT union (see note below) and the rather smaller UGT union (see note below), which was affiliated to PSOE. The PCE had been a small organization for years – less than a thousand members in 1931 – and at that stage had little support in Catalonia, Spain's most industrialized region. POUM had been formed in 1935 by breakaway Catalan communists and stood well to the left of the PCE. It rejected the idea of allying with bourgeois interests but was prepared to enter the Popular Front for electoral purposes. PSOE was itself split between two leaders, Largo Caballero and the moderate Indalecio Prieto, effectively functioning as two almost separate parties.

18 Partido Communista de España.

19 Partido Obrero de Unificación Marxista.

20 Confederación Nacional del Trabajo or National Confederation of Labour.

21 In Catalonia the CNT union had two million members and the UGT union had a million – see E.H. Carr, *The Twilight of the Comintern*, p290.

22 Unión General de Trabajadores or General Union of Workers.

23 E.H. Carr, *The Comintern and the Spanish Civil War*, Macmillan, London, 1984, p8.

24 Adherents of Carlism, for example, which demanded the reinstatement of a king, with succession from a different branch of the Bourbon dynasty.

25 One key player who refused to acknowledge the danger was Spain's prime minister, Santiago Casares y Quiroga, who, for example, 'shrugged off Prieto's [Indalecio Prieto, one of the leaders of the PSOE] warnings with the offensive comment "I will not tolerate your menopausal outbursts'" - Preston, p92. The government's refusal to heed warnings about the plotters made their task easier. See Preston, pp94–95.

CHAPTER 17

1 The Army of Africa was largely composed of indigenous North African troops commanded by Spanish career officers.

2 Hugh Thomas, *The Spanish Civil War*, Penguin Books, first published 1961, 1984 edition, p220–21.

3 A better word might have been 'enabling'.

4 Thomas, p220.

5 Browne was killed in August while taking part in an attempt to blow up a Francoist munitions train on the Aragon Front.

6 Quoted in Richard Baxell, *Unlikely Warriors*, Aurum Press, London, 2012, p83.

7 Chalmers (Terry) Trench, p126. Terry Trench believes his brother sent articles to ILP publications but because they were published anonymously or pseudonymously he could not identify them. Paddy Trench was invalided out of Spain in December 1936, after hospitalization with tuberculosis, which at times made him extremely poorly. He would have arrived back in England soon after Robert left.

Notes

8 In 1935, after Robert's departure for London, Fleming had delighted his goddaughter Deirdre by sending her a clock with a Mickey Mouse face.

9 Lionel Fleming, *Head or Harp*, pp169–70.

10 This threat was instigated by John Charles McQuaid, president of Blackrock College, as recorded in John Cooney, *John Charles McQuaid: Ruler of Catholic Ireland*, Dublin 1999, pp90–2, and cited in Barry McLoughlin and Emmet O'Connor, *In Spanish Trenches*, p11.

11 Helen Graham, *The Spanish Civil War, A Very Short Introduction*, Oxford University Press, 2005, p40.

12 A living, breathing Spanish revolution would have presented an unwelcome contrast with the tyrannies of Stalin's counter-revolution in Russia.

13 Felix Morrow, writing in 1937, tells us that: 'Delegations of Arabs and Moors came to the government, pleading for a decree [granting Moroccan independence]. The government would not budge. The redoubtable Abd-el-Krim [leader of the Riffian rebellion in North Africa during the 1920s against Spanish and French imperialist domination], exiled by France, sent a plea to Caballero to intervene with Blum [Prime Minister of France] so that he might be permitted to return to Morocco to lead an insurrection against Franco. Caballero would not ask, and Blum would not grant. To rouse Spanish Morocco might endanger imperialist domination throughout Africa.' See Felix Morrow, *Revolution and Counter-Revolution in Spain, (including The Civil War in Spain)*, Pathfinder, New York, 2023, p177.

14 On 7 October the Soviet delegate at the Non-Intervention Committee declared that 'unless violations of the non-intervention agreement are stopped at once [the Soviet government] will consider itself free from the obligations flowing from the agreement'. *Dokumenty Vneshnei Politiki SSSR*, xix (1974), 464, quoted in E H Carr, *The Comintern and the Spanish Civil War*, p25.

15 Richard Baxell, *Unlikely Warriors*, Aurum Press, London, 2012, p63.

16 At the same time as the launching of the International Brigades during late summer and autumn, the Comintern was instrumental in the government's cementing of control from the top down, for example by ending the independence of the militias, which were to be integrated with the newly created Popular Army. Morrow, pp98–103.

17 For a discussion of the 'divisive and controversial' nature of this decision to move the seat of government, the panic and chaos it left behind and the defeatism of the leaders who instigated it, see Preston, pp164–169.

18 'The gold was shipped from Cartagena on October 25, reached Odessa on November 6 and was safely deposited in the vaults in Moscow. The transaction was planned and carried out by Largo Caballero and the finance minister, Negrín, without – so far as the wisdom goes – any initiative from Moscow. Nobody suggested that it was in any way a counterpart of Soviet aid to Spain.' E.H. Carr, *The Comintern and the Spanish Civil War*, Macmillan, 1984, p26.

19 Preston, p150.

20 E.H. Carr, *The Comintern and the Spanish Civil War*, p28. In Paul Preston's words, Stalin was 'less concerned about the fate of the Spanish people than that

Notes

his cooperation with the democracies in the fight against Fascism should be sealed by an ostentatious Soviet readiness to keep social revolution in check.' Preston, p151.

21 Antony Beevor, *The Battle for Spain*, Weidenfeld and Nicholson, London, 2006, p109.

22 Gurney, p51.

23 All quotations in this and the foregoing paragraphs are from a letter to Robert written by Rosemary in September 1936, found among Rosemary's papers.

24 Trotsky had also challenged these doctrines and was exiled in 1929.

25 Gurney, *Crusade in Spain*, Faber and Faber London, 1974, p23.

26 Joe Jacobs, *Out of the Ghetto*, Phoenix Press, London, 1978, p148.

27 Gurney, p29

28 Jacobs, p145. Anti-fascist protests were not always big enough to forestall fascist and police violence; for example, in July 1935 a Communist Party-led counter-rally in Victoria Park Square, where Blackshirts mobilized on a regular basis, was viciously attacked by Blackshirts and police, with many arrests – Jacobs, p174.

29 See Jacobs, p237, which quotes in full the instructions printed in the *Daily Worker* of 30 September to go to Trafalgar Square on the afternoon of 4 October rather than East London, with an account of Jacobs's appalled reaction. The People's History Museum, Manchester, has an original of the CPGB leaflet advertizing the Trafalgar Square rally, which was to be followed by a belated march to the East End 'in opposition to the four meetings where Mosley will speak'. Printed crossways over this leaflet is the call the party was forced to make at the last minute: 'ALTERATION! RALLY ALDGATE 2pm.' Evidently the Party leadership bowed to the inevitable when it became clear that many members were about to vote with their feet.

30 These figures are estimates. Accounts of many Cable Street events are not clear cut or uncontested – see Tony Kushner, '*Long May its Memory Live!*', essay in *Remembering Cable Street*, ed. Kushner and Valman, Vallentine Mitchell, London, 2000.

31 Speech by Pat Devine at a Communist mass meeting in Hoxton Square on 4 October, 1936, quoted in Tony Kushner, '*Long May its Memory Live*', p119.

32 Baxell gives details of this process in *British Volunteers in the Spanish Civil War, The British Battalion in the International Brigades, 1936–1939*, Warren & Pell, Pontypool, 2007, p15.

33 Gurney, p38.

34 His arrival in Dunkirk is date-stamped on his passport.

CHAPTER 18

1 The Maison des Syndicats at 33 Rue de la Grange-aux-Belles had an annexe at 8 Avenue Mathurin-Moreau, and the two addresses are sometimes confused or conflated. Volunteers arriving at the Maison des Syndicats would receive a brief medical examination and their credentials would be checked before they were sent

Notes

off to catch the train to Perpignan. My thanks to Peter Verburgh for sending me this information.

2   Confédération Générale du Travail, or General Confederation of Labour.

3   Gurney, p41.

4   This postcard was found among Rosemary's papers.

5   Gurney, p42.

6   Tony Hyndman, eyewitness account in *The Distant Drum*, edited Philp Toynbee, Sidgwick and Jackson, London 1976, p123.

7   *TCD*, 27 May 1937, p175. We do not know how Robert managed to get this letter to England, but we do know it must somehow, eventually, have been brought to Rosemary. Andrée Sheehy-Skeffington states in her memoir of her husband Owen that the widow of 'R.M. Hilliard' 'sent Owen his last [*sic*] letter,' and goes on to give an accurate description of part of this letter's contents. As we know, this letter was not, chronologically, the last missive Robert sent to Rosemary. However, given her manifest desperation to hear any news of him between December 1936 and March 1937, and given also that it wasn't published until May 1937, it seems safe to assume it did not reach her until after she had heard of his death and had received his final postcard. See Andrée Sheehy-Skeffington, *Skeff – A Life of Owen Sheehy Skeffington 1909–1970*, The Lilliput Press, Dublin 1991, p83. The letter itself speaks of its being '*read in England*', which suggests Robert may have hoped the Communist Party would publish it, but by early 1937 the letter's discussion of Brigade discipline and authority and high praise for Wilfred McCartney would not have been welcomed in Communist Party publications, if indeed Rosemary ever offered it to them. Rosemary had long looked to Muriel Lester for advice about political matters. It's reasonable to conjecture that she consulted her on this occasion, and that Lester, a long-standing friend of Owen Sheehy Skeffington's mother Hannah, suggested sending the letter to him. A long excerpt eventually appeared in *TCD* in Dublin, over three months after Robert's death, with this explanation: 'We are fortunate in being able to print an extract from a letter written from Spain by the Rev. R M Hilliard (some-time editor of TCD). We regret to record that he has since been killed while fighting with the International Brigades.' Sadly, the contents of the unpublished parts of this letter are not known.

8   *TCD*, 27 May 1937.

9   George Orwell, *Homage to Catalonia*, Penguin Books in association with Martin Secker and Warburg Ltd, London, 2000, pp2–3.

10 Gurney, p52.

11 Gurney, p49.

12 *TCD*, 27 May 1937.

13 Gurney, p47.

14 Gurney, p47.

15 *TCD*, 27 May 1937.

Notes

16 Henry Buckley, *The Life and Death of the Spanish Republic, A Witness to the Spanish Civil War*, IB Tauris, London and New York, 2014 edition, p262.

17 Hugh Thomas, *The Spanish Civil War*, Penguin, London, 1990, p497.

18 Gurney, pp54–6.

19 Gurney, p55

20 See, for example, John Lochore's memoir anthologized in *Voices from War*, ed. Ian McDougall, The Mercat Press, Edinburgh, 1995, p116 and pp129–30.

21 Gurney, p56.

22 All quotations from Deirdre or information about Rosemary and the children in this chapter are from DHM unless otherwise stated.

23 According to Tom Wintringham the battalion was formed on this date. Tom Wintringham, *English Captain*, Faber and Faber, London, 1939, p40.

24 Richard Baxell cites, for example, Cyprus, South Africa and Australia in *Three Months in Spain*, a Len Crome lecture anthologized in *Looking Back at the Spanish Civil War*, edited by Jim Jump, Lawrence and Wishart, London 2010, p67.

25 Vincent Brome, *International Brigades*, Morrow, London, 1965, p17, cited in Fearghal McGarry, *Irish Politics and the Spanish Civil War*, Cork University Press, 1999, p74. McGarry also cites R Dan Richardson, *Comintern Army*.

26 Tom Wintringham, *English Captain*, Faber and Faber, London, 1939, p43: 'Springhall can size up a man in much less time than the rest of us ...'

27 National Unemployed Workers' Movement – see Chapter 16.

28 Gurney, p59.

29 Fred Thomas, *To Tilt at Windmills*, Michigan State University Press, East Lansing, 1996, p19.

30 Thomas, p19.

31 Gurney, p58.

32 Thomas, p19.

33 John Lochore, untitled essay anthologized in *Voices from War, Personal recollections of war in our century by Scottish men and women*, edited by Ian MacDougall, Mercat Press, 1995, p118.

34 Wintringham gives an account of an entertainment in the cinema while the 12th Battalion was stationed there, with a film and naked or semi-naked dancers; this was however before Robert Hilliard arrived. Wintringham, pp33–4.

35 Gurney, p65.

36 I was told this story when I visited the town in 2017. It's also recounted in Graham Davies, *You Are Legend, The Welsh Volunteers in the Spanish Civil War*, Welsh Academic Press, Cardiff, p46. A similar scene in which the village priest is executed after shooting at villagers appears in Ken Loach's film *Land and Freedom*. Attacks on churches, the killing of priests and friars, the desecration of nuns' graves and other such acts were political rather than anti-religious, a response to the active support given by the Catholic Church in Spain to the Francoist cause. As Paul Preston writes: 'With the exception of the Basque clergy, most Spanish priests and religious sided with the Nationalists. They

Notes

denounced the 'reds' from their pulpits. They blessed the flags of Nationalist regiments and some – especially Navarrese priests – even fought in their ranks. Clerics took up the fascist salute. As early as mid-August 1936, Bishop Marcelino Olaechea Loizago of Pamplona had already denounced the Republicans as "the enemies of God and Spain". After further examples, Preston goes on: 'The Jesuit provincial of León wrote to Rome on 1 September to warn against any peace initiatives by the Vatican: "Catholics see this war as a veritable religious crusade against atheism … Either it is won or Catholicism will disappear from Spain." ' The Spanish Catholic Church was a profoundly conservative institution which had for centuries opposed social change or any challenge to Spain's oppressive power structure. Because of this, attacks on churches and clerics were a feature of popular uprisings in Spain from the early nineteenth century onwards.

37 Wintringham, p47.
38 Gurney, p69.
39 Gurney, p71.
40 Lochore, p120. Lochore became attached enough to Robert to describe him as 'dear Hilliard' after his death.
41 Gurney, p69.
42 *TCD: A College Miscellany* – May 27th 1937, p175.
43 Wintringham, p26.
44 Wintringham, p42.
45 Wintringham, pp51–2.
46 Gurney, p61.
47 Kerrigan to Pollitt, Marx Memorial Library papers Box c 9/9, quoted in James K Hopkins, *Into the Heart of the Fire, The British in the Spanish Civil War*, Stanford University Press, 1998, p169.
48 Macartney had served a prison sentence for disclosing military secrets to Russia. As a condition of his release, he had to appear before the legal authorities at a particular date. The plan had been that he would do this and then return to his command in Spain.
49 Some accounts say it was the Black and Tans.
50 Fearghal McGarry, *Irish Politics and the Spanish Civil War*, Cork University Press, 1999, p65.
51 Spanish Civil War file, Irish Labour History Archives, quoted in Michael O'Riordan, *Connolly Column, The Story of the Irishmen who fought for the Spanish Republic*, New Books Publications, Dublin, 1979, p68.

CHAPTER 19

1 Gurney, p76.
2 When I visited Madrigueras in 2017 an elderly gentleman told me how vividly he remembered being carried as a toddler on the shoulders of the Brigaders when they walked up to practise at this range.

3   Wintringham, pp32–3, a passage notable among other things, as an example of Wintringham's casual stereotyping of this young man, who was Jewish: 'This plausible, sharp young Jew ... The good Jew's ability to endure the unendurable ...'
4   This plan was never realized and the Brigades remained a distinct body until 1939.
5   Wintringham, p46.
6   Wintringham, p46.
7   Wintringham, p47.
8   Gurney, pp64–5.
9   The suppression practised by the Comintern eventually undermined even the facade of democratic discussion. It is summed up in a memorably blunt passage in *The Spanish Cockpit*, by Franz Borkenau, written in 1937 following his second visit to Spain in January-February of that year. Borkenau, who had once worked for the Comintern himself, was appalled by the Communists' censorship of a press interview with moderate Socialist Defence Minister Indalecio Prieto, who had stated that the Spanish Popular Front government was Spain's last bulwark against 'Bolshevism' (meaning social revolution). Borkenau comments: 'The communists, less candid than Prieto, do not admit what is the notorious truth, namely that there is all the difference in the world between their policy in 1917 in Russia and their policy in 1937 in Spain; that they have ceased to be a revolutionary party and become one of the mainstays of the anti-revolutionary forces. ... unfortunately ... they prefer ... to deny that there has been a change. The result is that it is at present impossible in Spain to discuss openly even the basic facts of the political situation ... The concealment of the main political facts from the public and the maintenance of this deception by means of censorship and terrorism carries with it far-reaching detrimental effects, which will be felt in the future even more than at present.' Franz Borkenau, *The Spanish Cockpit*, Phoenix Press, London, 2000, p235.
10 Gurney, p144.
11 See Chapter 13.
12 Gurney, p69.
13 This opinion was given by Richard Baxell in an exchange of emails with myself, based on the fact that many of the other Irish volunteers who had not left for the Lincoln Brigade had been placed in this unit.
14 Rosemary's desperation at this point for news, any news, of Robert, and the lengths she went to in her efforts to find out where he was, indicate that the long letter she would send to Owen Sheehy-Skeffington had not yet reached her.
15 This paragraph draws heavily on Gurney's crisp summary of battalion leadership on p88 of *Crusade in Spain*. Details of Aitken's history as a Communist Party member, as recorded by MI5, are held in file KV 2/2492 at the National Archives, Kew.
16 Gurney, p83.
17 Lochore, p121. Lochore is one of several to record the emotional atmosphere among the crowd that gathered as they left.

Notes

CHAPTER 20

1   Anthony Beevor, *The Battle for Spain*, Weidenfeld and Nicolson, London, 2006, p209.

2   The Dimitrov battalion was mostly made up of exiled nationals from Balkan countries such as Greece, Bulgaria and Yugoslavia.

3   Each Brigade comprised infantry with artillery and tank units and its own medical, supply and transport organizations. As already noted, the armaments and materiel supplied were often of inferior quality, and in general the Republican side was very much less well equipped militarily than their adversaries.

4   Gurney, p86 and p88.

5   Gurney, p87.

6   Gurney, p87.

7   Gurney, p112.

8   Gurney, p99.

9   Like many who go there, I noticed the aromatic herbs growing on the site; likewise the blood-like appearance of the burst olives, recalled in the Christy Moore song about this battle, 'Viva la Quinta Brigada': 'Even the olives were bleeding'. Moore's song here quotes Irish socialist poet Charlie Donnelly, who reportedly uttered these words shortly before he was killed on February 27 1937, fighting at Jarama.

10   Gurney, p104.

11   Wintringham, operating without proper maps of the area (according to Gurney, p101), did not know until that morning that the Francoists had crossed the Jarama. Wintringham, p63.

12   Tony Gilbert, quoted in Richard Baxell, *Three Months in Spain*, anthologized in *Looking Back at the Spanish Civil War*, edited Jim Jump, Lawrence and Wishart, London, 2010, p76.

13   Gurney, p77.

14   The dread felt by those fighting on the Republican side was increased by the known brutality of the Army of Africa in its treatment of prisoners of war and of civilians in the areas conquered by the generals, a policy of deliberate terror imposed by the Army of Africa's Spanish officers and implemented under their command.

15   Gurney, p108.

16   Fred Copeman, *Reason in Revolt*, Blandford Press, London, 1948, p93.

17   Baxell, *Three Months in Spain*, essay in *Looking Back at the Spanish Civil War*, ed. Jim Jump, Lawrence & Wishart, London, 2010, p77.

18   Copeman, pp94–5.

19   '... attack followed attack throughout 13 February, as Varela became desperate to achieve his breakthrough.' Anthony Beevor, *The Battle for Spain*, Weidenfeld and Nicolson, London, 2006, p211.

20   Overton survived the battle and was later disciplined. He was killed at Brunete. Jason Gurney felt Overton had been unfairly maligned and that he was a loyal servant of the Republican side who should not have been given responsibilities that were beyond his capability.

Notes

21 Baxell, *Three Months in Spain*, p78.

22 'O.R.', recollections anthologized in *XV International Brigade, Records of British, American, Canadian and Irish Volunteers in Spain 1936–1938*, (first published 1938), 2003 edition, Warren & Pell Publishing, Pontypool, p56. 'O.R.' is thought to be Michael O'Riordan, an Irish volunteer who later wrote his own history of Irish volunteers for the International Brigades, *Connolly Column*.

23 'O.R.', p57.

24 'O.R.', p57.

25 Tom Wintringham, p82.

26 A graphic, detailed account of these three Jarama days under fire, and their aftermath, can be found in Ben Hughes, *They Shall Not Pass! The British Battalion at Jarama – The Spanish Civil War*, Osprey Publishing, Botley, 2011.

27 William Rust, *Britons in Spain*, Lawrence and Wishart, London 1939, p50.

28 'O.R.', p57.

29 Unattributed recollection anthologized in *XV International Brigade, Records of British, American, Canadian and Irish Volunteers in Spain 1936–1938*, Warren & Pell, p63.

30 No other first-hand accounts that I have been able to find support those given here, which is perhaps not surprising given the confusion of battle and the fragmentary, traumatized impressions that it leaves.

31 Imperial War Museum Sound Archive, interview 794, reel 2. My thanks to Richard Baxell for the correct reference for this interview.

32 Rosemary had no formal notification of the nature of Robert's wounds but somehow managed to find out that he was shot in the neck. I heard her mention this several times when speaking of his death. Deirdre believes that Tom Wintringham gave her this information.

33 The medical manager of this unit was Len Crome, a doctor who came to Spain with the Scottish Ambulance Unit. Crome saved innumerable lives during the Spanish Civil War and WWII. His story is told by Paul Preston in *No Soldier*, essay anthologized in *Looking Back at the Spanish Civil War*, pp31–44.

34 Lochore, p125, *Voices from War*, ed. Ian MacDougall, The Mercat Press, Edinburgh, 1995,.

35 Lochore, p126. The news referred to was of Robert's death, and Lochore heard it during his second week at the hospital, only a few days after it occurred. He also claims to have attended Robert's funeral. If he did, Lochore was definitely in Castellón, not Murcia. By his own admission, Lochore's sense of geography was extremely hazy – see later note.

36 Lochore, p125.

37 I have not been able to confirm that any bombing raid took place on this hospital at that date. Although it can reasonably be inferred that John Lochore was there, he does not mention any such raid. Neither Robert's death certificate nor the letter from General Stucker gives a bombing raid as the cause of death. The fact that no such raid

Notes

is mentioned in these sources does not prove that the raid didn't happen, but does make it less likely.

38 Stucker also mentions 'a letter of promotion', but no such letter appears to have reached Rosemary and none therefore now appears among Robert's papers. It's possible that the letter/article which was later printed in TCD, from which I have quoted extensively in these pages, was one of those in the wallet, though given its length and consequent bulk this seems unlikely.

39 The full title of the organization carrying the coffin was the Cuerpo Carabineros y Parque Mobil.

40 The location was disclosed to me by the archivist at the most modern of the three cemeteries in Castellon, as described in the Epilogue to this book.

41 *Voices from War*, ed. Ian MacDougall, p126. Soon after this, Lochore tells of being moved to Benicasim for convalescence, another clue that he was in fact in nearby Castellón rather than the much more distant Murcia. He writes (on the same page) of travelling 'south' from 'Murcia' to Benicasim, a further sign of his geographical confusion. Benicasim is located north of Murcia, not south – indeed, hundreds of kilometres north. Benicasim is also north of Castellón, not south. Benicasim had a convalescent centre to which patients hospitalized in Castellón like John Lochore were sent and it's reasonable to infer that Lochore was one of them. This self-evident confusion about where he was makes his inaccurate reference to 'dear Hilliard in his stony grave in Murcia' (p30) rather less surprising.

42 Lochore, p126.

EPILOGUE

1 Rosemary kept this copy of *the Daily Worker*, along with several others mentioned here, later passing them to my mother. Many of Pollitt's letters, with some of those he received, are held in the People's History Museum, Manchester, at CP/2ND/POLL/02/06. My mother holds the letter from Pollitt to Rosemary which appears in this chapter.

2 This passage is from a short unpublished piece Deirdre wrote about her father in 2004.

3 All quotations from Deirdre in the epilogue are – unless otherwise attributed – from DHM.

4 For example in July 1938 she went to London for a ceremonial 'Service in solemn Commemoration of the Victims of Fascist Aggression in Abyssinia, Spain and China' in St Clement's Church, Barnsbury. All the articles mentioned in this paragraph feature in copies of the *Daily Worker* and *News Chronicle* saved by Rosemary and kept by my mother.

5 Unforgettable eye-witness accounts of the terror imposed by the advancing Francoists are included in the first-hand testimonies collected by Ronald Fraser in his oral history: *Blood of Spain, The Experience of Civil War, 1936–193*, Penguin, Harmondsworth, 1981.

Notes

6 The only exception was the article-style letter published in TCD in May 1937, which she sent on to Owen Sheehy Skeffington.

7 He made me a bird-shaped glazed porcelain whistle when I was a child, painted in grey, black and white, with human-looking eyes, a feather pattern and my name in capital letters. Sadly the uncertain earnings of a potter and artist could not support a family, so he spent most of his life in other jobs.

8 Tim died in 1982.

9 Until her sight became impaired in later life, Deirdre was also a good painter, potter, portraitist and sculptor.

10 My mother understood from Davnet that she was offered the lead female role, which was eventually given to Virginia McKenna.

11 The Cementiri de Sant Josep, the Cementiri Municipal de Almassora, and the Cementiri Nou de Castelló.

12 His name is given as 'Robert Martin'. In Spanish nomenclature, the patronym follows the first name and the mother's name comes last and is sometimes omitted. The clerk making the entry therefore assumed that 'Hilliard' was Robert's mother's name and that 'Martin' was the surname inherited from his father. There is no doubt, however, that the person referred to was Robert Martin Hilliard, since the letter from General Stucker, which refers to this specific burial, could not otherwise have enclosed his personal effects.

13 Historian Guillem Casañ, with whom Alan Warren had kindly put me in touch (Alan is himself a most generous source of information and resources for those researching the Spanish Civil War), met me in Castelló, took time to show me round the old cemetery and gave me much of the information contained in this part of the Epilogue. I am extremely grateful to him.

14 An RTÉ programme screened in Ireland in 2006 showed viewers a different area of the cemetery, incorrectly describing it as the final resting place for Robert's body.

15 The campaign (long resisted by the political right) to excavate the graves of Spain's Civil War dead and those murdered during Franco's rule, is crucial to the task of recovering and honouring their memory and creating a truthful historical record. At the time of writing, for example, a mass grave holding fifty-one people killed by Francoist forces has recently been excavated in Castelló itself and work is underway to identify who they are.

ACKNOWLEDGMENTS

I've relied on the expertise of a great many archivists, librarians and others for access to documents, images and information while researching this book. I'd particularly like to thank Professor Cyril J Smyth, Fellow Emeritus, Trinity College Dublin, Aisling Lockhart and all the staff at Trinity College Dublin's Manuscripts and Archives Research Library, also all the staff at their Department of Early Printed Books and Special Collections, Jean Barber, archivist in the Heritage Team at St Anne's Cathedral, Belfast, Lois Overbeck, Director of the Letters of Samuel Beckett project at Emory University in Atlanta GA, Daniel Breen and Dara McGrath at Cork Public Museum, Eimhin Murgan-Fennessy at the GAA Museum in Croke Park, and the archivists and librarians at the Public Records Office Northern Ireland, The Irish National Archives in Dublin, the Cementeri Nou in Castelló, Kerry County Museum in Tralee, Jersey Archives, The National Archives in Kew, Archives New Zealand, People's History Museum in Manchester, the British Library and Killarney Library. Special thanks are due to those who helped with research in locations that I could not visit during the pandemic.

I'm deeply grateful to Alan Warren, who took me on tours of Madrigueras and Albacete, and to Caridad Serrano Garcia, Ángel Luis Arjona Márquez and a host of others in these two places and elsewhere who keep alive the

Acknowledgments

memory of resistance to Franco and of the International Brigades. Also to historian Guillem Casañ, for showing me the hospital and cemetery in Castelló and for researching and discussing with me Robert Hilliard's hospitalisation and burial.

Historian Alice St Leger, chronicler of Cork Grammar School and its successor schools, provided material relating to Robert Hilliard, while Liam Wegimont, Head of Mount Temple School, Dublin, welcomed me to the school and allowed access to its records. I'd like to thank them both, also Adrian Landen, Head of Ashton School, Cork, for permission to quote material and include images from the school's records.

Thanks, too, to Jimmy Clark for an afternoon of fascinating insights into the world of amateur boxing, and to labour historian Francis Devine, historian Brian Trench and GAA historian Donal McAnallen, each of whom supplied information no-one else could have given.

Thank you to my sister Jenny van Tinteren, who dug out and sent family records and photos as well as material relating to British colonial rule in Nyasaland (now Malawi).

Hilliard family members have contributed a wealth of information, photos, documents, encouragement and advice. Sadly Stephen Hilliard, Robin Hilliard, Richard Hilliard, Marlyn Hilliard in West Cork and Barbara Hall are no longer with us, but I remain deeply grateful to them. Thanks too to Martin Hilliard, Ken and Roberta Shellard, Alison Dunlop and Adrian Hilliard. Without the generous hospitality over many years of Marlyn and Martin Hilliard, Robert and Denise Hilliard and Roberta and Ken Shellard in Dublin, and Billy and the late Marlyn Hilliard in West Cork, staying in Ireland and researching this book would not have been possible. Warm thanks, too, to the late John Molyneux and to Mary Smith, who also generously put me up in Dublin while I carried out research.

Many individuals have read parts or the whole of this book and given valuable feedback and advice about necessary amendments or further sources. In particular I'd like to thank John Newsinger, John Borgonovo, Eugene Byrne, Martin Jenkins, Richard Baxell, Helen Graham, Lara Feigel, Ronnie Hess, John Keon, Mike Venner, Jane Creagh, Anita Cornwell and

Acknowledgments

Hilary Shaw. Eloy Bandin translated the newspaper article recording Hilliard's funeral. Edmund Gordon and the other Biographers' Club judges spurred me on in 2017 by shortlisting this book while still a work in progress for the Tony Lothian Prize. Sue Swingler, Rachel Bentham and Sarah Duncan, fellow members of a Bath Spa alumni writers' group that has lasted 25 years, have read and commented on successive drafts with endless patience. To the many others who have listened and helped, it was always appreciated.

At The Lilliput Press I received excellent support from Stephen Reid, Liam Maguire, Antony Farrell and Enejda Nasaj. I can't thank Séan Farrell enough for backing this book when I first submitted it.

Lastly, thanks to my children, sisters and cousins for the many kinds of encouragement they have given. For two family members it's been an especial labour of love. My mother, Deirdre Davey, has cherished Robert Hilliard's memory throughout a long life. Her carefully recorded recollections of her father and of her own early years are at the heart of this book and she has patiently listened to every chapter being read out loud while providing corrections and suggestions. My partner John encouraged me to begin this book and his advice and support have enabled me to write it.

INDEX

<u>Note:</u> Page locators containing 'n' refer to that particular note on the page in question.

Abrahams, Harold, 99
Act of Union (1800), the, 248n1
Aeschylus, 70
   Choephoroe, The (play), 110
Aitken, George, 202, 208, 277n15
Albacete, Spain, 189, 190, 201, 211
Alfonso XIII, King, 167
All-Ireland Amateur Boxing Championships, the, 94, 222
allowance for 'separation women,' 30–1
An t-Óglach (newspaper), 98–9, 101, 261n16
ancient Greece and the classicists, the, 70, 254n40
Anderson, Rev William, 53, 59–60
Anglo-German Naval Alliance (1935), the, 170
Anglo-Irish Treaty (1921), the, 68–9, 70, 76, 134, 241n33, 254n26, 255n54
   and Dáil vote on, 256n57
anti-Protestant sentiment in the Irish Free State, 108, 262n24
anti-Treatyite IRA, the, 69, 71, 72, 73, 74, 75, 90–1, 93, 254n32, 256n62, 256n69–70, 261n9
armaments and matèriel supplies, 179–80
arms raids, 38, 44, 69, 257n69
Armstrong, Rev Claude Blakeley, 34, 46, 47
Army Athletics Council, the, 95
army discipline in the International Brigades, 198–9, 208
Ashe, Thomas, 243n67

Asquith, Herbert, 22, 36
Aud, the (ship), 32, 33
Avoca School, Blackrock, Dublin, 105, 106, 223
Azana, Manuel, 179, 271n17

Baker, Cecil, 85
Baker, Charles, 79, 82
Baker, Edie, 79, 81, 217
Baker, Frances, 95, 263n14
Baker, Francie, 95, 263n14, 268n3
Baker, Madeline, 78, 79, 81, 103, 123, 217
Baker, Sir Robert, 79
Baker (née Cautley), Marianne, 79, 81, 82, 119, 145, 263n12
Baldwin, Stanley, 164
Balfour Declaration (1916), the, 72
Ballyseedy landmine massacre, the, 93
bank holiday weddings, 267–8n25
banning of nationalist gatherings and sports, the, 42–3, 245n21, 245n23
Barcelona, Spain, 49
   and the Spanish Civil War, 176, 177, 187–9, 200
Barcelona People's Olympiad, the, 177
Barnacle, Nora, 85
Barry, Tom, 53, 58–9, 251n38
Bass company, the, 110
Battle of Cable Street (October 1936), the, 182, 183–4, 273n29–30
'Battle of Patrick Street' (June 1917), the, 37
Beckett, Clem, 194, 207

Index

Beckett, Samuel, 130, 157, 158, 171, 264n16, 270n12–13
  More Pricks than Kicks (short stories), 66
  Murphy (novel), 157
Bill Sticker (cartoon character), 110
billeting of loyalist Protestant homes, the, 58–9
  at Moyeightragh, 59, 251n43–4
Black and Tans, the, 47, 48, 49, 51, 52, 85, 104, 246n45, 247n59, 259n23
blacking of Irish imports to the UK, the, 238n18
Blackshirts, the, 164, 182, 183–4, 273n28–9
Bloody Sunday (21 November 1920), 53–4, 249n18
  and enquiry, 54, 249n19
Blueshirts, the, 148, 149, 266n14
Blum, Léon, 272n13
Boer War, the, 81
Bolshevik Revolution (1917), the, 36–7, 83, 104
Borkenau, Franz
  Spanish Cockpit, The (book), 277n9
Bowen-Colthurst, Capt John C., 259
boxing tournaments
  Intervarsity Championships, 106, 109, 264n10
  Irish Inter-Varsity Boxing contest, 94
  zzDUBC Tournament, 109
Boycott, Capt, 12, 234n19
Breen, Dan, 51–2, 245n33
Brian Boru pipers' band, the, 39, 243n69, 247n55
Briskey, Bill, 192, 202, 207
British Army, the, 22, 199
  Argyle and Sutherland Highlanders, 166
  Auxiliary Division, 51–2, 53, 54, 55, 56, 195, 246n45, 250n21, 250n25
  Royal Defence Corps, 42
  Royal Munster Fusiliers, 31
  Territorial Army, 35
British boxing colour-bar, the, 92
British colonialism in Africa, 77, 258n2–5
British government, the, 60, 73
Brown, Norah C, 214

Browne, Felicia, 177, 271n5
Buchman, Frank, 122, 126, 149–50, 223, 241n39, 267n18, 267n20
Buckley, Henry, 189–90
BUF (British Union of Fascists), the, 182, 183–4
burnings of towns and property, 45, 47, 49, 53, 58, 73, 248n78, 266n27
  Cork, 54, 55, 250n21
  Customs House, Dublin, 252n53
  Dillon's Cross, 55
by-elections (1917), 36, 39, 243n70

Caballero, Largo, 167–8, 178, 179, 271n17, 272n15, 272n18
Cahill, Francis, 86
Cairo Gang, the, 52, 248n4, 249n5
capitalism and social justice, 163
Carpentier, Georges, 92
Carroll, Denis, 131
Carson, Sir Edward, 21, 33, 238n14–15, 240n27
Casañ, Guillem, 219
Casement, Sir Roger, 32, 240n20
Castellón, 210, 280n41, 281n15
  cemetery archives, 218–19, 280n40
  Cemetery of Sant Josep, 218–19, 224, 279n35, 281n13–14
  hospital, 211, 212, 224, 279–80n37
Castleisland Barracks, Co. Kerry, 69
Catholic Church, the, 107, 128–9, 147, 167, 177, 272n10
  and the feast of Corpus Christi, 108, 262n21
  and support for the Francoist/Nationalists, 193, 275–6n36
  and teaching on contraception, 143
Catholic Young Men's Society, the, 147
Catholics in Northern Ireland
  atrocities and violence against, 69, 71, 247n55
Caudwell, Christopher (Christopher St John 'Spriggy'), 194, 207
CGT, the, 186
Chaplin, Charlie, 67, 181
Chariots of Fire (film), 99

Index

Chelsea, London, 163
Christian Brothers' College, Cork, 30, 46, 241–2n44
Church of Ireland, the, 2, 5, 53, 128–9, 134, 140, 147, 149, 153, 236n38
(*see also* zHilliard, Robert M.)
Clark, Jimmy, 259n1
Clarke, Basil, 110, 262n30
class resentment in Ireland, 11–12, 236n37–9
Close, Bryson, 138
CNT union, the, 174, 176, 200, 271n17, 271n21
Cogley, Johanna Mary, 75
Cohalan, Bishop Daniel, 33, 243n2
Cohen, Nat, 177
Collins, Michael, 52, 53, 60, 61, 68, 72, 255n54
Come Back to Erin (film), 20
Comintern, the, 164, 165, 201, 262n1, 272n16
    and approach to the Spanish Civil War, 178, 198, 277n9
    Seventh World Congress, 168
    and the 'united front' tactic at the Fourth World Congress, 269n3
Communist Party of Great Britain, the, 163, 164, 165, 168, 169, 170–1, 182, 183, 184, 185, 213, 214, 215, 224, 257n72, 262n1, 268n11, 270n8, 273n28–9, 274n7
    and the Young Communist League, 178, 198
Companys, Lluis, 176
Connolly, James, 15, 20–1, 22, 31, 32, 33, 71, 106–7, 134, 236n39, 237n10–11, 238n18, 239–40n17, 240n22
conscription, 41–2, 43, 244n11–12, 245n25
Conservative Party, the, 263n1
contraception, 108, 120, 143
    and the Marie Stopes cap, 120, 143
Conway, Kit, 196, 202, 207
Cooper, Betty, 57
Copeman, Fred, 166, 197, 210

Cork, 30, 31, 33, 234n15, 239n8, 239n16, 240n25, 242n59, 243n69, 256n63
    and conscription and recruitment, 41–2, 43, 244n12
    and Empire Day, 33, 241n30
    and food prices and supply, 31, 40–1, 243n2–3
    and St Patrick's Day parades, 31
    and strikes and industrial unrest, 36, 37, 39, 42, 44–5, 48, 104, 140, 242n56, 256n59
    and the War of Independence, 46, 47, 48–9, 52, 54, 55, 59, 250n21
Cork Examiner (newspaper), 34, 74, 90, 93
Cork Gaol, 42
Cork Grammar School, Cork, 25, 29–30, 31, 34–5, 36, 37, 38–9, 45, 53, 55, 222, 239n1, 239n3–4, 241n30, 241n36, 242n44
    and corporal punishment, 45–6
    and drill instuction, 35, 242n47
    and the OTC, 35, 38, 41, 43, 46
Cornford, John, 177
Cosgrave, W.T., 107, 243n70
Costello, John A., 148–9
CPI (Communist Party of Ireland), the, 147–8, 149, 257n72, 266n9
Criminal Law Revision Committee, the, 263n11
Croke Park, Dublin, 53–4, 245n23
Crome, Len, 210, 279n33
cross-sectarian workers' unity, 139–40
Cuerpo Carabineros y Parque Mobil, the, 280n39
Cumann na mBan, 42, 240, 243n68, 255n46
Cumann na nGaedheal, 134, 148
    (*see also* Fine Gael)
Cunningham, Jock, 166, 192, 202, 208, 209, 213
Curragh mutiny, the, 22, 256n60
Curtin, John, 235–6n34

Dáil Éireann, 44, 45, 52, 69, 245n32, 246n50, 249n8, 251n39, 252n50, 259n24

Index

Daily Herald (newspaper), 81
daily Quiet Time sessions, 137, 141, 145, 150, 153
Daily Telegraph (newspaper), 189–90
Daily Worker (newspaper), 166, 169, 191, 195, 201, 202, 210, 213–14, 216, 270n11, 273n29, 280n1, 280n4
Daly, Daniel, 91
dance in the 1920s, 57, 250n31
Davey (née Hilliard), Deirdre (daughter), 80, 103, 108, 123, 124, 127, 128, 132, 133, 136–7, 141, 142, 143, 145, 146, 147, 150, 152, 153, 154, 160, 223, 254n41, 268n27, 272n8, 281n9
  and coping with separation from and death of her father, 3, 171, 172–3, 191, 214–15, 221, 263n13, 270n15, 280n2
  and eyesight, 145, 161, 173, 281n9
  and naming from James Stephens, 95–6, 121
  and relations with mother Rosemary, 9–10, 115, 120, 125, 131, 216, 218, 233n3, 263n13
  and schooling, 144, 161, 162, 173, 191
David, Rhys
  Early Buddhism (book), 206
Davis, Thomas, 70
Davitt, Michael, 234n17
de Valera, Éamon, 69, 72, 134–5, 148, 243n70, 251n39, 252n53, 255n54
deaths, 140, 146, 164, 170
  in Easter 1916 Rising, 33, 85, 259n22
  Irish Civil War, 91, 93
  Spanish Civil War, 3, 207, 208, 210, 213, 214, 216, 232n2, 271n5, 278n9, 278n20, 281n15
  in War of Independence, 45, 46, 49, 53, 54–5, 58, 60, 71, 240n29, 245n33, 246n49, 247n55, 249n18, 250n28, 251n39, 252n53, 259n23
  in World War I, 35–6, 53, 242n52
Debs, Eugene, 193–4
Deceased Wife's Sister's Marriage Act (1907), the, 233n5
Dill Medal for Classics, the, 43

Dimitrov, Georgi, 168, 170, 200–1
Doak, Houston Larmour, 47–8
Donnelly, Charlie, 278n9
DORA (Defence of the Realm Act, 1914), the, 31, 37, 39
Doyle, Maurice, 101
Dublin
  after the Easter 1916 Rising, 51
  decline and poverty, 51, 248n1
  and Merrion Square, 85, 86, 95, 222
  and Mountjoy Square, 52, 54, 57, 249n8
Dublin Castle, 45, 52, 53, 249n18
Dublin Lockout (1913), the, 21, 238n17–18, 240n22
Dublin Metropolitan Police, the, 75
Dublin Universities' and Hospitals Championships, the, 127
Dublin University Boxing Championships, the, 98
Dunlop, Alison (niece), 237n3, 237n7
Dwyer, Patrick, 101, 102

Easter Rising (1916), the, 25, 32–3, 51, 85, 240n22, 250n30, 259n24
  and executions of leaders, 33, 259n22
Eastern Command Boxing championships, the, 106
Editorial Services (PR agency), 110
Egypt and independence, 69–70
el-Krim, Abd, 272n13
election fraud, 72–3
electoral voting franchise, the, 23, 238n24
Empire Day in Cork, 33, 241n30
enlistment by Irishmen in the British Army, 36, 53
  motives to enlist, 30–1
Euripides, 70
  Bacchae, The (play), 71, 255n44–5
  Electra (play), 110
Eutychianism and divinity, 130–1

Fall, Louis Mbarick, 92
Falmouth, Cornwall, 173, 224
Famine, the, 40

288

Index

fascism and its rise in Europe, 148, 150, 164, 170, 173, 182–3
  and Comintern opposition to, 168–9
  (*see also* Franco, Gen Francisco; Hitler, Adolf, Mussolini, Benito)
Fenians, the, 11–12, 15, 234n15
Fianna Fáil, 134–5, 148, 149, 223
Figueras, Spain, 187
film and popular cinema in the 1920s, 67, 250n31, 253n16
Fine Gael, 148, 266n14
  (*see also* Cumann na nGaedheal)
Five-Year Plans, the, 270n6
Flaherty, Volunteer Daniel, 97, 98–9, 101
Fleming, Lionel, 65, 67, 74–5, 90, 119, 121, 130, 160, 177, 256n63, 272n8
food prices, 31, 41, 243n2, 244n6
food shortages, 40–1, 74, 90, 243n3–4, 244n7, 256n65
Ford, Henry, 267n20
Foreign Service, the, 213
Four Courts, Dublin, the, 72, 73
Four Horsemen of the Apocalypse, The (film), 67, 253n16
France, 170
  and arms supply, 179
  and the Comintern, 178
  and foreign policy in the Middle East, 72, 255n53
  and North African colonies, 179, 272n13
  (*see also* Olympic Games (Paris, 1924), the)
Franco, Gen Francisco, 1, 168, 177, 179, 187, 189, 204, 210
Francoist/Nationalist army, the, 179, 189–90, 193, 205, 207, 208, 209, 224, 280n5
  Army of Africa, 168, 175, 271n1, 278n14
Francoist strategy, 204, 205
Free State army, the (*see* National Army, the)
Freeman's Journal (newspaper), the, 93, 97, 106, 248n2
Freemasons, the, 136

French, Sir John, 43, 238n19, 245n25, 246n38
Frongoch prison camp, Wales, 33, 36
Fry, Harold, 202, 208
funding for Irish Olympians, 97, 98, 100, 101

GAA (Gaelic Athletics Association), the, 43
  (*see also* Croke Park, Dublin)
Gaelic League, the, 42
Gaelic revival, the, 14–15
Gaelic Sunday, 43, 245n23
Gal, Gen (János Gálicz), 209
Gallagher, Willie, 170
G.B. Britton, Bristol, England, 11, 235n22
Geehan, Tommy, 147
general election
  (June 1922), 72–3, 256n57
general elections
  (1918), 43, 245n28
  (1935, UK), 170, 270n10
  (February 1932), 135
  (February 1936, Spain), 174
  (January 1933), 148
  (May 1921), 60
general strikes, 60, 71, 73, 104, 107, 139, 140, 165, 240n18, 240n22, 252n50
  Belfast (January 1919), 44, 61, 246n36, 246n38
  in Cork, 36, 37, 39, 41–2, 44–5, 48, 104, 140, 242n56, 256n59
  Dublin Lockout of 1913, 21, 237n17–18, 240n22
  and government crackdowns on, 107, 261–2n12
  Limerick (April 1919), 44
  outdoor relief Committee strike (Belfast 1932), 139, 248n82, 265n25
  postal workers (1922), 107
  rail strike (1933), 146–7
  in the UK (1926), 117
George IV, King, 79
George V, King, 165
'German Plot' conspiracy allegations, the, 42, 246n38

289

Index

Germany
 and the Nazis, 270n9
 and World War I, 239n14, 244n8
Giral, José, 176
Gladstone, W.E., 236n38
GNR (Great Northern Railway) company, the, 146
government grants for boxing, 95
Goya, Francisco
 Disasters of War (print), 105
Great Depression, the, 134, 139, 158, 169–70
Great Unrest, the (*see* industrial unrest)
Greene, Graham, 117, 119
Grierson, Bishop Charles Thornton Primrose, 129, 136
Griffith, Arthur, 15, 61, 68, 74, 236n40
 Resurrection of Hungary, The (article), 236
gun-running, 32, 33, 240n20
Gurney, Jason, 163, 164, 166, 180, 182, 187, 188, 190, 192, 194, 195, 197, 200, 202, 206, 277n15, 278n20

Harrison, Jane, 70, 254n40
Hayden, Eve, 157, 263n14
health issues for Rosemary's children, 131–2, 172, 173, 191
Healy, Daniel, 38, 248n79
Healy, J.J., 99
Healy, Sean, 48–9, 239n7
Heraldo de Castellón (newspaper), 212
Hilliard, Billy, 233n7–8, 235n22–4, 235n26, 238n28
Hilliard, Davnet (daughter), 120, 131–2, 142, 143, 147, 172, 191, 214, 215, 217, 221, 223, 281n10
Hilliard, Ellen (Elsie) (step-sister), 10, 237n47
Hilliard, Geoffrey (brother), 17–18, 128, 136, 142, 145, 237n52, 266n4
Hilliard, John (uncle), 9, 13, 14, 15–16, 21, 71–2, 74, 235n21–2, 235n31, 236n35, 237n44, 237n48, 256n65, 266n27

Hilliard, Kit (Christopher) (son), 143, 147, 160, 172, 191, 214, 215, 217, 221, 262n32
Hilliard, Margaret (Marjorie) (sister), 17, 142, 145, 160, 266n4
Hilliard, Martin (nephew), 237n52
Hilliard, Phil (cousin), 24–5, 238n30
Hilliard, Phyllis (sister), 17, 127, 128, 142, 145, 171, 266n4
Hilliard, Richard, 250n25
Hilliard, Richard (grandfather), 10–11, 13, 133, 233, 234, 235, 237
Hilliard, Richard (uncle), 237n46
Hilliard, Robert M., 2–3, 5, 11, 33, 37, 55, 69, 74, 133
 and adolescence, 56–7, 59, 109
 and ambitions, 16
 and the Anglo-Irish Treaty, 69, 70, 72, 75, 90
 and anti-Protestant sentiment, 108, 262n24
 and the anti-Treatyite IRA and republicanism, 75, 256–7n69–70
 and burial records and plot, 218–19, 280n40, 281n12
 and the Church of Ireland, 5, 122–3, 128–9, 131, 134, 149, 150, 153, 162, 224, 267n24
 as pastor, 129, 136, 137–8, 140, 143, 144, 147, 149, 152, 200, 223, 266n1, 266n16, 267n25, 268n29
 as a copywriter, 110, 262n30
 and death, 2, 211–12, 214–15, 224, 274n7, 279n35, 280n39
 early years and childhood, 9–10, 19–20, 23–4, 25, 222, 255n45
 and education, 17, 18–19, 24–5, 29, 30, 34–5, 43, 45, 49, 51, 52, 56–7, 61, 65–7, 94, 105, 108, 109, 241n36, 250n30, 251n36
 'Corporal Punishment' (poem), 45
 'Daily Round, The' (poem), 47
 as a father, 124, 132, 141, 142, 145, 146, 152–3, 215–16, 219–20, 221
 and Fianna Fáil, 135, 148, 223, 267n20

290

and finances, 152, 153, 158, 160, 223, 224

as a freelance journalist, 117–18, 119–20, 121, 158, 169, 223, 270n11

In Praise of Baldness (newspaper article), 118

and gambling, 121, 122, 130, 263n16

and health and poverty, 268n11

influence of early exposures to Irish nationalism and workers' struggles, 36, 38, 39, 49–50, 52, 54, 56, 59, 61

and the International Brigades, 182, 185–7, 188–9, 190–1, 192, 194, 196–8, 199, 200, 201–2, 206, 224, 274n7

injury in battle, 210, 211, 224, 279n30, 279n32–3

and memories of, 220

and modernity and conservatism, 68, 91

and non-conventiality and non-conformity, 131, 200–1

and pomposity and censoriousness, 70–1

and reputation, 4–6, 138, 253n18, 265n7

and return to London, 154, 157–8

and Rosemary, 34, 50, 70, 76, 95–6, 103–4, 106, 108, 109, 110–11, 115–16, 180–1, 186, 222, 223, 241n38, 261n1, 262n24, 263n12

and correspondence with, 201–2, 212, 220, 270n16, 273n23, 274n7, 280n38

and married life, 116–17, 119, 120–2, 123–5, 127, 128, 132, 136, 137–8, 141, 142–3, 145, 146, 150, 151–4, 171–2

and separation from, 182, 187, 201, 224

and search for his place in life, 49, 140–1, 148, 149, 163, 182

and socialism, 49–50, 103–4, 149, 162, 163–4, 165, 168–9, 170–1, 184, 224, 266n9, 268n11, 270n8

and sport, 35, 46, 93, 257n75

and boxing, 76, 89–90, 93–5, 97–9, 100, 101, 102, 106, 109, 125, 127, 130, 186, 222–3, 257n69, 257n74, 260n23–4

and hurling, 93

and rugby, 35, 242n45

and TCD editorship, 129, 264n13

and Trinity College, 94, 105, 109, 126, 241n36, 241n39, 253n10, 254n35

and college debating, 67–8, 69–71, 72, 75–6, 91, 92, 104, 125, 126, 130, 135, 222, 250n31, 253n12, 253n14, 253n18, 253n20, 254–5n42, 254n39, 257n69, 257n72, 260n34, 262n19, 267n20

Divinity School, 123, 135–6, 223, 241n39

and editorship, 129–30, 135–6

Work and Progress in the Oxford Group (paper), 126

and women, 57–8, 68, 253–4n25

Hilliard, Robert Martin (father), 9, 10, 13, 14, 15, 17–18, 20, 23–4, 47, 59, 71–2, 108, 118, 129, 233n1, 233n4, 235n21, 235n27

and death, 132, 133, 223

and education of his children, 24, 30, 35, 39, 51, 52–3, 74

and estate valuation, 136, 142

on Home Rule, 22–3

as Justice of the Peace, 16, 58

and local business interests, 21, 74, 235n22, 236n35, 237n44

Hilliard, Robin (cousin), 23, 24, 111, 237n8, 238n27

Hilliard, Stephen (cousin), 5, 6, 59, 232n3, 232n6, 251n44

Hilliard, Tim (son), 3, 118, 119, 120, 121, 123, 124, 125, 127, 128, 132, 133, 136–7, 142, 143, 144, 145, 146, 152, 154, 159–60, 161, 162, 171, 172–3, 191, 212, 214–15, 217, 220, 221, 223, 263n12–13, 281n7–8

Hilliard, William (cousin), 13

Index

Hilliard, William (great-grandfather), 233n7

Hilliard, William (uncle), 11, 12–13, 234n10, 235n22–4

Hilliard (née Martin), Alice Eagar (mother), 9, 17, 18–19, 20, 30, 39, 47, 108, 133, 145, 160, 233n4, 266n4, 266n27
and husband Robert's estate, 136, 142
and Robert, 96
and support for Rosemary and grandchildren, 110–11, 158, 159, 160–1, 171, 172

Hilliard (née Martin), Mary Ann, 10

Hilliard (née O'Keeffe), Frances, 12–13, 235n22, 235n24

Hilliard (née Robins), Rosemary, 6, 50, 70, 76, 78, 79, 80–3, 95–6, 247n63, 248n83, 258n5–6
and Christmas 1935, 171–2
and contraception, 143
and creditors, 224
and death of father, 79, 80
and dog-breeding, 82, 217
and family life, 118, 119, 121, 125, 127, 131–2, 136–7, 141, 142–3, 144, 217–18, 263n12
and family support, 158–9, 160, 171, 218
and friendship with Muriel Lester, 84, 85–6, 259n24
and health, 223
and marital problems, 150–2, 153, 154, 158–60, 268n27
Midnight Flitting, The (essay), 162
and the Oxford Group, 123, 150–1, 223
and the Republican cause, 216, 280n4
and Robert, 95, 103, 104–5, 108, 110–11, 116–17, 119, 120–2, 123, 127, 149, 222, 223
correspondence with, 115–16, 180–1, 187, 191, 201, 212, 216, 220, 274n7, 280n1, 281n6
and death of, 214–15, 218
and efforts to hear news of, 213–14, 216, 277n14

and journalism, 118, 263n5–6
and life after separation from, 158–62, 171, 172, 173, 182, 270n15
and sexual mores, 86, 120, 263n14, 268n4
view of the Hilliards, 118–19, 145

Hilliard (née Saunders), Ellen (grandmother), 133, 233n7–8

Hitler, Adolf, 149–50, 164, 165, 170, 173, 178, 183, 217, 267n18, 270n9

Hogan's Lane, Killarney, 15, 235n31, 236n42

Home Rule, 14, 22–3, 33, 67, 237, 241n33
and the Home Rule Act (1912), 21, 22

Horace, 253n20

housekeepers and governesses, 143, 144, 233n2

hunger strikes, 39, 243n67, 247n66

hunting trophies from colonial Africa, 79, 258n7

Hyndman, Tony, 187

IABA (Irish Amateur Boxing Association) Championship, the, 98, 99

ILP (Independent Labour Party, UK), the, 164, 177

INAA (Irish National Aid Association), the, 33, 34

Incorporated Society for Promoting Protestant chools in Ireland, the, 251n47

industrial unrest, 20–1, 36–7, 44–5, 60, 83
in Russia, 36
in Spain, 174, 175–6
(*see also* general strikes)

Industrial Workers of the World (Wobblies), the, 193–4

infant mortality, 31, 83, 239n13

influenza pandemic (1918), the, 43

International Brigades, the, 2, 4, 43, 165–6, 179, 185, 190, 216, 272n16, 273–4n1, 276n2
battalions
Abraham Lincoln, 192, 195, 224, 232n2, 277n13

292

British, 166, 191–8, 202, 204, 205–6, 214, 224, 232n2, 275n23
 Dimitrov, 192, 205, 278n2
 Franco-Belgian, 192, 205, 207
 Thaelmann, 211
brigades, 278n3
 XI Brigade, 205
 XV Brigade, 166, 195, 205, 209, 224
and discipline, 198–9, 208
International Brigades Convalescent Centre, 211–12
journey for new volunteers, 185–8
and living conditions, 208, 209
and political commissars, 197–8, 199
International Brigades Memorial Trust, the, 220
International Lenin School, Moscow, 166
International Working Men's Association, the, 234n14
Internationale, the (song), 209
internments and deportations, 33, 42, 244n17
Invergordon Mutiny, the, 166
IRA (Irish Republican Army), the, 45, 46, 49, 52, 53, 55, 58–9, 134, 195, 246n49, 248n79, 251n39, 251n43–4
and Treaty split, 69, 71, 72
 (*see also* anti-Treatyite IRA, the; Irish Volunteers, the; War of Independence, the)
IRB (Irish Republican Brotherhood), the, 12, 32, 234, 240n22
Irish Bureau of Military History, the, 38
Irish Citizen Army, the, 32, 36, 240n22
Irish Civil War, the, 72, 73–5, 76, 90–1, 93, 134, 251n44
Irish Drapers' Assistants Association, the, 240n18
Irish Independent (newspaper), 55, 101, 127
Irish language, the, 15, 252n9, 253n14
Irish National Land League, the, 12, 14, 234n17–18, 236n37
Irish Olympic Boxing team, the, 97–102, 261n16

Irish Parliamentary Party, the, 14, 15, 22, 67
Irish People, The (newspaper), 234n14
Irish Socialist Republican Party, the, 15, 238n18
Irish tanning and leather industry, the, 11, 13–14, 15, 233n9
Irish Times, The (newspaper), 42, 72, 75, 94, 97, 98, 105, 106, 126, 130, 177
Irish TUC, the, 41, 245n28, 266n14
Irish Volunteers, the, 21, 31, 32, 33, 36, 37, 38, 40, 42, 238n22–3, 240n22, 243n5, 243n68, 243n71
and split, 22
Irish volunteers in the Lincoln Brigade, 195, 224, 232n2, 277n13
Italian occupation of Abyssinia, the, 170
ITGWU (Irish Transport and General Workers' Union), the, 20, 21, 31, 36, 44, 239–40, 242n56, 243n71

Jacobs, Joe, 169
Japanese occupation of Manchuria, the, 170
Jews, the, 267n20
 in Great Britain, 182, 183–4
 in Ireland, 236n40, 239n4, 249n14
 in Nazi Germany, 150
 in the Spanish Civil War, 191
Jones, Jack, 220
Joyce, James, 65–6, 85, 130
 Ulysses (novel), 57, 66

Kalem Film Company, the, 20, 22, 238n22
Kamenev, Lev, 181
Kasungu Mission, Nyasaland, the, 78
Keats, John
 Endymion (poem), 71
Kent, Thomas, 33, 240–1n29
 and attempted arrest of his brothers, 240n29
Kerrigan, Peter, 192, 195, 198, 202, 212, 213
Kerry People (newspaper), 69
Khayyam, Omar
 Rubaiyat (poetry), 103, 186

Index

Kid, The (film), 67, 253n16

Killarney, a Hundred Years with Hilliards (book), 234n10, 235n22

Killegy graveyard, Killarney, 133

Kilmainham Gaol, Dublin, 33

Kilmichael ambush, Co. Cork, the, 55

King Rehoboam (Old Testament figure), 122–3, 128–9

Kingsley Hall, Poplar, London, 83, 85

KPD (German Communist Party), the, 164

Ku Klux Klan, the, 91

L Coleman and Company, London, 165

La Scala Theatre, Dublin, 248n2

Labour Party (Ireland), the, 73, 135, 245n28, 256n58

Labour Party (UK), the, 83, 117, 164, 170, 198, 213, 270n10
in government, 104, 164, 262–3n1

Laidley, Kit, 111, 262n32

Lake Hotel (Castlelough), Killarney, the, 23–4, 90, 236n35
and farming out of Hilliard children, 15–16, 237n48

Land Act (1870), the, 236n36

Land Acts (1881–1903), the, 14, 236n38

land agitation in Spain, 167, 174

Land Wars, the, 12, 14, 234, 235–6n34

Lansbury, George, 83, 259n20

Lansbury, Minnie, 259n20

Larkin, Delia, 52, 249n6

Larkin, James, 20, 238n18

Le Carré, John, 76

Lee, Tancy, 95, 99, 260n33

leftist attitudes in Britain to the Spanish working class struggle, 177–8

Leggett, Adm Oliver, 79

Lemaans, Jack, 193

Lester, Doris, 83, 258n12

Lester, Muriel, 83, 84–5, 86, 117, 140, 172, 258n12, 259n20, 259n23–4, 264n17, 274n7

Leventhal, Gertrude, 111

Liberal Party (UK), the, 263n1

Liberator, The (newspaper), 133

Liddell, Eric, 99

Lloyd George, David, 33, 36, 42, 241n33

loan finances from shopkeepers and small business, 235n21

local government spending in London boroughs, 83–4

Lochore, John, 192, 194, 210–11, 212, 277n17, 279n35, 280n41

Loizago, Bishop Marcelino Olaechea, 276n36

Lund, Bob, 127

Lynch, Daniel, 91

Macartney, Wilfred, 192, 194–5, 198–9, 213, 274n7, 276n48

MacCurtain, Tomás, 46, 243n66, 243n69

MacDonald, Ramsay, 104, 164

MacDonogh, A.A., 105

MacNeill, Eoin, 32

Madrid, 176, 195, 202, 213, 216
and Francoist offensive on, 179, 189–90, 204, 210, 224

Madrid-Valenica road, the, 204, 205, 209, 214, 224

Madrigueras, Spain, 191, 192–3, 201, 203, 276n2

Mahaffy, John, 66–7, 252n9

Maison des Syndicats, the, 273n1

malnutrition and infant mortality, 31

Manchester Martyrs commemoration parade, the, 243n71

Mann, Tom, 140

marches and demonstrations
by the Blackshirts, 183, 273n28–9
in Cork, 33, 37, 38–9, 241n30, 241n32, 243n71

marital rape and English law, 120, 263n11

Markievicz, Constance, 85, 259n25

martial law and curfews, 55, 250n20

Martin, Margaret, 233n2

Martin family, the, 9, 10, 159, 233n4

Marx, Karl, 234n14

mass graves of Republican dead (Spain), 219, 281n15

Masters, Sam, 177

Index

Maundrell, Grace, 143, 151, 158, 161, 171, 172, 216, 217, 223
McCarthy, Helen Amy, 237n47
McGilligan, Patrick, 106
McGreevy, Thomas, 130, 264n16
McGrotty, Eamon, 232n2
McGuinness, Joseph, 243n70
Mcguinness, W.S., 92
McMahon family, the, 71–2
McTigue, Mike, 92
mechanization of shoemaking, the, 11, 13, 15, 234n10, 234n12, 235n29
Metropolitan Common Poor Law fund, the, 84
MI5, 214
Miaja, Gen José, 204
Midleton College, Co. Cork, 24–5, 222
Military Service Act (1918), the, 41, 244n11
military strength and complements, 204
Modern Times (film), 181
Monothelites and divinity, the, 130, 131
Monto district, Dublin, the, 57, 250n33
Moonlighter outrages during the Land War, 12, 14, 235–6n34
Moore, Christy
    'Viva la Quinta Brigada' (song), 4–5, 232n2, 278n9
Morrow, Felix, 272n13
Mosley, Oswald, 163, 177, 183, 184, 273n29
Mother and Baby Homes, the, 107–8
Mount Temple School papers, the, 251n47
Mountjoy Prison, Dublin, 48, 247n66
Mountjoy School, Dublin, 51, 52–3, 54, 56–7, 59–60, 222, 249n13–15, 251n36, 251n44
    and discipline and caning, 59–60, 251n47
    and the Matron, 57, 250n30
Moyeightragh residence and townland, Killarney, 23, 24, 59, 142, 233n1
    and feeding the local IRA, 59, 251n43–4
    and sale of, 145

Murray, Gilbert, 71, 110, 255n44–5
    Euripides and His Age (book), 70
Murray, Seán, 148
Murtagh, PC Joseph, 46
Mussolini, Benito, 148, 163, 170, 178

Nathan, George, 195, 208
National Army, the, 73, 74, 91, 93, 107
National Federation of Women Workers, the, 242n56
National Government (1931–35, UK), the, 164, 270n10
National Labour Organisation (UK), the, 270n10
National Sporting Club de France, the, 100
nationalist unrest in Cork after the Easter Rising, 33–4
Negrín, Juan, 272
New York Times (newspaper), the, 150
Newman, Alec, 75, 130
News Chronicle (newspaper), 191, 213, 216, 280n4
Nicholson, Barbara, 268n3
Non-Intervention Agreement (August 1936), the, 178, 196, 197, 272n14
NUWM (National Unemployed Workers' Movement), the, 165, 166, 192
Nyasaland (British Protectorate), Africa, 77, 258n2

Oblong, May, 57
O'Carroll, Richard, 259n23
O'Casey, Sean, 52, 65
OCI (Olympic Council of Ireland), the, 95, 97
O'Connor, Michael J., 240n17
O'Connor, Pat, 93
O'Higgins, Kevin, 107, 261n9
oil procurement in western Europe, 72
Olympic Games, the
    (Berlin 1936), 177
    (Paris, 1924), 95, 99–102, 222–3, 260n23–4, 261n15–16
        and funding for Irish Olympians, 97, 98, 100, 101
        and selection for, 97–8

Index

O'Riordan, Manus, 220
O'Riordan, Michael
  Connolly Column (book), 220, 279n22
Orwell, George, 188
  Animal Farm (novel), 270n6
  Keep the Aspidistra Flying (novel), 117
O'Sullivan, Michael, 40
Outdoor Relief Workers' Committee, the,
  139, 147, 248n82
Overton, Bert, 192, 202, 208, 278n20
Oxford Group, the, 122, 126, 129, 137,
  143, 149–51, 152, 160, 162, 172, 181,
  223, 267n18, 267n20

Parish of Derriaghy, Northern Ireland,
  129, 136, 223
Parnell, Charles Stewart, 234n17,
  236n37
partition, 60–1, 68–9, 71, 241n33
patronyms in Spanish nomenclature,
  281n12
PCE (Communist Party of Spain), the,
  174, 180, 188, 198, 200, 271n17
Pelagianism and divinity, 130, 131
Pemba, 78, 258n3–5
Perpignan, 186–7, 191, 274n1
Pertuzzo, Benjamin, 101
Petter oil machine, the, 235n29
Petty Sessions Court, the, 15, 236n35
Pingarron Heights, Spain, 205
Plunkett, George Noble, 243n70
political commissars in the International
  Brigades, 197–8, 199
Pollitt, Harry, 148, 165, 195, 201,
  214, 280n1
Poor Children's Milk Fund, the, 243n2
Poor Law hospitals, the, 83, 258n16
Poplar Borough Council, London, 83,
  84–5, 104, 258n15, 259n22
Popular Front, the, 174, 178–9, 188, 198,
  271n17, 277n9
Portobello Barracks, Dublin, 98
POUM (Marxist Workers' Unity Party),
  the, 174, 177, 188, 200, 271n17
poverty and social unrest in Belfast,
  139, 146

precepts and the local government rates
  system, 83, 84
Price, Mike, 90
Prieto, Indalecio, 271n17, 271n25, 277n9
proscription of Irish nationalist organisa-
  tions, the, 42–3
Protestant anxieties on partition, 69,
  254n28
Protestant exodus from Cork, the, 44
Protestant workers in Northern Ireland, 61
Provisional Government of the Irish Free
  State, the, 69, 73
PSOE (Spanish Party of Socialist Work-
  ers), the, 167, 174, 271n17, 271n25
PSUC, the, 180
Public Order Act (1936, UK), 184
Public Safety Act (1924), the, 148
Public Safety (Emergency Powers Resolu-
  tion) Act (1922), the, 74

Queen's University, Belfast, 94, 135
Quiroga, Santiago Casares y, 175, 176,
  271n25

R Hilliard and Sons, Killarney, 4, 10, 11,
  12, 13–14, 56, 234n10–13, 250n25,
  266n27
  and eviction of tenants, 15, 236n35
  and expansion, 237n44
raids on homes, 45, 246n45
railway network and the War of Independence, the, 37, 41, 42, 48, 55, 69,
  241n29, 250n22, 256n59, 256n63
  and sabotage in county Kerry, 90–1,
  247–8n71, 259n5
Ramsey, Frank, 263n14
Ramsey (née Baker), Lettice,
  85–6, 263n14
rates system in English local government
  boroughs, the, 83–4
'Red Train,' the, 186–7
Redistribution Act (1885), the, 238n24
Redmond, John, 22
Reid Sizarship Exam, the, 61
Representation of the People Act (1884),
  the, 238n24

Republican Army, the, 204, 205, 278n3, 278n14
Republican government of Spain, the, 174, 177
Republican strategy in the Spanish Civil War, 209–10
residences
   Heathery Hill Road cottage, Annalong, Co. Down, 160
   Kingswood Hanger, Surrey, England, 78, 79, 80, 82, 86, 102, 105, 106, 109, 125, 128, 137, 143, 258n9
   and the Visitors' Book, 261n1, 263n12, 263n14
   Kingswood Ruffs, Grayshott, Surrey, 116, 122, 223
   Knocknadona, Lisburn, Co. Down, 136, 137, 223
   Letchworth, Hertfordshire, 216
   Peaslake, Surrey, 217, 218
   Ravenhill Park, Belfast, 143, 223
   Tiverton, Devon, 217
   Weir Cottage, Ballinderry, Lisburn, 161, 162, 171, 172–3, 224
Resource (magazine), 5
Reynolds, Louis, 124, 128, 134, 264n17
RIC (Royal Irish Constabulary), the, 34, 37, 39, 42, 43, 45, 46, 47, 49, 52, 54, 240n29, 243n69, 243n71, 245n21, 245n35, 246n49–50, 248n75–6, 248n78, 249n19, 254n31
'shoot-to-kill' policy, 48
right-wing rebellion in Spain, 174, 176–7, 178, 179
   (*see also* Francoist/Nationalist army, the)
road maintenance in Kerry, 69, 254n27
Robins, Michael, 78, 79–80
Robins, Stephen, 77, 78, 79
Robins (née Baker), Rose Melicent, 77–81, 82, 120, 121, 154, 191, 217, 258n5
   and death, 217–18
   and Kingswood Hanger Visitors' Book, 103, 261n1
   as support for Rosemary and children, 127, 128, 137, 141, 144, 145, 151, 191, 217
Rochelle School, Cork, 47, 55
Ronan, Mike, 93

Roscommon by-election (February 1917), the, 36
Royal Navy, the, 32
RUC (Royal Ulster Constabulary), the, 139–40, 148
Russell, F., 109
Russell, George 'AE', 85
Russian matèriel supplies to Spain, 179–80
Rust, William, 210
RVG (Revolutionary Workers' Groups), the, 139, 147, 267n17
Ryan, Frank, 195–6

salmon fishing season, 13, 235n26
Samoyed dogs, 82, 111, 172
Schulze, Charles, 250n21
Scully, PC Timothy, 46
separation women, 30–1, 37
Shanahan's Pub, Foley Street, Dublin, 52, 249n9
Sheehy-Skeffington, Francis, 85
Sheehy-Skeffington, Hanna, 85, 259n23, 264n17, 274n7
Sheehy-Skeffington, Owen, 130, 187, 264n17, 274n7, 277n14, 281n6
Sheik, The (film), 67, 253n16
Shellard, Ken (nephew), 235n27, 237n8, 247n62
Shellard, Thomas, 149
Shellard (née Hilliard), Mary (Moll) (sister), 17, 19, 47, 55, 59, 68, 74, 136, 142, 149, 151, 159, 235n27, 237n8, 247n62, 266n4, 266n16
Siki-McTigue boxing match (March 1923), the, 92
Sinclair, Betty, 147
sinking of merchant shipping, the, 31, 239n14
Sinn Féin, 15, 36, 39, 42, 43, 44, 60, 61, 69, 75, 242n54, 243n5, 243n66, 243n69, 243n71, 245n21, 245n28, 245n32–3, 252n50
   as Cumann na nGaedheal, 236n40
   and the Democratic Programme, 245n32
   and the June 1922 election, 72–3
   and Treaty split, 69, 255n54

Index

Smyllie, Bert, 72–3, 130, 177, 256n55, 264n15
Smyth, DC Col Gerald, 48, 49, 248n73–5
social and economic life in the Free State, 106–8
social class and sport in schools, 241n44
Social Democratic Party (Germany), the, 164
social mobility and the Catholic middle class, 14
Socorro Rojo International (International Red Aid), 212
Soviet Trial, the, 181–2
soviets in Irish workplaces and towns, 37, 71, 73, 256n59
  and the 'Limerick Soviet,' 44
Spanish Army, the, 176
Spanish Civil War, the, 168, 175–9, 216
  Battle of Barcelona (July 19, 1936), 176, 177
  Battle of Jarama (1937), 3, 43, 195, 204–5, 206–10, 213, 224, 232, 278n9, 279n30
  Francoist Madrid offensive (November 1936), 179, 189–90, 204, 210, 224
Spanish gold reserves, 179, 272n18
Spanish monarchism and Carlism, 174, 271n24
Spanish Morocco, 175, 179, 272n13
Spanish Navy, the, 176
Spanish Red Aid, 213
Special Spanish Fund, the, 201
Spillane, Michael, 22, 40
Spock, Benjamin, 99
Springhall, Dave, 166, 198, 202, 213
St Anne's Cathedral, Belfast, 223
St George's School, Harpenden, England, 81
St James's Gate Harriers' Invitation Race (December 1923), the, 95
St Patrick's Anti-Communist League, 147
St Patrick's Day parade, Cork (1916), 31
Stakhanovism, 200–1, 270n6
  and worker productivity, 169
Stalin, Josef, 166, 168, 169, 178, 180, 181, 182, 217, 270n6, 272–3n20

Stearly, Garrett, 267n18
Stephens, James, 85, 95, 121
  Deirdre (tales), 95–6
Stopes, Marie, 120
strike warnings among unionized workforces, 37
Stucker, Lt-Gen, 211, 215, 216, 279n37, 280n38, 281n12
Suez Canal, the, 72
Sunday Independent (newspaper), 32
Swanzy, DI Oswald, 243n69, 247n55
Sykes-Picot agreement, the, 72

Tate, Sir Robert, 95
TCD (college magazine), 67, 68, 70–1, 92, 93, 126, 187, 223, 254n38–9, 254n42, 264n13, 267n20, 274n7, 280n38
  and editorship of Robert, 129–30, 135–6, 233
territorial division in Spain, 176
Thomas, Fred, 192
Thomas, Hugh, 175, 176
Thomson, Basil Home, 44, 258n13
Thrift, Harry, 65–6, 105
Timberton Follies, The (stage musical), 82
Times, The (newspaper), 117
Tone, Theobald Wolfe, 235n20
Town like Alice, A (film), 217
Trades Council of Limerick, the, 44
train drivers' boycott of the British Army, the, 48, 55
training, 197, 205
Transport and General Workers' Union (UK), the, 201
Treacy, Sean, 245n33
Treaty of Brest-Litovsk, the, 244n8
Treaty of Versailles, the, 170
Trench, Paddy, 75, 95, 121, 157–8, 164, 173, 177, 222, 263n14, 268n3–4, 269n18, 270n13, 271n7
Trench, Shamrock, 260n35
Trench, Terry, 121, 158, 263n14, 268n9, 271n7
Trench, Wilbraham, 263n14

Trinity College, Dublin, 61, 65–8, 69–71, 91–2, 109
  Classical Society, 254n39
  Divinity School, 123, 128
  Historical Society, 75–6, 253n12
  Neophyte Debating Society, 76, 92, 106, 257n72, 262n19
  OTC (Officers' Training Corps), 75, 257n69–70
  and resources for the Irish Olympic boxing team, 97
  and Sizarships, 61, 222, 252n57, 254n35
  and TCD (DUBC) Boxing Club, 76, 93–4, 106, 109, 222, 260n28, 264n10
  and TCD Hurling Club, 93, 135
  Theological Society, 130, 134
  Thomas Davis Society, 67, 253n10
  and women, 66, 68, 253–4n25
Tripoli, Salvatore, 101
Trotsky, Leon, 273n24
TUC (Trades Union Congress), the, 117, 213, 238n18
Twomey, Con, 38

U-Boats, 31, 244n7
UGT (General Workers' Union), the, 167, 174, 176, 271n17, 271n21
Ulster Covenant, the, 238n15
Ulster Special Constabulary (B Specials), the, 60, 71, 139, 252n55
Ulster Unionists, the, 69, 237n12, 238n15
unemployment, 60, 252n49
  and the Great Depression in Belfast, 139–40
Unionist opposition to Home Rule, 21, 22, 33
University College Dublin, 94
unwed mothers in the Irish Free State, 108
US Army, the, 192
US Navy, the, 242n59
USSR and the Spanish Civil War, 272–3n20, 272n14
  (see also Comintern, the)

UVF (Ulster Volunteer Force), the, 21, 22, 252n55

Valencia, Spain, 189, 210
  and the Madrid-Valencia road, 204, 205, 209, 214, 224
  as seat of the Spanish government, 179, 204
Valentino, Rudolph, 67, 253n16
Varela, Gen, 204–5
Victoria Barracks, Cork, 30, 33

Wall Street Crash (1929), the, 134
War of Independence, the, 44–5, 46, 47, 48–9, 51–2, 53–6, 58, 60, 85, 251n38–9, 252n53, 254n36
  and human shields, 58, 251n37
  and the Soloheadbeg ambush, 44, 245n33
  and the truce, 61
  (see also railway network and the War of Independence, the)
Warner, Jack (Horace John Waters), 85, 259n21
Waters, Doris, 85
Waters, Elsie, 85
Waters, Horace John (Jack Warner), 85
weaponry, 197, 203, 205, 207
  Colt machine gun, 202
  Maxim machine gun, 202
Wegimont, Liam, 249n14
Weissmuller, Johnny, 99
Wells, H.G., 258n12
Wilde, Oscar, 85, 238n14
Willey, Deborah, 15
Williams, Alexander, 16
Wilson, Sir Henry, 42, 73, 256n60
Wintringham, Tom, 166, 192, 195, 198, 199, 206, 208, 209, 275n23, 275n34, 278n11
women in the Irish Free State, 107–8
  and Trinity College, 66, 68, 253–4n25
worker militancy and perceived threats of communism, 139, 140, 147

Index

workers' insurrections in Spain, 167–8
  and surrender of control of collective
    structures, 180
Workers' Union of Ireland, the, 147
World War I, 22, 35–6, 80, 244n8
  and Armistice Day, 43, 80
  Battle of the Somme, 36, 242n52
  Gallipoli campaign, 31, 36

Yeats, W.B., 85
Young Ireland movement, the, 67

Zinoviev, Grigory, 181
  and the Zinoviev letter, 117, 262n1–2